# Sites of Memory in Spain and Latin America

# Sites of Memory in Spain and Latin America

## *Trauma, Politics, and Resistance*

### Edited by Aída Díaz de León, Marina Llorente, and Marcella Salvi

LEXINGTON BOOKS
Lanham • Boulder • New York • London

Published by Lexington Books
An imprint of The Rowman & Littlefield Publishing Group, Inc.
4501 Forbes Boulevard, Suite 200, Lanham, Maryland 20706
www.rowman.com

Unit A, Whitacre Mews, 26-34 Stannary Street, London SE11 4AB

British Library Cataloguing in Publication Information Available

**Library of Congress Cataloging-in-Publication Data**
The hardback edition of this book was previously cataloged by the Library of Congress as follows:

Sites of memory in Spain and Latin America : trauma, politics, and resistance / [edited by] Marina Llorente, Marcella Salvi, and Aída Díaz de León.
pages cm.
Includes bibliographical references and index.
1. Memory--Political aspects--Spain. 2. Memory--Political aspects--Latin America. 3. Political atrocities--Spain--Historiography. 4. Political atrocities--Latin America--Historiography. 5. Government, Resistance to--Spain--Historiography. 6. Government, Resistance to--Latin America--Historiography. 7. Spain--Politics and government--Historiography. 8. Latin America--Politics and government--Historiography. 9. Spain--Intellectual life. 10. Latin America--Intellectual life. I. Llorente, Marina. II. Salvi, Marcella. III. Díaz de León, Aída.
DP63.S58 2015
946--dc23
                              2015025003

ISBN 978-1-4985-0780-6 (paperback)
ISBN 978-1-4985-0778-3 (cloth)
ISBN 978-1-4985-0779-0 (electronic)

# Contents

*Contents*

*I*

# Introduction

# The Politics of the Past and the Fragmentary Present

*Locating Memory in Spain and Latin America*

Aída Díaz de León

On a clear night in the Atacama Desert, two planes of vastness converge at the horizon. One is a dark, velvet mantle encrusted with stars that hold the physical traces of our cosmic history. As our eyes travel downwards, the expanse of the desert emerges as the symmetrical reflection of that infinite sky. Astronomers gather here to reconstruct the memory of the universe through state-of-the-art telescopes. The deferred light, though millions of years from its originating event, bears the clues that will complete the narrative. Others confront a more daunting task. To this day, Chilean women continue to search in this spectral landscape through the lens of their mourning for remains of their loved ones—those who fell decades ago during Pinochet's dictatorship. Compelled by the prison of their trauma, relentlessly looking backwards to that elusive origin of their loss in an attempt to understand, they are indeed walking, breathing memorials to their dead. In his haunting reflection on memory, the 2010 documentary *Nostalgia de la luz* (*Nostalgia for the Light*), Patricio Guzmán draws parallels between two processes set in motion by irrevocably lost, violent origins: the birth of the universe and the cataclysmic onset of Pinochet's regime.

I mention Guzman's film because no other work in recent years has so evocatively captured the power and fragility of memory, and its counterpart, oblivion. The essays found in this volume are informed by the belief that the relentless disappearance of the present into the past can only be understood in its opposite movement: the intrusion of the past in the present. Examining those links that bind the past and the present is never a solitary endeavor; it

1

is, Walter Mignolo notes, "a communal and dialogic enterprise" (5). Whether individual or collective, remembering (re)constitutes an image of the past through structures of visibility available in the present, or in Maurice Halbwach's words, through the "social frameworks of memory" (38) and the "frames of collective memory" (39). The past, cautions Halbwachs, "is not preserved but is reconstructed on the basis of the present" (40). The work of memory, therefore, is subject not only to the erasure of forgetting, but also to the refracting yet fundamental practices and tools of memory. In other words, the very frameworks constituting and preserving its meaning inexorably alter the significance of the past as well as that of the present. In this context, mnemonic processes become particularly fraught in geographies that have been drastically transformed by violence and conflict. For all their diversity, the studies gathered here offer insights into how witnessing, trauma, and testimony speak to the urgency of truth and justice; historical memory, therefore, becomes ultimately a political act.

As in other parts of the world, Latin America and Spain have seen in the last decades a dramatic shift from authoritarian regimes to (more or less) democratic participatory governments. In the transition to democracy seen in the 1980s, new political orders have emerged as the disenfranchised—whether through racial, political, or economic circumstances—have advanced toward the centers of power to contest the paradigms that brought about unbearable economic disparities and a blatant disregard for human rights violations. Many political analysts thought that the robust and widespread drive of the social movements of the 1980s was an expected but temporary response to the authoritarian regimes of the 1960s to early 1980s. Nonetheless, rather than subsiding, the resistance movements have continued up to the present day, in part as a reaction to the "advance of neoliberal globalization within processes of nominal democratization that often mean competition among elites without significant participation or substantive social justice" (Stahler-Sholk et al. 2). New forms of activism have consequently reimagined the notions of citizenship, government, and democracy. With the election of governments more receptive to the investigation of human rights abuses—as well as the proliferation of NGOs, grassroots movements, and human rights organizations—survivors and family members of victims have in some cases been the recipients of transitional justice reparations for atrocities carried out by prior regimes through the workings of Truth and Reconciliation tribunals, as has been the case in Chile, Argentina, and Spain. These Truth and Reconciliation tribunals, however, have encountered obstacles. Incapable of fully revisiting the disturbing, shameful national past, the political and economic realities were deemed more critical to the advancement of the country. As Idelber Avelar has written about the Argentina of the 1990s, the "country was now being asked to forsake the dreams of the 'impossible future' and embrace the 'realism' of the market" (*The Untimely Present* 61).

Insofar as the memory of the political struggles of the last two decades of the twentieth century has animated contemporary activism, citizens have confronted their government's inability or outright unwillingness to act on behalf of its people. After all, this form of "grassroots memory mobilizing," writes Katherine Hite and others, "seems to be defined in direct opposition to the expressed views of state actors and institutions" (Hite et al. 7). The examples are far and wide: from the Venezuelan protests of 1989 against the neoliberal restructuring of the country, a movement that was silenced with a massacre perpetrated by Carlos Andrés Pérez's government, to the attempted revolution in 1994 by the Ejército Zapatista de Liberación Nacional (Zapatista Army of National Liberation), who revolted against the North American Free Trade Agreement (NAFTA). The early 2000s saw the *guerra del agua* (water war) in Bolivia, where the poor inhabitants of Cochabamba protested against the privatization of the drinking water, which made this vital resource virtually inaccessible to them. In Argentina, numerous riots were waged by people of all economic levels who poured into the streets of Buenos Aires to demonstrate against rampant unemployment and the collapse of the country's government and economy. Furthermore, the economic claims catalyzing these protests were concomitant with human rights issues. From the Chilean marches that led to the 1987 plebiscite and signaled the end of Pinochet's regime to decades of activism undertaken by the mothers, grandmothers, and then children of the disappeared demanding information and accountability in Argentina, social protests and political mobilization brought an end to the state of terror. Sidestepping the oblivion embraced by their government, in the year 2000, Spanish citizens founded the Asociación para la Recuperación de la Memoria Histórica (Association for the Recuperation of Historical Memory) to pursue the exhumation of bodies and compile forensic evidence that could be used to bring to justice the perpetrators of crimes under the Francoist regime. Thus, the political dimension of memory began to act as a democratizing force.

The essays here focus on the variety of mnemonic instruments—from the most concrete to the performative—that resist forgetting and unite individuals against hegemonic memory. The volume's title alludes to *Lieux de mémoire* (1981–1992), the monumental seven-volume collaborative work on French national identity and memory that was edited by Pierre Nora. The work did not become available to English speakers until Nora's introduction was translated and published as an article, "Between Memory and History: *Les Lieux de Mémoire*," in 1989. Notwithstanding Nora's idealized, nostalgic conceptualization of the permanency of memory in the past as "real memory" (7)—those shared recollections that assured the continuity of a collective identity—the contributors to our volume find useful Nora's identification of the forms assumed by the materialization of memory. Furthermore, while Nora laments the "rupture of equilibrium" and waxes nostalgic for the "warmth of tradition" and "the silence of customs" (7), these essays defiantly inquire whose *tradition,* whose *custom*, and whose *equilibrium* does a monological narrative about the past (pre)serve. More than concerning themselves with what exactly constitutes a *lieu de mémoire*—or "site of memory"[1]— contributors to this project have shown how the concept can be built upon to account for a variety of historical memories. The studies gathered share the recognition of the plurality of social and political identities and their founding narratives—configurations that are in continuous flux in accordance with the "historical-political moment." As Katherine Hite has succinctly expressed, "Historical memories are the less conventionally institutionalized dimensions of politics-symbols and sites for contestation, associations, palpably expressed through representations, testimonials, imagery, the media, public opinion, and diverse political discourse" ("Historical Memory" 1078).

The volume comprises four thematic sections that focus on Chile, Spain, Argentina, Venezuela, Mexico, Peru, and the Dominican Republic. Keeping in line with the concept informing this collection, that the past returns politically to haunt the present, the four sections move from the contemporary context to the colonial and pre-Columbian eras in Latin America.

## FROM THE *REPERTOIRE* TO THE *ARCHIVE*: MEMORY IN CHILE AFTER PINOCHET

The inauguration of the Museum of Memory and Human Rights in Santiago, Chile, in 2010 marked a seminal moment in a process that began, as Liliana Trevizán discusses in her essay, under the Pinochet dictatorship in the day-to-day hardships to survive and keep alive the democratic ideals that had no time to flourish during Salvador Allende's all-too-brief mandate. Since those imprisoned, tortured, and disappeared by Pinochet's regime were mostly men, women were essential to the survival of the dreams of social and economic justice pursued by the Allende administration. Slowly but relentlessly, the momentum of the underground movements grew to occupy once more the national landscape in the vociferous and galvanizing plebiscite of 1987, which democratically ended the authoritarian government of Augusto Pinochet. Although the political alliances forged to oppose the regime—a center-left coalition of opposition parties that came to be known as Concertación por la Democracia—successfully carried four presidential elections from 1990 to 2010, the elected heads of state were caught between the narration of a reconstructed, rule-of-law-abiding nation with a vigorous economic scenario on the one hand, and a general tendency toward collective amnesia on the other. Emphasizing the performative dimension of the Chilean fight for democracy, Trevizán delineates a genealogical memory of strategies of political denunciation that have informed resistance movements in Chile to the present day.

To understand the embodiment of political memory enacted in the public space by these activists, we turn to Diana Taylor's discussion of the *archive* and the *repertoire*. On one hand, the *archive* comprises the institutionalized forms of memory conservation: "documents, maps, literary texts, letters, archaeological remains, bones, films"; in other words, media that are traditionally perceived as more "resistant to change" (*The Archive and the Repertoire* 19). On the other hand, the *repertoire* encompasses a type of remembering produced through the body itself, located in the very vessels of memory, in the performative dimension of the individual in society. As embodied presence, it imparts through the performative its truth-telling power. In this vein, Taylor includes in the *repertoire* all acts considered "ephemeral, nonreproducible knowledge"—such as "performances, gestures, orality, movement, dance, singing" (Taylor, *The Archive and the Repertoire* 20); that is, all those acts that take place in the public realm and are meant to be viewed, therefore reappearing only ephemerally in their performativity. Whether these are religious rituals, cultural traditions, sports events, or political rallies, to name a few, the underlying constitutive force of the *repertoire* is the notion of "embodied memory," which, "because it is live, exceeds the archive's ability to capture it" (Taylor, *The Archive and the Repertoire* 20).

From the public protests demanding accountability for the disappeared and tortured under Pinochet's dictatorship to the collective movements calling attention to the income gap further dividing Chilean society and the ongoing student protests contesting the government's restructuring of the education system, "performative protest" (in Taylor's words) has been instrumental in the struggle for transparency in the political machinery in Chile. When the Museum of Memory and Human Rights was inaugurated, the performative dimension of resistance entered symbolically the *archive* in the space of the museum; in doing so, this space of remembrance has emerged as a symbol of the nation's political will to articulate counterhegemonic forms of representation of the past and to confront competing recollections. With Ricardo Brodsky at the helm of the museum, the site has become an international model for other countries. In an interview with Brodsky included in this volume, Oscar Sarmiento and Liliana Trevizán posed incisive and challenging questions, thus drawing responses that reveal the difficulties, as well as the accomplishments, in the creation of such a space of national dialogue that at once recognizes the victims of the Pinochet era and invites differing points of view—an approach that reflects the "shared memory" Brodsky underscores. The archival artifacts in the museum function to provide elements for consideration by the visitors without insisting on foregone conclusions. Instead of *museum as temple*—a locus of transcendental monological truth—Brodsky's conceptualization reflects Edward Linenthal's discussion of the *museum as forum*, as a space that urges a sustained reflection on the "complicated motives . . . actions and consequences often hardly considered at the moment of the event itself" (9–10). Brodsky's emphasis on engagement dovetails with the genealogy of performative memory of democracy delineated by Trevizán: democratic institutions require work, engagement, and commitment to forge and maintain the delicate thread of memory at its core; to enact the present and secure the future, the past must be confronted and represented.

## LITERATURE AS MEDIA OF MEMORY IN SPAIN AND LATIN AMERICA

As Aleida Assmann explains, cultural memory as a form of historical memory "includes works of art that retain more ambivalence and allow for more diverse interpretations" than political memory, which is mediated by symbolic signs attributed with meanings that are "clear-cut" and "charged with high emotional intensity" in order to draw "individuals into a tight collective community centered around one seminal experience" (221). Literature, a medium of cultural memory, resists this uniformity. One of the principle effects of literary tools, "such as allegory, metaphor, symbolism, and intertextuality, is the bringing together and superimposition of various semantic fields in a very small place" (Erll 145). For the work of memory, particularly in a political context, the results prove generative in the contiguity of irreconcilable meanings and antagonistic interpretations of shared experiences in the textual space, as discussed by Marcella Salvi, Marina Llorente, Steven White and Mallory Craig-Kuhn.

In contrast to Chile and Argentina, Spain did not actively pursue the investigation of human rights violations committed under Franco upon the conclusion of the dictatorship. In fact, the journey to the Ley de Memoria Histórica (Law of Historical Memory) of 2007 has been long and fraught.[2] When Franco died on 20 November 1975, the country was poised to break with the past, only to find itself continuing the legacy of the dictatorship, in part through the efforts of the reformist factions within the Left and the Right. With the Ley de Amnistía (Amnesty Law) of 1977, members of the regime achieved their goal: never to be held accountable for any crimes committed for political reasons. Thus, the pardons paved the way for the ratification of the 1978 Constitution. The price for these concessions was steep, though; national unity could only come about, it seemed, through a bargain with the devil, the *pacto de olvido* ("pact of oblivion"), in effect sweeping under the rug the human rights violations in order to focus the country's attention on the refashioning of its political, economic, and cultural identity through the period known as La Transición. The Partido Socialista

Obrero Español (Spanish Socialist Workers' Party [PSOE]) governed the country through the four mandates of Felipe González (1982–1996), which saw a general improvement of Spain's image buoyed by its entrance into the European Union in 1986. Nonetheless, disappointed with rampant corruption, parapolice violence, and economic woes, the citizenry voted in 1996 to oust the Socialists and bring back the old (albeit revamped) guard by electing José María Aznar of the Partido Popular (People's Party [PP]).[3] Then, when the PSOE's candidate José Luis Rodríguez Zapatero won the elections in 2004, he was able to fulfill one of the promises central to his campaign: to pursue the investigation of victims of the civil war and the dictatorship. In 2007, the Spanish Parliament passed the Law of Historical Memory, which, as many critics have noted, has not been as effective as originally envisioned.[4]

As in the case of Chile discussed earlier, the rights to remember and to mourn, then, can only be exercised through the enactment of democratic practices. As Llorente underscores in her research on contemporary Spanish poetry elsewhere, "Without a national reconciliation with the bellicose past that divided Spain into winners and losers and installed a long military dictatorship, it will be very difficult to look ahead as a true democratic society" (*Poesía en acción* 46–47).[5] In a sense, Salvi's and Llorente's readings in this volume exemplify the function of literature as a "media of memory" (Erll 144) capable—to a certain extent—of mending the fragmented narratives about the Spanish Civil War and its aftermath, and in the process (re)building communities of memories. Salvi underscores the dialogic nature of Carmen Martín Gaite's semiautobiographical novel *El cuarto de atrás* (*The Back Room*), which was published in 1978, three years after Franco's death. *El cuarto de atrás* transcends the silences imposed by the Francoist regime as the narrator-character one night recalls her life experiences, from Primo de Rivera's dictatorship through Franco's burial. Within the vigorous interaction of voices emanating from a number of sources of popular culture— romance novels, gazettes, songs, and domestic and international films, for example—juxtaposed with contrasting propagandistic messages originating in indoctrinating brochures and state-run media, the dueling utterances create a multivocal text where the past meets the present. Salvi draws our attention to the veils rendering opaque the back room of the subconscious, to those "screen or concealing" memories—to borrow Freudian terminology (243)— that conceal repressed, more disturbing memories of a traumatic political past. Commenting on the Spanish contemporary memory novel, Hans Lauge Hansen writes that with the progressive disappearance of the generations that witnessed the civil war, the country is currently undergoing "an intense intergenerational postmemory transfer, driven by an affiliative compromise with the memory of the civil war and postwar repression on the part of the generation of the grandchildren of the victims" (98). As a Spaniard, Martín Gaite herself occupies the genealogical succession identified by Hansen; her novel represents the symbolic constitution of a moment in this genealogy.

As a symbolic system, moreover, literature creates a locus where elements that would otherwise be anachronous and incompatible in reality freely mingle in this condensed space. Through this "compression of several complex ideas, feelings or images into a single, fused or composite object," Erll explains, "many different associations about the past can converge in one condensed mnemonic object" (145–146). In a similar fashion, time and space collapse in Antonio Crespo Massieu's collection of poems *Elegía en Portbou* (*Elegy in Portbou*) (2011) portrayed by Llorente here as a textual space where poetry encounters testimony. Throughout these verses, the figures of Walter Benjamin (1892–1940) and Spain's emblematic poet Antonio Machado (1875–1939)—both victims of fascism—stride side-by-side the thousands of Spaniards who tried to escape the violent reprisals of Franco's army at the conclusion of the civil war. Namely, the infamous *retirada* ("retreat") is reenacted in the allegorical procession of forced exile not only from the homeland but from *life* itself. The scenario of exile and death is repeated: the cemetery of Portbou, where Walter Benjamin is buried, coexists with the cemetery of Collioure, Machado's final resting place. The phantasmatic landscape becomes more populated as Crespo Massieu invokes the hundreds of Spaniards buried along with Machado and who died in the deteriorated castle at Collioure, which was transformed into the concentration camp that spawned "the most notorious horror stories of all of French concentration camp history" (Cate-Arries 49).[6] The ghosts haunting Crespo Massieu's verses call to mind the thousands who fell during the civil war and its aftermath and who still await legal recognition in the mass graves that cover the Spanish topography. Hansen provides chilling numbers: "there are still more than 88,000 victims waiting to be exhumed from the 2,246 mass graves around the country that though identified have not yet been exhumed: numbers that give Spain the world's second highest total of unidentified victims scattered around in the landscape, a position second only to Cambodia" (92).

Buried truths, therefore, are disinterred, brought forth by the testimonial impulse of Crespo Massieu's poetry. Poetry textualizes the traces of experience, which in turn attests to survival. Testimony reveals the lingering traces of an event whose tragic dimensions defy narrativization, even by the eyewitness, who often becomes ensnared in the prison of trauma. Testimony holds the capacity to transform reality, as does a speech act, as Shoshana Felman writes: "Testimony is, in other words, a discursive *practice*, as opposed to a pure *theory*. To *testify*—to *vow to tell*, to *promise* and *produce* one's own speech as material evidence for truth—is to accomplish a *speech act*, rather than to simply formulate a statement" (17).[7] With regards to literary works, testimony actuates reality through the intimate engagement between the writer who testifies and the reader who witnesses, thus establishing a succession of witnesses. In this collection, Steven White's investigation of the role of the translator speaks to the testimonial power of this art form. As we have learned through the various ardent translating enterprises in Latin America, many civilizations have indeed survived oblivion through the reterritorialization of that culture in the symbolizing system of the colonizing powers.[8] The translator's task therefore resists the impulse to forget. In the contemporary context, the translator, as White notes, is capable of participating in witnessing. His translation of social conscience poetry, for example, disseminates forms of recall of the Spanish Civil War, the fall of Salvador Allende, the Sandinista Revolution, and other similar politically tumultuous events. In this manner, the boundaries of the *archive* (to use Taylor's term) must cede as the translated texts multiply exponentially the chain of witnesses. Drawing on Walter Benjamin and Emmanuel Levinas, Sandra Bermann concludes that "the translator's task is inevitably an ethical one. In attempts to translate, we become most aware of linguistic and cultural differences, of the historical 'hauntings,' and of experiential responsibilities that make our languages what they are and that directly affect our attitudes toward the world" (6).

As Salvi, Llorente, and White have discussed, literature provides a framework of meaning for unconstituted discourses concerning the past. In the same vein, Mallory Craig-Kuhn focuses on Osvaldo Soriano's novel *Una sombra ya pronto serás* (1990) to discuss allegory's mechanism, which compensates for the limits (as well as the ideological obstacles) of realism, in order to represent a nation emerging from the grips of authoritarian rule, this time in Argentina. Though published in 1990, Soriano's novel foreshadows the political, social, and economic deterioration that culminated in a national crisis at the end of the twentieth century. After the brutal dictatorship 1976–1983, the democratically elected governments of Raúl Alfonsín (1983–1989) and Carlos Ménem (1989–1999) purported to return Argentina to its prosperous and stable past. Following in step with their contemporary counterparts in Chile and Mexico, these presidents privatized the nation's public assets in order to sell off its valuable resources to the highest bidders—in most cases, foreign investors. Awash in foreign money and delusively secure in the inflated value of goods, the corrupt politicians and banking elites sacked the state's coffers, and in the process even further destabilized the economy. Keeping in mind that the theatrics of capitalism reside on the display of perceived value, we can read Osvaldo Soriano's recurrent motif of *el truco* ("the game")—rife with secret signals, deception, and daring bluffs—as a lucid literary symbolization of the economic machinations characteristic of rampant neoliberalism. Lacking a past and incapable of imagining a future, Soriano's characters wander aimlessly in a land that has been deterritorialized by the loss if its spatial, temporal, and therefore historical moorings. Craig-Kuhn reads *Una sombra ya pronto serás* as illustrative of a crisis of memory and identity emerging from the debris of the military dictatorship in Argentina. Notwithstanding the return to democracy with the Alfonsín and Ménem presidencies, the state's institutions embraced the organized narration of a reconstructed, rule-of-law abiding nation instead of dealing with the fragmented, open-ended stories of individual victims. "By 1990," Taylor writes, the "new efforts in nation-building under Ménem were based not just on commonality and shared experience, but on communal forgetting" (*Disappearing Acts* 16). Therefore, from the truth-seeking momentum of the early Alfonsín years to the series of acquittals carried out in the name of peace and reconciliation by his government and then Menem's, the country continued to struggle to reconstruct its recent past and represent the truth in the historical record. Politics could no longer ignore the persistence of national memory.[9]

## THE STRUGGLES OF MEMORY IN THE GLOBAL MARKET: VENEZUELA AND MEXICO

George Ciccariello-Maher investigates the reimagining of the "Bolivarian revolutionary process" through the various deployments of the memory of the massacre that occurred in Venezuela at the end of the 1980s. In 1989, when Venezuela's president, Carlos Andrés Pérez, caved in to the demands of the IMF and the Washington consensus, the poor disproportionately suffered the impact of the neoliberal policies set in motion. Seemingly overnight, economic reforms slashed the budget of social programs while the cost of basic goods and vital services, such as public transportation and utilities, soared. The disenfranchised—predominantly dark-skinned citizens—poured into the streets of downtown Caracas on the morning of February 27, in an event that would be remembered as the *Caracazo* or *Sacudón* of 1989. Needless to say, the looting and protests were met with violence; though no one is certain, the number of victims of the massacre may well have reached the thousands.[10] In this manner, the "Bolivarian revolutionary process" was born out of violence. Three years later, Hugo Chávez mobilized the memory of the Caracazo to rally support for his failed coup of 4 February 1992; in 1999 he finally emerged as the leader of the nation through the electoral ballot. The ghosts of the martyrs of the Caracazo have served to further galvanize political movements: Chávez strategically cited the martyrs as he defended his administration during the 2002 failed coup against his own government; and in his 2013 presidential campaign, Nicolás Maduro, Chávez's chosen successor, promised to bring about the changes that were yet to be fulfilled by the Bolivarian revolution. The road to the future, as Ciccariello-Maher demonstrates, was paved by the ghosts of those who had fallen for the potentiality of that very future.

Perhaps in no other space do we observe the forces of the global market and the neoliberal paradigm as at the US-Mexico border, where transnational business now determines the perimeters of the political, economic, and social realities of its inhabitants. Since the implementation of the North American Free Trade Agreement (NAFTA) in 1994, the border has become the duty-free and free trade zone designed by the transnational capitalist class, where the conditions of production remain optimal—no matter the human cost—for the unimpeded flow of investment and goods between Mexico, the United States, and Canada. The *maquiladora*—the foreign-owned factory whose low-cost Mexican labor guarantees the production and exportation of goods at a high rate of profit return—mostly employs women, who in the recent decades have increasingly become the target of horrific crimes. The incidence of feminicide—a "gender-based violence that is both public and private, implicating both the state . . . and individual perpetrators" (Fregoso and Bejarano 5)—has risen dramatically in the last two decades. Ciudad Juárez has become particularly dangerous for young women. As Martha Chew Sánchez and Alfredo Limas Hernández discuss in their contribution to this volume, memory at the border competes with (and often loses to) economic interests.

What is left of the bodies of these female victims—attractive dark-skinned girls and young women of poverty stricken areas—bear the marks of mutilation, torture, and rape. Their bodies—dumped in nonplaces, desert highways, construction sites, garbage dumps, city streets, parking lots, and other liminal spaces of transit—are inscribed with the violence of the system of production. These bodies are the detritus—the *abject* in Kristevan terms—of the capitalist machinery. Nonetheless, to hallow a space that is continuously traversed by economic and political interests, the families of the victims build clandestine cemeteries and makeshift memorials marking the place their daughters were last seen, dead or alive. The mothers have also taken to marking telephone poles with black crosses as well as other public sites. Because the Mexican government immediately dismantles these "fleeting representations" (Portillo 220), the documentarian Lourdes Portillo describes the mothers as agents of "collective memory . . . [for] they are the keepers of memory" (222).[11] Once more, the *repertoire* comes alive as the family members chant the names of their beloved and wear magnified pictures of their daughters on their chests—as if these images were enormous scapulars—to challenge the Mexican government's erasure of the crimes and their lack of accountability. To borrow Taylor's words, the victims' survivors participate in "[e]mbodied and performed acts [that] generate, record, and transmit knowledge" (*The Archive and the Repertoire* 21). These manifestations of "performed evidence" (Taylor 170) are particularly important when the institutions representing the *archive*, such as the judiciary, the police, and government, promote oblivion. Therefore, to combat this structural violence, the female fragmented bodies and effaced identities are reconstructed through the many forms of social protest at the border; in this manner, the victims regain meaning as a unified body with a reconstituted narrative. This is their only chance to become visible in legal discourse.[12]

Clearly, as Chew Sánchez and Limas Hernández demonstrate, this web of structural as well as physical violence at the border reduces its inhabitants to noncitizens, beings that are neither here nor there, unable to take root in a place to create community, and, by extension, memory. Forgetting, as Connerton observes in modernity, emerges as a result of the "processes that separate social life from locality and from human dimensions" (5). We can view the eroding processes at the border as an example of the profound alterations of the practices structuring collective memory: "There is some kind of deep transformation," Connerton states, "in what might be described as the meaning of life based on shared memories, and that meaning is eroded by a structural transformation in the life-spaces of modernity" (5). In an effort to counteract the forces that undermine the notion of place while reinforcing the individual's ties to a community, a number of solidarity groups, artists, and filmmakers regularly come together in marches and protest events in an attempt to recover the social fabric, and most importantly, in order to remember.[13] The chant *Ni una muerta más* ("Not one more dead woman") has become the battle cry against forgetting at the border.

## THE PALIMPSEST OF MEMORY: RECONSTRUCTING RACE, CULTURE, AND RELIGION FROM COLONIAL TIMES TO THE PRESENT IN PERU, MEXICO AND THE DOMINICAN REPUBLIC

Erasures of another nature, but no less significant, preoccupy the essays by Beatriz Peña, Selfa Chew, and Juan José Ponce Vázquez, whose interests lie in the religious, cultural, and racial deletions in the development of national identity in Peru, Mexico, and the Dominican Republic since the colonial era. The three contributors share an archaeological approach to memory as they delve deep into the layers of the past to reveal something that should have remained concealed. Their methodologies also coincide in the investigation of overlapping layers of discursive forms—hence the reference to the palimpsest-like structure in this section. Peña painstakingly reconstructs the ancestral identity of the *piedras campanas* ("bell stones")—phonolites known for their remarkable quality of producing a bell-like sound when struck—which used to sit on Morro de Eten on the northern coast of Peru, in Lambayeque. Following a chain of allusions that preserves the memory of these wondrous boulders, Peña uncovers the various transmutations of the identity of these boulders as it traversed different symbolic systems; from the oral and ritualistic traditions of the pre-Columbian cultures living in the area of Lambayeque hundreds of years before the arrival of the Spaniards to colonial accounts that invested the site with Christian meanings. A "miracle" in the seventeenth century (conveniently) eradicated the ancestral origins. Then, with the nineteenth-century's ideological projects to construct uniform national identities founded on racial, religious, and linguistic commonalities, the site suffered its final reterritorialization. When Ricardo Palma included the legend of the Christian miracle as "Las campanas de Eten" ("The Bells of Eten") in his *Tradiciones peruanas* (*Peruvian Traditions*), the site entered with a Christian garb the institutionalized memory of the national literary canon. Sadly, written accounts now exist in place of these natural wonders.

In a similar vein, Chew follows the evolution of the legend of La Mulata de Córdoba to demonstrate how this trajectory reflects the racial anxieties formulated at defining moments in Mexico's history as a nation. Despite the black presence on Mexican territory from the very beginning of European colonization in the sixteenth century, the various configurations of the legend, as Chew explains, have reflected the racial and sexual proscriptions of the colonial society, through the nineteenth-century's national movements touting the (alleged) homogeneity of its people, and then the twentieth-century practitioners of storytelling. According to Chew, the modern day formulation of the legend bears no vestiges of the historical circumstances of the black presence in Mexico and the contributions of this ethnic community to Mexican identity.

Racial and cultural anxieties once more define the development of national identity, as Ponce Vázquez discusses in his article concerning the infamous *devastaciones de Osorio* ("Osorio's devastations"). In 1605, the governor of Hispaniola, Antonio de Osorio, obeying Felipe III's mandate, began a year-long campaign to punish the population living on the western part the island for engaging in contraband and other commercial activities with the French, English, and Dutch, beyond the Spanish trade monopoly. The memory of this scorched-earth campaign has survived through the centuries as *las devastaciones de Osorio*; ironically, this purging and population displacement cleared the path for further occupation of the western side of the island by the French with its expansion of the sugar plantation system and the importation of black slaves. The division of the island and the consequent birth of Haiti have been seen by some as a direct consequence of the *devastaciones* and the founding moment of "the deformation of Dominican identity and of the body it inhabited" (Altagracia Espada 157).[14] Looking to excise the *contagion*—meaning the black presence—from the national body and "Dominicanize" the border, Rafael Trujillo launched a murderous campaign termed *el corte* ("the cutting"). Thousands of Haitians were killed during the Parsley Massacre, named so because the soldiers would ask suspected non-Dominicans to pronounce *perejil* in Spanish. Ponce Vázquez identifies the various textual forms and political uses of the memory of the *devastaciones* in the national collective memory throughout the past five centuries. The yearly commemoration of the massacre, through which the memory of the *devastaciones* is also mobilized, vividly exemplifies the use and misuse of memory.[15]

## CONCLUDING REMARKS

At the end of *Nostalgia for the Light*, the center of the galaxy passes slowly, indifferently, above Santiago de Chile at night. The city's amplitude eerily mirrors that of the night sky. Memory, according to Patricio Guzmán, exerts the power of a fundamental force structuring the universe itself: "I believe that memory has a gravitational force. It always pulls us. Those who have memory are capable of living in the fragile moment of the present; those who don't live nowhere" (*Nostalgia for the Light*).[16] Oblivion and amnesia thus dislocate the individual, both within himself as well as within the community. Individual or social, identity can only be actualized by retrieving and enacting memory. Identity, then, depends on being located, on being a *witness*, on assuming an anchoring point within the temporal structure of the *present*. The opposite is oblivion. As psychoanalyst Dori Laub has written: "This loss of the capacity to be a witness to oneself and thus to witness from the inside is perhaps the true meaning of annihilation, for when one's history is abolished, one's identity ceases to exist as well" (67).

The work of memory, however, can never restitute the past; hence, the radical *othering* of the past, which is inevitably subsumed by systems of representation. "The past," Walter Mignolo warns us, "cannot be rendered in a neutral discourse" (5). Every system of representation is historical; it is linked to power. For every form of record keeping, there lies dormant a corresponding silence. For all its diversity, the researchers' interdisciplinary methodology displayed in this collection brings to light processes that would otherwise have remained illegible under a more narrow interpretative approach to historical memory.

## NOTES

1.  For overviews of critiques of Nora's work, see Erll (22–27) and Wertsch (125–126). The Vietnamese historian Hue-Tam Ho Tai writes a scathing criticism of the ideological framework of Nora's research: "I write this review from the margins of both French history and of the French nation, as a historian (not of France but Vietnam) and as a postcolonial subject" (907). Also, in contrast to Nora's idealization of "real environments of memory (7)" in the past, Paul Connerton offers another perspective on memory concerned more with the separation of "social life from locality and from human dimensions"—the radical alteration of time and space in the modern global age (*How Modernity Forgets* 5).

2.  Interestingly, Pierre Nora has expressed his disapproval of Spain's Law of Historical Memory. In an interview conducted by Salvador Martínez Mas in 2009, Nora deemed the Rodríguez Zapatero administration's advocacy for the Law a serious error: "Principally, be-

cause the departure of the dictatorship occurred miraculously, without bitterness or violence. Spain thus avoided the settling of the score thanks to a miracle of history. With the debate over the victims of the Francoist repression, however, Spain is living a civil war of memories" (73). ("Principalmente, porque la salida de la dictadura en España se realizó de manera milagrosa, sin amargor, ni violencia. España evitó entonces el ajuste de cuentas gracias a un milagro de la historia. Sin embargo, con el debate sobre las víctimas de la represión franquista, España vive una guerra civil de memorias" (73). Further on in the interview he compares the Law to a Pandora's box; this type of legislature, Nora argues, threatens the apaciguamiento ("appease-ment") achieved during the transition to democracy (73). Unless otherwise noted, all transla-tions are mine.

3. We must remember that the precursor to the Partido Popular was the Alianza Popular (People's Alliance) founded in 1976 by Manuel Fraga, a former minister in the Francoist government.

4. For the shortcomings and difficulties of the Law, see Hansen (93) and the Association for the Recuperation of Historical Memory website.

5. "Sin una reconciliación nacional con el pasado bélico que dividió a España en gana-dores y perdedores y que arrastró a una larga dictadura militar, es muy difícil que se pueda seguir adelante como una verdadera sociedad democrática" (*Poesía en acción* 46–47).

6. We can add another layer of memory sedimentation to Crespo Massieu's text. More than four centuries before the erasure of the lives of the victims of fascism, Collioure had been the scene of another banishment, one imposed by the Catholic monarchy, at the end of the fifteenth century: refusing to convert to Christianity, the last remaining Jews left Spain in 1493. A plaque at the castle memorializes the diaspora.

7. Shoshana Felman has lucidly written about testimony within the framework of litera-ture, law, and psychoanalysis. See "Education and Crisis, or the Vicissitudes of Teaching."

8. We need only to think of the survival, though not without its controversy, of the Nahuatl and Mayan languages through the efforts of Motolinía and Diego de Landa, respectively. Nonetheless, the annihilation of the very systems of representation of these civilizations—such as the systematic destruction of the Mayan and Aztec codices and the violent suppression of these civilizations' languages—was fundamental to the European colonial expansion. See Mig-nolo.

9. When Ménem grants sweeping presidential pardons to hundreds of officers who would have faced charges for various reasons—ranging from human rights abuses during the 1976–1983 dictatorship to treason for their involvement in the Falklands War fiasco or the Carapintada rebellions—Ménem confronts his critics retorting: "Argentina lived through a dirty war, but the war is over. The pardons will definitely close a sad and black stage of Argentine history" (qtd. in Taylor, *Disappearing Acts* 14)

10. See Grainger.

11. After finishing her documentary *Señorita extraviada* (*Missing Young Woman*, 2001), Lourdes Portillo returned regularly to Ciudad Juárez to document the struggles of the families to find their daughters. Due to the psychological toll of filming, however, Portillo stopped doing so in 2011. The collected footage is kept under the director's name in the Stanford Archives (Portillo 221).

12. One strategy to fight feminicide is to render the crime visible through legal discourse, a process that the Mexican government has been less than willing to facilitate. Tellingly, the first official Mexican report on feminicide did not appear until 2006, as the result of the creation of the Comisión Especial para Saber (Special Commission to Know). This commission has been essential for the General Law of Women's Access to a Life Free from Violence, a piece of legislation that declared feminicide a crime against humanity, an issue of human rights. As an active member of the Chamber of Deputies from 2003 to 2006, Marcela Lagarde y de los Ríos fought tirelessly to craft and get the law passed. Since the day it went into effect on February 2, 2007, the General Law is "the only law in Mexican legal framework in which women are recognized as juridical subjects and in which the legal interest protected is the life of women" (Lagarde y de los Ríos xxiv). Unfortunately, only nine of Mexico's thirty-two states legally recognize feminicide as a crime (Ramírez Carreño 5–6).

13.  Barrio Nómada (Nomadic Barrio), a youth urban collective, regularly holds artistic events in the city streets and parks with the purpose of inviting the people—especially women and their children—back into the streets with the promise of their protection. The hip-hop group Batallones Femeninos (Female Battalions) tirelessly works to raise awareness about the victims of violence at the border and the Mexican government's lack of political will to confront the issue. Cultural events are the tools of Pacto por la Cultura (Pact for Culture), which tries to mend the collective imaginary through the arts. The organization's spokesperson provides a disturbing fact: Ciudad Juárez only has four theaters while it boasts 321 maquiladoras (Pastrana). Similarly, documentaries such as *Señorita extraviada* (*Missing Young Woman*, 2001) by Lourdes Portillo, *La carta* (*The Letter*, 2004) by Rafael Bonilla and Patricia Ravelo Blancas, and *Performing the Border* (1999) by Ursula Biemann, and literary texts, such as Roberto Bolaño's posthumous novel *2666* (2004), resist oblivion by raising awareness of these issues of human rights.

14.  In his assessment of Manuel Arturo Peña Batlle, one of the historians that contributed ideologically to Trujillo's ethnic cleansing, Altagracia Espada states, "The history of the Devastaciones is key to Peña Batlle's narration; for this historian, those events caused the deformation of Dominican identity and of the body it inhabited" (157). ("La historia de las Devastaciones es clave para la narración de Peña Batlle; esos acontecimentos fueron los que para este historiador originaron la deformación de la dominicanidad y del cuerpo en el que habitaba.")

15.  The border between Haiti and the Dominican Republic is the scene of the yearly commemoration of the Parsley Massacre. For the inhabitants' perceptions of the event and its memorialization, see "La masacre que marcó las relaciones de Haití y la República Dominicana."

16.  "Yo creo que la memoria tiene fuerza de gravedad. Siempre nos atrae. Los que tienen memoria son capaces de vivir en el frágil tiempo presente. Los que no la tienen, no viven en ninguna parte" (*Nostalgia for the Light* 1:26:52–1:27:15).

# WORKS CITED

Altagracia Espada, Carlos Daniel. "El cuerpo de la patria: imaginación geográfica y paisaje fronterizo en la República Dominicana durante la era de Trujillo." *Clío* (Enero–Junio 2004) 167: 147–202. Web. 21 Oct. 2014. http://www.clio.academiahistoria.org.do/ipad/index.htm.

Assmann, Aleida. "Memory, Individual and Collective." *The Oxford Handbook of Contextual Political Analysis*. Ed. Robert E. Goodin and Charles Tilly. Oxford: Oxford University Press, 2008. 210–224.

Asociación para la Recuperación de la Memoria Histórica. Web. 15 Oct. 2014. http://www.memoriahistorica.org.es/joomla/.

Avelar, Idelber. *The Untimely Present: Postdictatorial Latin American Fiction and the Task of Mourning*. Durham: Duke University Press, 1999.

Bermann, Sandra. "Introduction." *Nation, Language, and the Ethics of Translation*. Ed. Sandra Bermann and Michael Wood. Princeton: Princeton University Press, 2005. 1-10.

Caruth, Cathy. "Trauma and Experience: Introduction." *Trauma: Explorations in Memory*. Ed. Cathy Caruth. Baltimore: Johns Hopkins UP, 1995. 3–12.

Cate-Arries, Francie. *Spanish Culture behind Barbed Wire: Memory and Representation of the French Concentration Camps, 1939 – 1945*. Cranbury: Rosemont Publishing, 2006.

Collins, Cath, Katherine Hite, and Alfredo Joignant. *The Politics of Memory in Chile: From Pinochet to Bachelet*. Boulder: First Forum Press, 2013.

Connerton, Paul. *How Modernity Forgets*. New York: Cambridge University Press, 2009.

Erll, Astrid. *Memory in Culture*. Trans. Sara B. Young. Hampshire: Palgrave Macmillan, 2011.

Felman, Shoshana. "Education and Crisis, or the Vicissitudes of Teaching." *Trauma: Explorations in Memory*. Ed. Cathy Caruth. Baltimore: Johns Hopkins University Press, 1995. 13–60.

Fregoso, Rosa-Linda, and Cynthia Bejarano. "Introduction." *Terrorizing Women: Feminicide in the Americas*. Ed. Rosa-Linda Fregoso and Cynthia Bejarano. Durham: Duke University Press, 2010. 1–42.

Freud, Sigmund. "The Material and Sources of Dreams." *The Basic Writings of Freud.* New York: Random House, 1938. 238–318.

Grainger, Sarah. "Victims of Venezuela's Caracazo Clashes Reburied." *BBC News Latin America and Caribbean.* 27 Feb. 2011. Web. 4 Oct. 2014.

Guzmán, Patricio, dir. *Nostalgia de la luz (Nostalgia for the Light).* Icarus Films, 2011. DVD.

Halbwachs, Maurice. *On Collective Memory.* Ed. and trans. Lewis A Coser. Chicago: University of Chicago Press, 1992.

Hansen, Hans Lauge. "Auto-reflection on the Processes of Cultural Re-memoration in the Contemporary Spanish Memory Novel." *War: Global Assessment, Public Attitudes and Psychosocial Effects.* Ed. Nathan R. White. New York: Nova Science Publishers, 2013. 87–122.

Hite, Katherine. "Historical Memory." *International Encyclopedia of Political Science.* Ed. Bertrand Badie et al. Thousand Oaks, CA: Sage, 2011. 1078-1082.

Hite, Katherine, Cath Collins, and Alfredo Joignant. "The Politics of Memory in Chile." *The Politics of Memory in Chile: From Pinochet to Bachelet.* Ed. Katherine Hite, Cath Collins, and Alfredo Joignant. Boulder: First Forum Press, 2013. 1–29.

Lagarde y de los Ríos, Marcela. "Preface: Feminist Keys for Understanding Feminicide." *Terrorizing Women: Feminicide in the Américas.* Ed. Rosa-Linda Fregoso and Cynthia Bejarano. Durham, NC: Duke University Press, 2010. xi–xxv.

Laub, Dori. "Truth and Testimony: The Process and the Struggle." *Trauma: Explorations in Memory.* Ed. Cathy Caruth. Baltimore: Johns Hopkins University Press, 1995. 61-75.

Linenthal, Edward T. "Anatomy of a Controversy." *History Wars: The Enola Gay and Other Battles for the American Past.* Ed. Edward T. Linenthal and Tom Engelhardt. New York: Henry Holt and Co., 1996. 9–62.

Llorente Torres, Marina. *Poesía en acción.* Tenerife: Baile del Sol Ediciones, 2014.

"La masacre que marcó las relaciones de Haití y la República Dominicana." *BBC Mundo.* 13 Oct. 2012. Web. 15 Nov. 2014.

Mignolo, Walter D. *The Darker Side of the Renaissance: Literacy, Territoriality, and Colonization.* 2nd ed. Ann Arbor: University of Michigan Press, 2003.

Nora, Pierre. "Between Memory and History: Les Lieux de Mémoire." *Representations* 26 (Spring 1989): 7–24.

———. Interview. "Pierre Nora: España vive una guerra civil de memorias." By Salvador Martínez Mas. *Pasajes* 31 (2009–2010): 70–75.

Pastrana, Daniela. "Los vivos de Juárez." *Magis.* Iteso. Universidad Jesuita de Guadalajara. 1 June 2011. Web. 27 Sept. 2014. http://www.magis.iteso.mx/content/los-vivos-de-juárez.

Portillo, Lourdes. Interview. "Feminicide and the Disintegration of the Family Fabric in Ciudad Juárez: An Interview with Lourdes Portillo." By Alice Driver. *Studies in Latin American Popular Culture* 30 (2012): 215–25.

Ramírez Carreño, Sandra Milena. *Feminicide and the Politics of Representation: Media Perpetuating and Normalizing Gender Violence in Mexico.* MA thesis. Development Studies International Institute of Social Studies Erasmus The Hague, The Netherlands. Nov. 2012. Web. 29 Aug. 2014. http://thesis.eur.nl/pub/13200/.

Stahler-Sholk, Richard, Harry E. Vanden, and Glen David Kuecker. "Introduction." *Latin American Social Movements in the Twenty-First Century: Resistance, Power, and Democracy.* Ed. Richard Stahler-Sholk, Harry E. Vanden, and Glen David Kuecker. Lanham, MD: Rowman & Littlefield Publishers, 2008. 1–15.

Tai, Hue-Tam Ho. "Remembered Realms: Pierre Nora and French National Memory." *The American Historical Review* 106.3 (June 2001): 906–22.

Taylor, Diana. *The Archive and the Repertoire: Performing Cultural Memory in the Americas.* Durham: Duke University Press, 2003.

———. *Disappearing Acts: Spectacles of Gender and Nationalism in Argentina's Dirty War.* Durham: Duke University Press, 1997.

Wertsch, James. "Collective Memory." *Memory in Mind and Culture.* Ed. Pascal Boyer and James V. Wertsch. New York: Cambridge University Press, 2009. 117–37.

*II*

# From the *Repertoire* to the *Archive*: Memory in Chile after Pinochet

*Chapter One*

# Performing Memory and Democracy in Chile

## Liliana Trevizán

In an attempt to examine the current notion of democracy at work in Chile, this chapter explores how the scope of public discourse has expanded with the entrance of female actors into mainstream politics, thus producing today's strong consensus on memory and human rights. This arduous consensus, which has not turned out as definitive as the victims would have wished, has nevertheless produced a tacit agreement on democracy as the systematic protection of the citizen's most basic human rights. Only now—twenty-five years after the end of Augusto Pinochet's dictatorship in 1990—is Chile addressing the democratic turbulences that have threatened to destabilize a hard-fought-for political consensus; and in doing so, the country is embracing a renewed political and cultural awareness upon which a solid and inclusive democracy may develop. To discuss this transformation in contemporary Chilean society, I draw on William E. Connolly's observation that it is not unchanging stability, but contested, challenged scenarios that produce the necessary reconfigurations signaling the inclusive call of democracy:

> Democratic turbulences disturb established commonalities: it shows them to be complex contrivances; it brings out elements of contestability within them; it exposes possibilities suppressed and actualities enabled by contestable settlements. [Thus] democracy disturbs the closure of self-identity and, sometimes, provides a medium for modifying the terms of collective identity. [. . .] It increases pressure to revise the contours of the social form so that its institutional tolerance for democratic agonism can expand. (200)

The complicated course of events by which the country in the twentieth century went from being one of the most solid democracies in the Americas to installing a brutal dictatorship that lasted seventeen years, and then recuperating democracy, is a process that indeed resulted in the loss of many lives. I want to claim, however, that the numerous movements and events constituting this process also broadened democracy in the region. At the end of the day, democracy became more desirable for Chileans than before it had been tested and violently destroyed by Pinochet's regime. The years of struggle have demonstrated that a democratic memory remained alive even during the darkest times in the everyday practices of those who opposed the regime. Among them, women and other nontraditional social actors played a significant role. Because politicians and union leaders—who were mostly men— were targeted, jailed, and killed, women activists exercised their right to speak up, to organize, to publish and disseminate dissenting news, and to keep political parties, unions, and social movements functioning, even when it was illegal to do so. In the limited spaces for political action available to them, women learned nontraditional ways of doing politics by performing democratic practices more democratically and closer to the people, since much dissenting political action occurred at a small scale. These two factors—the presence of more women in the public political space and this new and distinct form of political practices—were energizing forces during the struggle to recuperate democracy. Furthermore, these same forces seem at play again today, when—after a sad and cautious mourning period informed by traditional politics—the uncontested, exclusionary "pragmatic" views of the neoliberal system are being challenged. Significantly, this form of participatory politics that legitimates new political actors played a key role in President Michelle Bachelet's decision to create the Museum of Memory and Human Rights at the end of her first term, in 2010. The decision to build such a museum emerged as a clear sign of the state's strategic commitment to memory and human rights. A close reading of that key junction brings to the surface political features that, though often overlooked by analysts, merit attention to understand how democracy brings about stability and development. Aware of a gap in people's understanding of democracy, the president seized this opportunity and signed the document that officially mandated the creation of the museum. By using the authoritative gesture of an executive order, President Michelle Bachelet represented a state that vowed recognition and reparation to the victims of state terror and their families. Tellingly, the hand that signed that document was not simply the hand of a chief of state but the hand of a victim, a tortured political prisoner, daughter of an assassinated army general, and a socialist militant exiled from her homeland for more than a decade.

How did this powerful phenomenon, this commitment to secure the binding intersection between the memory of human rights abuses and democratic values, come to take place? At first sight, it may seem to have come from nowhere. After its return to democracy, Chile had been presented internationally as the exemplary economic success story of an underdeveloped country seriously invested in its speedy rise to a solid neoliberal status. The country's achievement, in this view, would have its citizens—and the world—forget the horrors and hardships of sixteen years of military rule. However, the commitment to human rights that the creation of the museum signaled did not take by surprise an international community that had acknowledged Bachelet's presidency in Latin America as emblematic of reparation for victims of decades of state violence. In fact, soon after her election in 2006, she attended the 61st session of the United Nations where she gave a speech that reflected such a commitment: "I come from Chile, a country that has learned from its history. We Chileans lived through difficult times, and this organization knows it. The learning curve has been difficult, but productive. From suffering came hope, and after profound divisions we have been able to reach great consensus. I come from a country that today is under the rule of law, and where the rights of people are respected and promoted" (345).[1] Further on, the president stated, "Looking back at the past doesn't intimidate us" (345), thus repeating what was to become an important accomplishment of her administration: its commitment to memory. Tellingly, just days after taking office, one of her first public appearances involved the inauguration of a memorial to the victims of one of the most infamous crimes of the dictatorship, the beheading of three influential communist leaders by the Carabineros, Chile's national police force, in 1985.[2]

In this same speech, Bachelet elaborated on a notion of memory that at the time was still viewed as risky, even dangerous by many, including notable leaders of her political coalition. Recalling the "horror that was our reality" and the significance of having gone from "a nation of enemies to a nation where its children live together in peace," she emphasized "a peace that is not founded on forgetting, one that is not based on the avoidance of that which does not make us proud as a society, but a peace founded on the memory of our people, on the remembrance of our pain, and on the memory of the hope that never left us. [. . .] I am convinced that memory is *the pillar* on which we are building a much better country" (550).[3] Evidencing her personal investment, this statement also reflected the president's clear resolution to ensure that her term in office would contribute to the arena of human rights. In this way, she was fashioning a marked difference from the three previous democratic presidents' agendas.[4]

Moreover, memory and human rights were inscribed in the body and politics of Michelle Bachelet, and for this reason the Chilean people understood her candidacy as highly symbolic from the very beginning. This, in turn, helped her to win the election. The emblematic value of the body politics of Michelle Bachelet explains, in part, the creation of the Museum of Memory and Human Rights in 2010. The symbolic effect of her figure on the nation's imagination also reveals the importance of strong cultural changes that have triggered deep political transformations in Chile. Some of those changes have translated into a more inclusive notion of democracy, a more democratic conception of citizenry, and a definitive commitment to memory and human rights. This pledge to human rights embedded in an inclusive notion of democracy guarantees the basic consensus on the nature of its defining practices, such as free and transparent elections. One must credit this transformation to a strong, important set of cultural practices that—albeit ignored and disparaged in the preceding past decades—sustained the very core of what Chileans realized they had lost when the military took power and disrupted democracy.

Two particular cultural trends that grew out of the struggles of the anti-dictatorial movement help explain, in part, the central role human rights has played in this refashioning of democracy. These two tendencies continued to develop within the ranks of the center coalition Concertación por la Democracia, which elected four presidents between 1990 and 2010.[5] Active members in Concertación persevered against all odds to locate human rights and memory at the foundation of their conception of democracy and to change the traditionally hierarchical understanding of politics. Therefore they re-charged, rejuvenated, and invigorated the Chilean understanding of the democracy itself.

Many of these same political actors—including members of the New Left[6]—became part of the first democratically elected government. Pinochet's overwhelming presence overshadowed the reconstruction of democracy practically until his death in 2006. These actors strove hard, though; first under the urgency of fighting the dictatorship, and then later on during the negotiated transition to democracy that embroiled them in bureaucratic entanglements and spiteful interactions. Once democracy was achieved, the most prominent appointments in the administration went to seasoned politicians who had been part of Frei's (1964–1970) and Allende's (1970–1973) cabinets or who had held a seat in congress. With a few outstanding exceptions, the advent of democracy made a definitive generational and gender cut, one that excluded from governmental posts many of the most vocal activists who had fought in Chile against the Pinochet regime for almost two decades. Notable politicians returned from exile in the last years of the dictatorship and passionately dedicated themselves to the transition to democracy. Their respectability lent name recognition in the public sphere when they were appointed to the Cabinet or sought seats in the newly elected Congress. In light of the influential role the women's movement had played in fighting the dictatorship, the absence of female representatives was noticeable. The pressing political circumstances of the times that had led to this lack of representation also brushed aside most of the cultural changes (for instance, the advancement of leaders through the process of political struggle and the creation and embracement of nonpartisan platforms) that the social movements had brought to politics during the 1980s.[7]

Women, as well as other political actors, learned much from a decade of organizing and protesting.[8] The extenuating efforts to survive and to keep alive political and social organizations that would prove crucial later on in rebuilding the social fabric at all levels, taught them lessons that had been long forgotten about public trust, accountability, and generosity. The political left, in particular the party of Salvador Allende, underwent a bitter process of self-critique, which for almost a decade mostly consisted in laying blame on one or another faction of Allende's party. However, by the early 1980s there were several leaders and different clusters of the Left in the country, as well as among the organized groups in exile, that had in effect begun to articulate a powerful New Left discourse. Women's voices were emerging within the Socialist party, and notable feminists were part of a process that lasted until the plebiscite of 1987, when political affiliation was no longer banned as it had been for seventeen years.[9]

As expected, the majority among Socialists had defined democracy in traditional terms, in an antidictatorial rhetoric. The citizen's loss of the most basic civil rights, nevertheless, had shed new light on people's limited appreciation of the practices defining democracy. Now that all citizens had been denied their rights to vote, to assemble, to hold elections, to convene Congress, to hold public office, and to unionize, to name a few, Chilean people surprised themselves by suddenly placing a vigorous premium on the most formal and ritualistic aspects of democracy. The so-called bourgeois democracy, which in the revolutionary discourse of the 1960s had been shredded to pieces, now encapsulated a deep yearning for all those basic individual rights that had been denied, namely, the freedom of speech and association and the right to a fair trial in a court independent from state power. Members of the Left who at first stepped forward with a vindication of the term "democracy" in their public discourse were called *los renovados* (the Renewed Left)[10]; their activism, which energized social movements, left a strong imprint on political practices. These militants' understanding of democracy led to the forging of transparent political practices whose vital traces, though obscured by the weight of politics-as-usual that returned after 1990, are salient in today's struggles, more specifically, in the impressive street demonstrations that regularly make the news. Nowadays, the memory of these underground practices is alive in the strategies and tactics employed by the current student movement, as well as others. Addressing the Arab Spring and the value of performance, Judith Butler observes that when bodies assembly in the streets they are exercising "one of the most basic presumptions of democracy, namely that political and public institutions are bound to represent the people [. . .] those bodies enact a message, performatively, [. . .] they are refusing to become disposable" (196–97). In the case of Chile, it is precisely the memory of the social movements exercising democracy and representing the people that allowed the resistance movement against the dictatorship to organize, struggle, and finally prevail.

While it would be easy to dismiss the idea that genuine democratic practices can take place when democracy has been co-opted, and is therefore no longer operational, the Chilean process suggests otherwise. What happened to the individuals involved in underground politics of the 1980s in Chile can be best described by what William Connolly sees as the process of identification with the state, a process by which "one's self-identification as a free individual is bound up with a common belief in the capacity of the state to promote publicly defined purposes" (198). The Chilean people believed in the state and its capacity to recover itself from the corrupted military and the far-right masterminds that had held it captive. Several years prior to the 1987 plebiscite, which signaled the political defeat of the dictatorship, the social movements—in particular the women's movement—enacted democratizing practices that captured the political drive of and erased the fear in the vast majority of Chileans. Fear slowly eroded as the number of grassroots organizations, NGOs, and activists increased; this momentum continued until a democratic project took shape through the collaboration and dialogue of major political parties. The enactment of democratic practices that took place within social movements forced politicians to articulate a more flexible and inclusive political vision, which in itself became empowering. In doing so, these actors fully permeated the public sphere, altered traditional political tactics, and changed the overall understanding of democracy. According to Jane Jacquette:

> Because the mobilization of women and the growth of feminist awareness took place during this extraordinary political period of transition to democracy, women's agendas and strategies are different from what they would have been had they developed in an environment of democratic continuity. Women's groups were formed in a political climate that rewarded cooperation, mobilization, and direct negotiations between women and the state. As a result, Latin American feminist analyses of politics differ from those of other regions. South American feminism reflects transitions politics: it is closely linked to human rights, defines its goals in moral and political terms, and is anti-authoritarian. (205)

Women and other new political actors—students, gays and lesbians, for instance—understood democracy within an antiauthoritarian framework, and they were instrumental in crafting the delicate articulations of those alternative voices that comprised the fabric of Chilean public discourse.

Twenty years later, Concertación is still relevant, but its luster has worn out as a result of the difficult task of governing what is still today an underdeveloped country starkly divided by a wide income gap between the poorest and the wealthiest of its citizens.[11] Severe limits imposed by the constitution Pinochet put in place, in addition to difficult political negotiations that contributed to ending Pinochet's regime, also hindered governing with clarity and transparency. This maneuvering, in turn, tired Chilean citizens and made the government appear weak when confronting the political opposition. By the end of President Bachelet's first term, a strong student movement protesting the poor quality of education—a legacy of the dictatorship—overtook the streets of Santiago for months, gaining support from parents and a large part of the population that demanded structural changes that the government had no resources to enact. Concertación was unable to survive a new election—although the president herself had an approval rating of almost 80 percent when she left office in 2010—and thus the conservative businessman Sebastián Piñera was elected president.

There is no doubt as to how much women's commitment to justice has shaped the public discourse on human rights. Spouses, mothers, daughters, and sisters of the mostly male victims of state terror were the first to bring attention to the illegal detentions, the false accusations, and the disappearance of persons. Also, family members assumed that women could approach more safely police departments and military sites without risking their lives. This perception may not have been completely accurate, but in the end it proved effective and empowering. Reflecting on their untiring drive to find out and publicly expose what had happened to their relatives, one of the mothers of the detained-disappeared said in an interview, "the mistake they [the military] made was to leave us [the women] alive."[12]

Less known than the more recognizable Madres of Plaza de Mayo Association of Argentina, the Association of Relatives of the Disappeared Detainees in Chile comprised mostly, but not exclusively, of women. As vocal leaders, they were the first who took to the streets of Santiago to demand an answer to the atrocities and the crimes of the dictatorship. Much as the Greek chorus, these women appealed to the national consciousness and their valiant defiance became the standard by which the opposition had to measure itself if it wanted to win over the public's trust. They may not have brought about the end of the Pinochet regime by themselves, but their dignity became the face of the opposition while their human rights claims mobilized millions to change the state of affairs in the country. By 1990, their demand, "Where are they (the *desaparecidos*)?" became the call of the majority of Chileans. President Patricio Aylwin acknowledged the relatives in front of the cameras at the National Stadium, during the welcoming ceremony on the first day of democracy. Signifying their loss and their demand for justice, some of these women danced alone the traditional *cueca*[13] in the middle of the National Stadium that day, while people read the names of the 3,200 disappeared displayed on a giant marquee. From their homes, the mesmerized citizens watched the ceremony unfold on TV. Then, the compelling *Nunca Más*

(Never Again) slogan appeared after the last name. One year thereafter, President Aylwin appointed the Commission for Truth and Reconciliation to investigate thousands of cases of human rights violations. A report containing details of 2,115 individuals who were disappeared was released. Thousands of other cases were investigated, and only those that could be legally substantiated in court made it to the final report. For almost two decades the Vicariate of Solidarity run by the Catholic Church had kept thousands of files and legal documents pertaining to individual cases of human rights abuses. The country as a whole was shocked by that official first report, and the families were able to see their truth—this time disclosed as a reality of national proportions—in the news for the first time. Then the whole nation heard President Aylwin pronounce: "Therefore, in my role as President of the Republic, and assuming the representation of the entire nation, I dare ask the victims' families for forgiveness."[14]

Twenty years later, in 2010, President Michelle Bachelet responded to that historical trajectory of the country and created the Museum of Memory and Human Rights. It would be perhaps appropriate to suggest that by the time the museum was actually built and made part of the National Registry of Libraries, Archives, and Museums (DIBAM), Chileans had modified their collective memory by assuming the unavoidable task of recognizing a collective responsibility for the truth of what had happened in the country. Interestingly, Connolly suggests that in addition to sharing a territory, people who identify themselves as citizens of a given country share not only proclivities but also repugnancies: "In sharing a culture, a set of institutionalized rules, and a language, we share, albeit, variably and imperfectly, a set of preliminary understandings, proclivities, and repugnancies that infiltrate the structure of perception, judgment, and decision" (199).

The museum's mission clearly evidenced the change in perceptions that had taken place in the country. As the museum's website explains, the purpose of this institution is "to draw attention to human rights violations committed by the Chilean state between 1973 and 1990. Its mission is to elicit dignity for the victims and their families, stimulate reflection and debate and to promote respect and tolerance in order that these events never happen again."[15] Because it was constructed thirty years after most of the crimes were committed, and because many cases had been brought to justice, the creation of the museum infused a sense of compassion into the public sphere and generated an overall claim for justice. The same way that Susan Sontag sees war photography as compelling people to care for the suffering of others, a museum of this nature has contributed nonverbal manifestations of a public discourse that cares for the pain of others, thus disturbing the general narratives of individual success.[16]

As is the case with the current democratically elected presidents of Brazil, Argentina, and Uruguay, Michelle Bachelet was a victim of a military dictatorship. In her case, she endured prison, torture, and exile, as well as the death of her father, a Chilean Air Force general. This historical weight leads us to read Michelle Bachelet's body as the embodiment of a paradoxical moment in Chile's democratic narrative at which state and victim are both one and the same. The presidential signature that sealed the decree creating the Museum of Memory and Human Rights as an act of reparation fulfilled one of the measures recommended two decades earlier by the Rettig Commission, which was established by President Aylwin in 1990 to investigate the cases of the disappeared between 1963 and 1990. When it made public its first reports in February 1991, the Commission presented the documented cases of 2,279 persons killed for political reasons by the military regime. [17]

Those who had been carrying the weight of memory and the pain of the loss of their loved ones for many years now had the right to have a say in the museum's mission. There were no more legitimate voices to represent the memory of Pinochet's victims than those of the people—mostly women—who had spent their lives keeping alive the memory of their family members, and who, time and again, made public the atrocities that were committed in the name of the state. For this reason, from the very inception of the museum, they were represented on the board of the foundation that the government had created to enforce the reparation measures. The nation as a whole, or at least the majority of its citizens, needed to understand and accept that the call to memory—that *Never Again*—and the defense of human rights were not only the responsibility of the mothers, wives, and daughters of the victims, but of all Chileans. It has been, therefore, the country's responsibility to ensure that human rights are respected. A female president in Chile was, and is now, only possible because of the strong history of the women's movement and the substantial cultural changes that feminism imprinted on the country's imaginary after decades of underground—and then public—work organizing and building political momentum.

Thus, what seems to be the most evident link between Michelle Bachelet and the Museum of Memory and Human Rights—namely her past as a victim of Pinochet's regime—may be less significant for Chilean democracy than the current social movements, which have challenged an exclusionary, inflexible, and rigid narrative unable to respond to the needs and the changing identities of its citizens. The majority that supported Michelle Bachelet for two terms in office is proud of her background as a political prisoner. In fact, many of her supporters share a similar history. Today, when one hears scorching debates about abortion laws on the radio—and women know they may not yet have enough votes to pass reproductive rights laws in a mostly Catholic country—the echoes of the 1980s' feminist slogan *Democracia en el país y en la casa* (Democracy in the country and at home) still resonate true. Those echoes most certainly resonate among those that are now in the streets posting *2014 El Machismo Mata* (2014 Chauvinism Kills) campaign posters; they know that much work remains to strengthen democracy in Chile. Interestingly, at the present time, the recent election of a female president is less momentous than the existence of a critical mass of the electorate avid to participate, ready to voice its demands, and eager to hold accountable the actual implementation of its representatives' agendas. Indeed, her election seems less relevant than the sustained student movement led by many who saw Bachelet elected when they were ten or twelve years old.[18] In fact, the president made the student-led organized demands for educational reform an important part of her electoral campaign. Her government had to contend with a strong student movement that generated strikes and paralyzed schools in 2006 and 2008.

Without a doubt, the process by which Chile will be able to envision itself as a thriving democratic community is rooted in the day-to-day work that the ritual of electing presidents requires. In addition, democratic practices are reinforced when citizens challenge their government to act on its democratic values and to fight for the welfare of its weakest. Perhaps Bachelet's present urgency to deal with an empowered social movement during her second term in office will produce enough social energy to disrupt the existing state of affairs and make room for further transformations in the democratic system. After all, both the will to prosecute those involved in crimes against humanity and the will to secure basic living conditions for Chilean citizens stem from the basic pursuit of justice. The ghosts of Chile's past will inevitably bring back the unfulfilled dreams of those who sacrificed their lives in the struggle for justice.[19] People understand that the work of social justice has not yet completely begun in Chile, and justice for the victims of human rights abuses is, at the moment, only partial. Hard work and agreement are necessary for the Chilean social imaginary to broaden and for an inclusive democracy to prosper. If memory is crucial to developing democracy, as historian Peter Winn emphasized in a radio interview in Santiago, citizens need to vividly remember the ideals that informed the democratic struggles of the past: the quest for a more just society and for a democracy that would offer opportunities to the underprivileged.[20] Driven by the pain of the cruel injustice of the victims' deaths, this form of remembering honors their unfulfilled dreams for a democratic Chile to come. Thus, a refashioned culture would have a chance to become stronger by sharing a common repugnancy to abuses and exclusions of all kinds and by sharing in the ideals of social justice of the past. In the case of Chile, expanding the country's understanding of democracy will take time; this process will require a different performance of politics by its citizens. The student movement, which once again in 2014 has actively mobilized to contest the educational reforms of Bachelet's government, is proof of the significant changes that citizens' activism can enact in a country. It's not only the victims of human rights abuses in the past who are deserving of compassionate politics; it is the millions of poor and disenfranchised from Chile's economic success and progress.

Finally, Tzvetan Todorov has suggested that although the road to punitive justice will take a long time and will be delayed by obstacles, justice is indeed necessary to bring about a democratic society in Chile—one that will achieve stability, move forward, and avoid returning to violence and terror. What Todorov calls "restorative justice" is imperative in the Chilean context: "Its purpose is not to protect an impersonal order, but to enable former perpetrators and former victims to live side by side. It seeks not to punish but to restore relations that should never have been interrupted" (66). In this new scenario, a stronger public presence of women and other actors has introduced more transparent ways of doing politics, which in turn, have challenged the hegemonic discourse. Remembering the long struggle that paved the way for these achievements will certainly define the relationship between the Chilean state and its citizens in the future.

## NOTES

1. "Vengo de Chile, un país que ha aprendido de su historia. Los chilenos vivimos días difíciles. Esta asamblea lo sabe. El aprendizaje fue duro pero fecundo. Del dolor nació una esperanza. Los grandes disensos dieron paso a grandes consensos. Vengo de un país donde hoy impera el Estado de Derecho, donde los derechos de las personas son respetados y promovidos. [. . .] Chile, *sin temor de mirar al pasado*, construye su futuro" (Bachelet 345). Unless otherwise noted, all translations are mine.

2. The three victims were members of the Communist Party: José Manuel Parada, a sociologist and staff member of the Catholic Church's Vicariate of Solidarity; Manuel Guerrero, a teacher and union representative of the National Teacher's Federation (AGECH); and Santiago Nattino, a painter and member of their underground bureau. The memorial is called Las Sillas (The Chairs); it features three monumental chairs erected at the site where the bodies of Parada, Guerrero, and Nattino were found in Quilicura, a rural community near Santiago.

3. "Ese horror era una realidad. [. . .] El país del odio, 'la nación de enemigos' como decía un autor, ha quedado atrás. Hoy nuestros hijos conviven en paz. Pero no en cualquier paz, y eso es quizás lo más importante que podamos señalar de este momento, es que es una paz fundada no en el olvido, no fundada en colocar debajo de la alfombra aquello que no nos orgullece como sociedad, sino que fundada en la memoria de los nuestros, en la memoria del dolor, en la memoria de la esperanza que nunca se perdió. [. . .] Soy una convencida de que sobre la base de la memoria estamos construyendo los pilares para un país mucho mejor" (Bachelet 550).

4. In fact, most studies have described the Chilean transition to democracy as one based on a pact of silence that was part of the negotiations that ended the dictatorship. When the first three democratically elected presidents (Aylwin, Frei, and Lagos) appointed commissions to investigate "the truth," the official policy was silence and oblivion. Activists and families resisted this, even after they had received financial reparation benefits. Analyses of this situation can be found in several books. Most relevant is Steve Stern's trilogy, of which *Reckoning with Pinochet: The Memory Question in Democratic Chile, 1989–2006* (2010) is the last book.

5. The current Chilean Constitution (which is still a source of debate since it was ratified during Pinochet's time and includes several measures to prevent transparent elections, such as the binominal system) doesn't allow for consecutive presidential terms. Therefore, Bachelet—the only president to be re-elected—did so after a hiatus of four years during which the political right was able to elect the conservative Sebastián Piñera as president. Piñera made an official visit to the Museum of Memory and Human Rights on April 20, 2012, and made positive

comments to the press. His visit encouraged many more public schools to include visits to the museum as part of their curricular activities. See "Piñera visita el Museo de la Memoria y habla de la importancia de 'recordar.'"

6. I am using the term New Left not as the name of a specific political party affiliation but as a phenomenon that was characterized by several iterations of political tendencies that operated within the framework of the various political parties situated to the Left in the political spectrum and mostly within the parameters of the Chilean Socialist Party. The New Left was often referred to as *la izquierda renovada* (the renewed left) or *los renovados* (the renewed ones). Many of these politicians—Jorge Arrate, Oscar Guillermo Garretón, María Antonieta Saa, Enrique Correa, and Carlos Montes, for example—were instrumental in the creation of the coalitions that culminated in the victorious Concertación por la Democracia that ended the military rule in 1990. These political actors contributed significantly by introducing the themes of civil liberties, feminism, social movements, and participatory democracy in the discourse of the Left in Chile.

7. Katherine Hite analyzes this phenomenon in *When the Romance Ended. Leaders of the Chilean Left, 1968–1998.*

8. The Chilean women's movement of the 1980s was greatly influenced by its feminist leaders, as well as feminist movements in other Latin American countries. To a great extent, the women's movement was and still is today characterized by its staunch defense of human rights. See Silva. Furthermore, the relationship between feminists and the political parties in the Left has been close, difficult, and somewhat controversial. See Kirkwood.

9. Tomás Moulian has published several studies of the Chilean Socialist party. Most pertinent here would be *Contradicciones del desarrollo político chileno, 1920 – 1990.* For further discussion on the issue, see Hardy.

10. This political phenomenon is very similar to what was called the New Left in the United Kingdom and United States in the 1970s and 1980s.

11. The income gap has widened in the last decade, despite the increase in the middle-class and its opportunities. As reported by the Paris-based Organization for Economic Cooperation and Development on its Web page, "Chile also has the highest level of income inequality and the 4th highest level of relative poverty in the OECD area."

12. See *In Women's Hands*, the documentary by Rachel Field and Juan Mandelbaum.

13. The *cueca*, the traditional Spanish-Chilean colonial dance with a vibrant melody and quick steps, is officially recognized as the national dance of Chile. Women of the Relatives of Disappeared Detainees Association formed a musical group, and they often performed it as a somber 'solo' evoking the absence of a dance partner. It became widely known as *la cueca sola* (the lonely cueca). Inspired by this, the British musician Sting composed the song *They Dance Alone*, first performed in 1988 at an Amnesty International Concert in Buenos Aires. In a concert in Santiago in October 1990, Sting performed it as the women carried the pictures of their love ones.

14. "Por eso es que yo me atrevo, en mi calidad de Presidente de la República, asumir la representación de la nación entera para, en su nombre, pedir perdón a los familiares de las víctimas" (Aylwin Azócar 132). For information on Pinochet's response to the findings of the Commission for Truth and Reconciliation created by President Aylwin, see Long.

15. "About the Museum."

16. In *Regarding the Pain of Others*, Sontag discusses the notion of photography as facilitator of compassion in the public discourse of the twentieth century.

17. The work of the Rettig Commission (officially known as the Commission for Truth and Reconciliation) has had a profound impact on the public sphere by producing and making available the documentation that has empowered families to press charges and initiate legal proceedings for the first time. Close to a hundred perpetrators have been jailed, including some prominent members of the Pinochet regime, for example General Manuel Contreras, chief of the secret police (CNI). In 2004, the Valech Commission investigated other human rights abuses including torture.

18. The current leaders of the student movement saw Bachelet elected when they were 10–12 years old. Today, the presidents of all the student organizations in the major universities

(FECH and FEUC) and in the secondary schools (FESES), as well as the presidents of the National Federation of Workers (CUT) and of the Senate, are all women.
  19.   Jacques Derrida elaborates on the deconstructive figure of the ghost in *Specters of Marx*.
  20.   Winn has stated in a recent interview that the official policy of the Chilean government has been one of providing some financial reparations to the families of the victims, only to then "turn the page." This tendency, Winn observes, is not conducive to a democratic society: "It's impossible to build a solid democracy while maintaining all those silences at its base." ("Es imposible construir una democracia sólida manteniendo todos esos silencios en la base.")

## WORKS CITED

"About the Museum." Museo de la Memoria y los Derechos Humanos. Santiago, Chile. Web. 17 June 2014.

Aylwin Azócar, Patricio. *La Transición chilena. Discursos escogidos marzo 1990–1992.* Santiago: Andrés Bello, 1992.

Bachelet, Michelle. *Presidenta Michelle Bachelet: Discursos escogidos 2006. Contigo mejor país.* Santiago, Chile: Secretaría de Comunicaciones, Palacio de la Moneda, 2007.

Butler, Judith. *Precarious Life. The Powers of Mourning and Violence.* London: Verso, 2004.

Butler, Judith, and Athena Athanasiou. *Dispossession: The Performative of the Political.* Cambridge: Polity, 2013.

Connolly, William E. *Identity/Difference. Democratic Negotiations of Political Paradox.* Ithaca: Cornell University Press, 1991.

Derrida, Jacques. *Specters of Marx: The State of the Debt, the Work of Mourning, and the New International.* Trans. Peggy Kamuf. New York: Routledge, 1994.

Hardy, Clarisa, et al. *Reflexiones socialistas sobre Chile.* Santiago: Ediciones La liebre ilustrada, 1996.

Hite, Katherine. *When the Romance Ended. Leaders of the Chilean Left, 1968–1998.* New York: Columbia University Press, 2000.

*Informe Rettig.* Informe de la comisión nacional de verdad y reconciliación. Programa de Derechos Humanos. Ministerio del Interior y Seguridad Pública. Web. 28 Oct. 2014.

*In Women's Hands.* Dir. Rachel Field and Juan Mandelbaum. PBS, 1992. DVD.

Jaquette, Jane. *The Women's Movements in Latin America: Feminism and the Transition to Democracy.* Boulder: Westview Press, 1991.

Kirkwood, Julieta. *Ser Política en Chile: Las feministas y los partidos.* Santiago: FLACSO, 1986.

Long, William R. "Former Dictator Expected to Dispute Rights Report: Chile: Pinochet is preparing a response to finding that 2,115 victims died or disappeared during his ruling." *Los Angeles Times* 26 Mar. 1991. Web. 29 July 2014.

Moulian, Tomás. *Contradicciones del desarrollo político chileno, 1920–1990.* Santiago: LOM-ARCIS, 2009.

Museo de la Memoria y los Derechos Humanos. Web. 6 June 2014.

Organization for Economic Cooperation and Development. "Society at a Glance 2014 Highlights: Chile OECD Social Indicators." Web. 30 July 2014.

"Piñera visita el Museo de la Memoria y habla de la importancia de 'recordar.'" 20 de Abril 2012, 17:18. Web. 29 July 2014. http://www.emol.com.

Quevedo, Vicky. *Una agenda política de la sociedad civil.* Santiago: Cuarto Propio, 2003.

Silva, María de la Luz. *La participación política de la mujer en Chile: Las organizaciones de mujeres.* Buenos Aires: Fundación Friedrich Neuman, 1987.

Sontag, Susan. *Regarding the Pain of Others.* New York: Picador, 2003.

Stern, Steven. *Reckoning with Pinochet: The Memory Question in Democratic Chile, 1989–2006.* Durham, NC: Duke University Press, 2010.

Sting. "They Dance Alone (*Cueca sola*)." YouTube. Web. 17 June 2014.

Tzvetan, Todorov. *Hope and Memory. Lessons from the Twentieth Century.* Princeton, NJ: Princeton University Press, 2003.

————. *Memory as a Remedy for Evil*. London: Seagull, 2010.
Winn, Peter. "Académico destacó la importancia de la memoria histórica en la democracia."
     Cooperativa, Santiago. 7 Aug. 2014. Web. 17 Sept. 2014.

*Chapter Two*

# Memory in Chile:
# A Conversation on Democracy

*Interview with Ricardo Brodsky Baudet, Executive
Director of the Museum of Memory and Human Rights
in Chile (December 3, 2013)*

## Oscar D. Sarmiento and Liliana Trevizán

The Museum of Memory and Human Rights is housed in an impressive modern building that is located in a most accessible and traditional neighborhood of Santiago, Chile. The museum is currently a thriving place, where its numerous visitors and students can watch films and attend academic seminars and theatrical and musical performances. Most important, the museum serves as the site of a permanent exhibition that portrays the truth of the human rights violations that took place in Chile during the military dictatorship of Augusto Pinochet (1973–1990). According to its own mission statement, the creation of the museum responded to the need to have a space to recover the memory of the victims as well as the actions undertaken to protect and defend human rights in Chile between September 11, 1973, and March 11, 1990.[1] President Michelle Bachelet inaugurated the museum on January 11, 2010, two months before the end of her first term in office. The timing of the inauguration underscores the symbolic legacy of the museum, not only as an accomplishment of the president herself but as an action that brought legitimacy to the legacy represented by four presidential terms for Concertación por la Democracia (Coalition for Democracy), the political coalition that transitioned Chile back to civilian rule.[2]

Ricardo Brodsky, executive director since May of 2011, has led the museum on its current path as a solid institution and the public voice on human rights and memory in the country and abroad. [3] Presently the museum is also an educational space with the capacity to shape a high-level discourse on ethical issues that tests the strength of Chilean democracy. In a lecture during the commemoration of the fortieth anniversary of the coup d'état of 1973, Alain Touraine stated, "human rights are fundamental (only) if we understand them as radical; radical in the sense that they are pillars of democracy. [This is] democracy understood (then) as an agreement in which all actors have a commitment to behave responsibly and to be responsible as actors; (thus, at the end of the day, we think) that all actors are always more important than their ideas or goals."[4] There is no doubt that the museum contributes significantly to promote this kind of perspective in Chile and, though it may seem contradictory, it is clearly evident that the political scenario set up by a conservative government has not been an obstacle to Brodsky's work. Along with a solid group of professionals—including a person of the stature of Maria Luisa Ortiz,[5] who oversees the museum's collections—Brodsky leads an institution crucial to the development of Chilean democracy. Reflecting on the impact of the museum's creation, Katherine Hite has said that the museum struck a chord in the Chilean public's imagination, establishing the possibility for memory dialogues that had been rather limited prior to its creation (361). Through sustained efforts, the museum has institutionalized itself in a few years and, more importantly, it is currently in the process of becoming a beacon for the defense of human rights in the Latin America of the twenty-first century. In the transcript of this interview, the interviewers, Oscar Sarmiento and Liliana Trevizán, are abbreviated OS and LT, respectively. The interviewee, Ricardo Brodsky Baudet, is abbreviated RB.

LT&OS: In 2014 the museum commemorates four years of existence since its inauguration on January 10, 2010. What are the most important moments that have contributed to establish its reputation as a sound institution?

RB: I can think of several important moments in these four years. First, we need to mention the museum's inauguration, which was attended by the last four presidents of Chile. This event attained an important state-like connotation. Second, a series of significant art exhibit openings broadened the museum's audience and placed it well within Chile's cultural landscape. For instance, along with the University of Berkeley, we exhibited Fernando Botero's paintings on torture at Abu Ghraib. This exhibit, which represented a tremendous challenge for us, is valued in the millions of dollars.[6] We next exhibited works by Chilean artist Gonzalo Díaz, who brought back to Chile his *Lonquén* show, which had been at the Reina Sofía museum in Spain. These were truly relevant exhibits that positioned the museum as an authoritative space within the museum world. Third, we need to mention the visits by Tzvetan Todorov on November 7, 2012, and by Alain Touraine on September 6–7, 2013. The presence of the two scholars placed the museum in a global perspective of reflection. The international significance of their visit was surprising to the Chilean community. Fourth, we must mention a moment that was perceived by the public as a crisis: the debate between the museum and the most conservative sectors of the political right, which was represented by Magdalena Krebs, the director of Dibam (National Center of Libraries and Museums), and historians such as Sergio Villalobos.[7] People took sides and either defended or attacked the museum. In turn, this triggered a sort of identification with the museum among political and social communities. And the fifth decisive moment was the commemoration of the fortieth anniversary of the coup d'état of 1973, in which the television was involved, plays were staged, and debates took place. The museum became the very location where the press and the people would come to ask for information. We had more than twenty itinerant exhibits traveling through Chile.

LT&OS: At the opening ceremonies, President Bachelet described "the Museum as a place where Chilean society meets and comes together again. It is a place where society confronts its own history, where we are trying to draw moral lessons from a difficult period, lessons which should, in turn, reinforce the foundations of a life in freedom."[8] To what extent has it been possible to translate that description into the actual reality of the museum and its operation?

RB: The victims of human rights violations were the result of the Chilean state's intervention. The museum, in performing an act of reparation at the symbolic and moral levels, elicits the possibility of the reconnection between the state and the victims. Now the state performs acts of recognition and solidarity with them. Thus, a reconnection is made possible. The museum also fulfills an important role educating the youth that did not go through the experience. The topic is hard to discuss in schools: teachers do not get to teach this segment of Chilean history and they avoid it so as not to engage the conflict. The museum forces people to look at this past and thus it becomes a pedagogical resource for Chilean formal education. In this sense, its role brings to mind the expression: "To face the future, one needs to confront the past."

LT&OS: The institutional framework of any museum is didactic and pedagogical in its strictest sense; the Museum of Memory and Human Rights is not the exception. However, a museum of this nature has to grapple with a unique ontological conundrum: If the teachings that stem from it are of an ethical, instead of an aesthetical, historical or natural order, how does the museum promote the ethics of the slogan "Never Again," without becoming dogmatic and ruling out dissidence?

RB: The answer is two-fold. On the one hand, the discourse of the museum seeks to elicit the visitors' empathy with the experience of the victims. This is the starting point, to elicit empathy through the museological resources that appeal to the sensibility of the spectator and to combine both emotional as well as rational elements residing essentially in the archival work. In this way, the history of this period gets constructed. Ours is, then, not simply a goal but a sustained effort at approaching the victims. It is a shared memory. From this interplay of historical moments the audience starts drawing an ethical lesson. How could something like this happen in our country? How did we come to this? Leaving the question open, the museum does not provide visitors with an answer but lets them draw their own conclusions. Now we also use, in particular with the youth, a number of criteria used in Germany. For example, we do not overwhelm the audience with a tragic and violent story; instead, we mix hard moments with other more removed moments. We do not seek to present a frontal proposal. A guide introduces conversations so that the youth construct their own versions based on those conversations. We try to avoid a sort of obscenity of violence that could turn seductive for the youth. We are not interested in promoting either a sadistic or a voyeuristic encounter with the past. We try our best to avoid this so that the exercise is useful, and people draw as a conclusion that this cannot be repeated, that one must take care of the respect for the other and for democracy. In this sense, our discourse is located more at an ethical than at a political level.

LT&OS: How did the museum conceive its participation in the "Cátedra de la Memoria y los Derechos Humanos" ("Symposium on Memory and Human Rights") it instituted in November of 2012 and that elevated the debate to a high level of reflection? Internationally recognized intellectuals who are rigorously informed on the topic—such as Tzvetan Todorov, Alain Touraine, Steve Stern, and Katherine Hite—participated in this event.

RB: The symposium emerged from the very beginning at the initiative of the museum, which in its capacity as the organizing institution extended an invitation to a number of scholars. It is important to identify another important actor of reflection who not only brought prestige to the symposium but also contributed to the funding of the event: the Universidad Diego Portales. Our connection to Georgetown University helped us bring American presenters to the event. All participants came as a result of the museum's call. The museum, then, has become a space where discourse is produced; it is where we do our best to place ideas on Chile's public agenda and create opportunities for reflection for the youth, college students, and people who feel motivated by the world of ideas. We then publish these lectures and disseminate them. It is an intellectual task whose aim is to add a number of concepts to the Chilean debate.

LT&OS: During his participation at the "Symposium on Memory" of September 2013, in the session "Politics of Memory at Forty Years of the Coup d'état" at the Universidad Diego Portales, historian Steve Stern stressed the importance of "memory" over the "human rights" component in determining the role of the museum. To what extent, and how, does the museum see itself in the context of such a debate?

RB: Stern's scholarly work focuses on the construction of the political subject in relation to memory. The struggle he sees between antagonistic memories does not have human rights at its core. This is not the memory we are interested in. We want to foster human dignity and the lessons one must draw from a traumatic experience and, concerning this, human rights are at its core. Our role is not to uphold the memory of the Chilean Left before the coup or the political ideas of the victims. This is rather what sites of memory such as Villa Grimaldi, academic institutes or political parties do, but not the museum.

LT&OS: Many specific cases of human rights violations became known and were constantly present due to the national significance of the individual in question or the international repercussion of the case; however, the majority of victims did not achieve the same sort of relevance in the sites of memory. Can one say, without any doubt that the museum, as an institution that understands itself as diverse and inclusive, has made sure to make room for the memories of all sectors or all victims equally, and that differences of class, race, sexual orientation, and ethnicity among all victims are equally respected?

RB: We work with a specific concept of victim: these are individuals included in the Rettig and Valech reports.[9] One finds in these reports information about all of them: poor, wealthy, tall, short, professionals, peasants, homosexuals, civilians, and also police officers. We have the obligation to treat all victims equally. That said we always receive demands from groups to give more importance to their specific grievances; for instance, women, indigenous peoples, community leaders, and students. We try our best to respond to these demands through specific exhibitions when we have enough information. Now we are working on an itinerant exhibition, which will take place next year, focusing on victims of the dictatorship from indigenous communities. We need to do more research and conduct more interviews. We must construct a narrative that is not haphazard but real. We patronize a considerable number of itinerant exhibitions, and from these we gain important information that we add to our permanent collections. In the permanent exhibition all victims are represented equally, and in the temporary ones we concentrate on more specific groups. Through the Oral Archive, we also broaden both the cases and the coverage of situations that affected less prominent individuals in rural areas and in different regions of the country. And so far we have been successful. People who could have felt excluded did not criticize us. There was a comment by an artist that accused us of being homophobic. But none of the gay organizations in the country—with which we jointly organize events—have backed up what we consider unfair criticism.[10]

Initially, the organizations of relatives of the detained–disappeared questioned the creation of the museum because they felt that an unknown entity, led by a board of directors that did not sufficiently represent them, was appropriating their memory. They thought that the museum should represent their memory. This occurred at the beginning when the museum was created, but that tension began to disappear shortly after. Nevertheless, there are still criticisms: The Agrupación de Familiares de Detenidos Desaparecidos (Association of Relatives of the Disappeared Detainees) does not support the inclusion in the permanent exhibition of the armed attack to Augusto Pinochet that shows his murdered escorts.[11] Due to their disagreement with the Rettig Report—which makes no distinction among victims of political violence resulting from actions undertaken either by state agents or by political actors in the opposition—they do not see these escorts as victims. But the Association is not arguing with the museum; this disagreement only means that each organization is doing what it is supposed to do. In fact, the Association values our broad audience. The museum has two hundred thousand visitors per year. And the Association also values the inclusion in our work of sessions and educational activities of, among other institutions, the PDI, Policía de Investigaciones (Chilean Bureau of Investigation) and the Escuela de Carabineros (Police Officers Academy).

LT&OS: To what extent is the museum linked to the museological world in Chile and abroad? Do you think the museum has contributed something in this regard?

RB: In Chile, in terms of a museological perspective, ours is probably the most interesting museum. To begin with, it is the most modern museum. This is evidenced by its programmatic focus: it responds to the project of establishing a very clear and direct relation with current debates in Chilean society. For instance, we recently connected decisively with a very controversial issue in Chilean society: the fortieth anniversary of the coup d'état of 1973. Rooted in these debates, the programmatic focus of the museum allows people to discuss and adopt positions on controversial matters such as this one. Our museum has gained attention in other latitudes—particularly in Latin America. We have received official delegations from Peru, Colombia, Brazil, Argentina, and all of them have been extremely interested in replicating our experience in their respective countries. It is clear that at the present time each of these societies is embarking on memory-themed discussions. During their visits these delegations are not only interested in the content or in specific concepts—matters that are at the center of what I, as executive director, do at the museum—but they also request lectures and consultation on aspects pertaining to our more specific museological work. They have wanted to know, for instance, how we have shaped our collections and how one develops the educational project that we have. In this sense, we are having an impact on the training of professionals in the field. I have also been officially invited to Europe, to Bilbao, to Liverpool, to Paris, even to Taiwan, to explain the programmatic focus of the museum, how it was built, what were the founding principles behind its inception, and how we put together the collections and the archives. In fact, the museum has been achieving a more international presence and gaining prominence among sites of conscience around the world. The Museums Association in the United Kingdom holds each year a congress, and this year (2013) they decided to invite us to open the congress. So, representing the Museum of Memory and Human Rights, I presented at the inaugural session where more than eight hundred museum professionals were in attendance. Our concept of the museum appealed to Europeans, perhaps the English in particular, because this is a museum that significantly contributes to debates in society; it is a museum that has not been conceived to showcase a past already set in stone but, on the contrary, one that inserts itself well within the debates that permeate our society. Though these European museums, unlike ours, were not created as a result of a traumatic event, and even though they look at museological work from perspectives and cultural parameters that are not exactly as our own, they find what we do here salient and provocative. This new concept that we work with, of course, also takes place in other contemporary museums: the concept of a museum not separated from but inserted well within current conversations across society.

LT&OS: The introduction to your Spanish translation of Tzvetan Todorov's 2013 lecture "The Uses of Memory" ends with the following quote: "Giving moral lessons has never been a virtuous act. It is not possible to understand the evil others do if we refuse to ask whether we ourselves would be able to do such evil."[12] How does this apply to the work of the museum?

RB: The quote responds, first of all, to the goal of avoiding a unilateral reading. At the museum we work with young people by trying to elicit informed conversations so that youth develop a complex understanding of history, one in which the simplistic scenario of good versus evil no longer applies. Victims are not models of virtue, they are not saints, but that does not deprive them from their condition as victims. We do not present a Manichean view of history. We do our very best to show a complex view, and this we do, most of all, in our educational programs for students from middle and secondary schools that participate at all levels in our programs; we try to teach the need to see the complexity of the topic.[13] To understand this, one needs to be able to see both victims and victimizers as human beings in all their complexity; clearly, this is not easy to accomplish in societies emerging from traumatic events. Personally, I would be suspicious of those who pontificate on moral matters, particularly on controversial issues that are still vigorously debated in society. We cannot present unilateral nor simplified perspectives on multilayered issues. An institution such as ours makes sense and finds its reason for being in not presenting the world divided between good and evil. I personally take to heart Todorov's words in the quotation you are referring to. One way or another, I take this quotation to be a guide for the work we all do here at the museum. We cannot weigh the issues and pontificate while refraining from keeping a vigilant eye on our own work.

## NOTES

1.   The museum's *Strategic Definitions* conveys its mission statement: "To shed light on the systematic violation of human rights by the Chilean State in the period 1973–1990, so that as a result of the ethical reflection on memory, solidarity and human rights, the nation's resolve shall be strengthened and Never Again will similar events take place." ("Dar a conocer las violaciones sistemáticas de los derechos humanos por parte del Estado de Chile entre los años 1973–1990, para que a través de la reflexión ética sobre la memoria, la solidaridad y la importancia de los derechos humanos, se fortalezca la voluntad nacional para que Nunca Más se repitan hechos que afecten la dignidad del ser humano" [*Definiciones Estratégicas*]). Unless otherwise noted, all translations are by Oscar D. Sarmiento and Liliana Trevizán.

2.   The Center-Left Political Coalition successfully ruled the country since the transition period that ended the dictatorship in 1990. Four presidents were elected under the Coalition: Patricio Aylwin, P. (DC), Eduardo Frei, E. (DC), Ricardo Lagos, R. (PS), and Michelle Bachelet (PS). However, in 2010 the Coalition lost the presidential election to the conservative candidate Sebastián Piñera (2010–2014). In 2014 Michelle Bachelet was re-elected for a second term.

3.   Ricardo Brodsky Baudet (Santiago, Chile, 1956) has been the executive director of the Museum of Memory and Human Rights since May 2011. He has a masters in literature from University of Chile. Brodsky has also served as head of the Program for Indigenous Policies of Corporation Proyectamérica (2010–2011); head of the Inter-ministerial Coordination Division of the Ministry General Secretariat of the Presidency of Chile (2007–2010); Ambassador of Chile to Belgium and Luxemburg (2000–2004); head of the Division of Social Organizations at the Ministry General Secretariat General of Government (1993–1997); and cabinet head for the president of Chamber of Senators (1990–1993).

4.   "Los DDHH son fundamentales (sólo) si es que se los entiende como radicales; radicales en el sentido de que son fundamento de la democracia. La democracia (que es de ese modo) entendida como un acuerdo en el que es responsabilidad de todos los actores el comportarse y ser responsables como actores, (entendiendo) que los actores son siempre más importantes que las ideas, o los objetivos."

5.   María Luisa Ortiz Rojas holds the positions of head of Collections and Research at the Museum of Memory and Human Rights and master archivist librarian. She has a Masters in Literature from the University of Chile. She is a member of the Association of Relatives of the Disappeared Detainees.

6.   See Roberta Smith's "Botero Restores Dignity of Prisoners at Abu Ghraib."

7.   See Claudia Urquieta's article "La histórica irritación de Magdalena Krebbs con el Museo de la Memoria."

8.   "[En] este Museo [es] donde se encuentra y se reencuentra la sociedad chilena. Donde la sociedad enfrenta su propia historia, donde se busca extraer las enseñanzas éticas de un período difícil, a partir de lo cual se trata de reforzar los cimientos de la vida en libertad" (1).

9.   The Patricio Aylwin administration (1990–1996) created the National Commission on Truth and Reconciliation, which presented its findings in the Rettig Report on February 8, 1991. Thereafter, the Ricardo Lagos administration (2000–2006) formed the National Commission of Political Prison and Torture, which presented the Valech Report on February 8, 2010.

10.   In May of 2013, for instance, the museum held a cultural event named "Social Dialogue on Human Rights, in remembrance of people who had died as a result of VIH/AIDS." The museum is also the venue of the B-Movie Festival, whose focus is on gay and lesbian cinema.

11.   The failed attack against the dictator took place on September 7, 1986, in the outskirts of Santiago, at Cajón del Maipo, while the general was returning from his house at El

Melocotón. The attack, which was perpetrated by the guerrilla organization Frente Patriótico Manuel Rodríguez (FPMR), resulted in eleven deaths, five wounded, Pinochet untouched, and the last strong repressive response by the military and the secret police that lasted at least a year. In the end, this action had an important political impact because it triggered unity among opposition leaders and precipitated several prior iterations of what finally became known as Concertación por la Democracia, a coalition that led a viable political exit to the sixteen years of dictatorship.

12. "Dar lecciones de moral nunca ha sido un gesto virtuoso. No es posible entender el mal que llevan a cabo los otros si nos negamos a preguntarnos si seríamos capaces de cometerlo nosotros también" (12).

13. The museum grants a certificate (diploma) on education of human rights, which has been tailored to high school teachers, and it has also established an annual award to the best thesis on the topic of memory written by a graduating senior from any Chilean university. The museum has also established the Annual Contest on Books and Arts. *Memorias eclipsadas*, poet Jorge Montealegre's book about the Chacabuco concentration camp, received the award in 2013. In addition, the museum offers competitive, unpaid internships at the graduate and undergraduate levels, and in the last three years more than eighty students from Chile and abroad have benefited from these opportunities

# WORKS CITED

Bachelet, Michelle. "Discurso de S.E. la Presidenta de la República, Michelle Bachelet, en inauguración del Museo de la Memoria y los Derechos Humanos." Museo de la Memoria y los Derechos Humanos. Santiago. 11 Jan. 2010. Inaugural Address.

Botero, Fernando. "'Abu Ghraib.'" Catalogue of March 16–June 2012 art exhibition. Museo de la Memoria y los Derechos Humanos. Web. 29 July 2014.

*Definiciones estratégicas*. Museo de la Memoria y los Derechos Humanos. Web. 29 July 2014.

Díaz, Gonzalo. *Lonquén*. Description of June 26-August 12, 2012 art exhibition. Museo de la Memoria y los Derechos Humanos. Web. 29 July 2014.

*Fundamentos. Comisiones de verdad*. Museo de la Memoria y los Derechos Humanos. Web. 29 July 2014.

Hite, Katherine, and Mark Ungar, eds. *Sustaining Human Rights in the Twentieth Century. Strategies from Latin America*. Baltimore: Johns Hopkins University Press, 2013.

Montealegre, Jorge. *Memorias eclipsadas. Duelo y resiliencia comunitaria en la prisión política*. Santiago: Asterión, 2013.

Smith, Roberta. "Botero Restores Dignity of Prisoners at Abu Ghraib." *New York Times* 15 Nov. 2006. Web. 30 July 2014.

Todorov, Tzvetan. "Los usos de la memoria." Cátedra de la memoria y los derechos humanos. 7 Nov. 2012. Lecture in French translated into Spanish. Five video segments. YouTube. Web. 28 July 2014.

———. *Los usos de la memoria*. Trans. Ricardo Brodsky. Santiago: Museo de la Memoria, 2013.

Touraine, Alain. "Chile, 40 años después." Cátedra de la memoria y los derechos humanos. Seminar. 5 Sept. 2013. Inaugural lecture. YouTube. Web. 29 July 2014.

Urquieta, Claudia. "La histórica irritación de Magdalena Krebbs con el Museo de la Memoria." elmostrador.país. 29 June 2012. Web. 29 July 2014.

*III*

# Literature as Media of Memory in Spain and Latin America

## Chapter Three

# Everything is Coming to Light

*Reappearance of Lost History in Carmen Martín Gaite's*
El cuarto de atrás[1]

## Marcella Salvi

In recent years, literary critics have been focusing on the ways in which the historical memory of the Spanish Civil War (1936–1939) and the subsequent forty years of dictatorship (1939–1975) has been represented in different fields and disciplines. As a response to this interest, in 2008, the *Journal of Spanish Cultural Studies* dedicated a volume titled *The Politics of Memory* to the topic of historical memory.[2] Founded on an interdisciplinary approach, this volume represents a significant contribution to the recent debates surrounding the issue of historical memory in contemporary Spain.[3] This impulse to recover the memory of those years responds to the need of certain sectors of contemporary Spain to break the *pacto de silencio* (silence pact) established during the years of the transition toward democracy. The political constituencies involved in the process of transition to democracy deliberately decided not to confront the violent past of those years by reaching a negotiated consensus that implied the dismissal of all the atrocities committed during the War and Postwar eras (Golob 127).[4] Many thought that this silence was vital for Spain to move forward into the future. As Stephanie Golob explains, "[k]eeping individual memory out of the public sphere and collective memory in the 'deep freeze' was widely viewed as the formula which produced the Spanish success story: reconciliation without truth, transition *without* transitional justice" (127).[5] Once Spain moved past the transition toward becoming a strong democracy, the issue of the suppressed past began to surface; the importance of recalling and confronting the past, therefore, has emerged as fundamental to achieving a true democracy.[6]

*El cuarto de atrás* (*The Back Room*, 1978), by the Spanish author Carmen
Martín Gaite (1925–2000), could be read through the lens of this interest in
historical memory in contemporary Spain. Although this novel was written
and published well before these recent debates, it portrays and anticipates the
necessity of twenty-first century Spain to finally acknowledge and recognize
the past that the transition to democracy tried to suppress.[7] Literary critics
generally are in agreement in considering *El cuarto de atrás* as a *libro de la
memoria* (a memoir). In fact, Shirley Mangini deems it one of the best
examples of this literary trend of the 1970s, when writers "began to 'revise'
their memories and tried to contextualize their impressions of the War and
Postwar" (33, translation is mine).[8] However, *El cuarto de atrás* goes beyond
the personal memory of the historical accounts of the years of the Spanish
Civil War and the subsequent repressive aftermath. As we will see, Martín
Gaite rewrites history from different perspectives, voicing all kinds of private
and collective emotions—loss, scarcity, and lack of freedom—associated
with those years. Private and collective memories, therefore, are intimately
connected in the recollection of her past. Her childhood perception of the
events alternates with her analysis of the past from a contemporary adult
perspective, which inserts the personal memory into a shared collective context.[9] In other words, the novel confirms the collective need for Spaniards of
all generations, past and present, to confront and process the silenced past.

In a 2006 seminal study on the depiction of the Civil War in some of the
Spanish novels written in Spain during the 1980s, Carmen Moreno-Nuño
stresses the importance of literature as a catalyst for the reappearance of lost
memory. Following the French historian Pierre Nora's theory on *lieux de
mémoire*, Moreno-Nuño defines the Spanish literature of the first years of
democracy as "a cultural space for the creation of a *lieu de mémoire* or space
of memory of the Civil War" (15, translation is mine).[10] In this context,
considering the role that literature, among other disciplines, has played in the
debates on recovering the silenced memory of the past, this chapter explores
how literature together with other mass cultural products—such as radio
songs, cinema, popular tales, and romantic novels—play a central role in *El
cuarto de atrás* as a means to recuperate and express Martín Gaite's own
memory of the period encompassing the Spanish Civil War to the end of
Francisco Franco's dictatorship. *El cuarto de atrás*, in fact, could also be
inserted in the representative group of novels written between Franco's death
and the beginning of the 1980s as an example of how historical memory can
be recalled and processed through literature. In *El cuarto de atrás*, literature
and mass cultural products become, in Pierre Nora's terms, *lieux de mémoire*
(places of memory), which help the author to articulate her private memory
in a collective context.[11] Through a metareferential discourse Martín Gaite
establishes a relationship between art and life, which allows her to reflect on

the nature and role of literature while questioning the dominant ideology of that particular historical moment.

The reader of *El cuarto de atrás* witnesses the creation of the novel, which is written while a conversation takes place between the narrator-pro-tagonist—identified as C. and alter ego of the same author—and a mysteri-ous man described as "the man in black" (46).[12] We know from their conver-sations that C. is not satisfied with her previous attempts to write about history (49). She is trying to get away from traditional historiography and the literary trends of her time. She is searching for her own way to recover and process past events. She, in fact, declares to her interlocutor, "I'm waiting to see whether I can hit on some entertaining way of stringing my memories together" (124),[13] and their discussions on literature will help her remember and analyze events of her childhood and adolescence during the Civil War and Postwar. The novel, thus, builds on the narrator-protagonist's memories stimulated by her exchanges with the man in black. As the narrator-protago-nist reminds us several times, after each conversation with the man in black, the pages of *El cuarto de atrás* magically appear under the hat he has left "like a temporary paperweight, on top of a pile of papers laying next to the typewriter" (23).[14] Their interactions are necessary to encourage the recalling of past memories; she wishes that he continue speaking since his words, she says, "have the same hypnotic effect as those of a *story*. . . . There is no telling what he may produce from underneath that hat" (97–98, emphasis is mine).[15] The man in black, therefore, is symbolically associated with the world of literature because his words, "as those of a story," have the power to trigger memories, which in turn are the core of the novel (literature) being created under the hat. Through their interactions, C. is able to fulfill the need of "rescuing [her memories] from oblivion" by "telling . . . them aloud" (15).[16] These personal memories, as mentioned before, contribute to unbury the silenced past the author shares with generations of Spaniards.

The episode of the trip to Burgos, for instance, is a good example of how literature and popular culture stimulate personal memories, which in turn become collective memories. The narrator-protagonist travels with her father, uncle, and cousin to Burgos in order to search for her father's car, wrecked during the Civil War and "buried" in an automobile graveyard. The reappearance of this particular memory was sparked by the recollection of different cultural products such as a "conjuro" (incantation) Cervantes quoted in his *Novelas ejemplares* (*Exemplary Novels*) (95) and the popular tale of *Pulgarcito* (*Tom Thumb*) (100). Those cultural products help the narrator-protagonist summon her memories while at the same time the pages of the novel are piling up under the hat of the man in black (96).

From the perspective of the young C. and her cousin, the trip to Burgos was exciting, similar to the adventures of the characters played by the actress Deanna Durbin—best known for her work in the late 1930s and 1940s in

Hollywood—whose characters often wander in cities, such as Manhattan or Los Angeles, where freedom reigns (108). In fact, the night before the recovery of what was left of her father's car, C. and her cousin left the hotel without permission and ventured into the city. They felt a real happiness; one that, according to C., had nothing to do with the one imposed on women during the regime for "having done our duty nor [was it] the happiness considered appropriate to display in order to set an example of moral courage and fortitude." It was, instead, she continues, "a wild happiness, inappropriate and selfish, stemming from the fact that they had left us by ourselves" (105).[17] The fun and excitement experienced by the girls were, hence, a transgression and contrast with the adult perspective of the same event. The adult perception of the episode is clearly evident in the scene of the recovery of the car where C. alternates her memories as a child experiencing the event with her father's and uncle's emotional reactions to the same experience. As we will see, this particular memory evokes the collective memories of many of the victims of the War and Postwar. It is interesting to note that Pierre Nora in his study on the *lieux de mémoire* lists the cemetery, among others, as a place where memory resides. In fact, in *El cuarto de atrás* the recalled experience of the narrator-protagonist as a child in the automobile graveyard, symbolizes the collective memory of the devastation left by the Civil War.

Here is how C. recalls the experience in the automobile graveyard that took place the day after her adventurous experience of freedom:

> All they could talk about was going to recover the remains of the car, as though they were about to attend a ceremony that was something like a funeral . . . The city had lost all its strangeness. The automobile graveyard was on the outskirts of town. It was a sort of very large shed, with a huge pile of skeletons of vehicles that were charred, riddled with holes, or split in half, lying any which way, in whatever position they had fallen, as in a garbage dump . . . [I]t took them a long time to find it, because everything was all mixed up there, because the war had mixed up everything. The two of us followed the others at a certain distance, threading our way, with the sort of religious fear that keeps one from treading on grave markers. (108–109)[18]

C.'s words conjure images of the mass graveyards, where the anonymous remains of the victims of the violence of the regime still lie. Years after the publication of Martín Gaite's novel, the issue of mass graveyards has finally been addressed. Golob notes that along with the efforts of the Ley de la Memoria Histórica (Law of Historical Memory) to obtain a posttransition justice, the work of individuals and groups has been vital to promote "a shared 'post transitional justice' political agenda" (133). In particular, the author mentions the efforts of groups of citizens (Association for the Recovery of Historical Memory [ARMH], for example) "focused on exhuming the remains of victims of Francoist repression buried in mass graves throughout the country. This growing movement is multi-regional, as well as *intergenerational*, an important characteristic because of the enforced silences that made open recognition of Republican allegiances impossible even within families, as fear and shame persisted even after the transition" (134).

The reaction of Uncle Vicente to his brother's grief confirms the association of the automobile graveyard episode mentioned above with the violence of the War and the regime. He, in fact, encourages his brother—who was grieving "motionless in front of the *corpse* of the late-model Pontiac, very nearly in tears" (110, emphasis is mine)[19]—to count his blessings; after all, neither of them were killed by the regime for being a socialist as their brother Joaquín was (111). C.'s childhood memory stimulates the recollection of a collective historical memory, therefore confirming the importance of memory in the reclamation of history. As Christina Dupláa explains, historical memory is "the union between a re-reading of Spanish historical events of the last fifty years and the experience of the collective memory of those who experienced it" (29, translation is mine).[20] In this regard, Labanyi emphasizes the shortcomings of official historiography, which disregards the role of personal memory in the "objective" recollection of historical facts:

> [S]uch an opposition [memory vs. history] conceives of memory in purely private terms, as something that individuals engage in. This negates the existence of collective memory as a bridge providing a continuum between personal memories and what happened in the past—for the two do not, and cannot, exist in isolation from one another. Indeed, without the "social frameworks" (Halbwachs's term) provided by collective memory (the sum of understandings of the past that circulate in any given society), individual memories could not be recounted, since narration requires the insertion of data into a narrative structure (or mix of narrative structures) drawn from an available repertoire. (121)[21]

The official historiography is openly criticized in *El cuarto de atrás*. The author expresses her detachment from official history and proclaims allegiance to literature as a mean to retrieve her childhood and young adult memories. Talking about her previous historical research projects she says, "I was aware that I was going astray, deserting dreams in order to come to a compromise with history, forcing myself to put things in order, to understand them one by one, out of fear of being shipwrecked" (49).[22] The order in which historical events are recounted in historical sources does not help the narrator-protagonist to recover her own memories.[23] She is not even able to differentiate between her recollections of the War and Postwar years, as her memories do not follow a chronological order. Besides being unsatisfied with historiographical methods, the author also wants to take distance from the literary trend originated by Franco's death. The end of the regime, in fact, as we learn from C., provoked the proliferation of many books of memoirs:

"They're a real epidemic now, and in the final analysis that's what discouraged me, the thought that, if other people's memories bore me, why wouldn't mine bore other people?" (124).[24] Historiographical and canonical literary trends, therefore, will not help the narrator-protagonist recuperate her own memories. Literature, however, which the man in black defines as "a defiance of logic" (49),[25] could help her recall a past she perceives as disorderly, as "a homogeneous block" (129).[26] What C. finds intriguing about literature "is [its] contradictory versions. They are the very basis of literature. We are not just one being, but many, exactly like real history is not what is written by putting dates in their proper order and then presenting it to us as a single whole" (166).[27] Literature, therefore, can help recapture the variety of voices and perspectives silenced by official historiography. Hence, when she decides to write on the forty years of the regime, she decides to disregard official news of the time. In her own words:

> [W]hat I was trying to recapture was something far more difficult to grasp. What I was after were the crumbs, not the little white pebbles [here she is referring to the tale of *Tom Thumb*]. That summer I also reread a great many romantic novels. The role that romantic novels played in shaping the sensibilities of young girls growing up in the forties is very important. And songs, the part songs played in our life seems fundamental too. (135)[28]

In the romantic novels, songs, tales, and literature, therefore, reside the memories of those years. The novel *Robinson Crusoe* by Defoe, for instance, helps recapture the "scarcity" of the War and Postwar years. As was the case for Robinson Crusoe, in those years of scarcity in Spain, "[n]ecessity [was] the mother of invention" (179).[29] From the perspective of children, invention was necessary to compensate for the lack of toys. Consequently, with one of her friends, C. created the island of Bergai where everything was possible and where the two girls could escape reality. C.'s friend used to tell her, "[A] person can invent riches the way Robinson did" (183)[30]; and so together they created the island and began writing a novel during those years of scarcity.

From this personal childhood memory, C. starts recalling what "scarcity" meant in more general terms, inscribing the concept in a collective context. She explains how the War and Postwar years affected the daily speech of both adults and children. She states that words like "*amortize, requisition, ration, hoard, camouflage* . . . were on everyone's lips from morning to night and [that] it was impossible to ignore them" (184).[31] At the same time, the back room in her childhood home in Salamanca undergoes a radical transformation. Before the War, *el cuarto de atrás* (the back room) was considered the children's space where, she notes, "disorder and freedom reigned. We were allowed to sing at the top of our lungs, move furniture around as we pleased . . . it was a kingdom where nothing was forbidden" (187).[32] In the year 1936, however, the back room was taken away from the children and transformed into a storeroom. In particular the cupboard, which was a space for children's toys and anything they wanted to store, became a symbol of the repression and scarcity brought on by the War:

> Its essential nature as a sideboard constituted the first pretext that was resorted to for *the invasion*. When the hoarding of articles of prime necessity started, my mother cleared out two shelves and began putting packages of rice, soap, and chocolate on them because she couldn't find room for them in the kitchen. And *the conflicts* began, first of all over the problem of how to keep in order our various possessions that had been left without a home, and after that *the violation of our freedom*, since at the most inopportune moment almost anybody might walk in the back room as though he or she owned the place. . . . Then after that came strings of sausages hanging from the ceiling, and butter, and so on until we ceased to have a room to play because the articles of prime necessity *had shoved our childhood aside* and *driven it into a corner*. Play and subsistence cohabited in bitter *disharmony*, amid *incompatible* smells. (188–89, emphasis is mine)[33]

It is clear that the description of the gradual transformation of the back room recalls images of conflict, repression, loss, and defeat associated with War and Postwar periods in Spain.

The shortage of basic goods of those years echoes throughout the novel. The transformation of the back room is the beginning of a long period of material scarcity epitomized by her father's words during family meals: "We're eating money" (185).[34] The lack of articles of prime necessity also corresponded to an intellectual stagnation. The narrator-protagonist mentions the "ignorance and repression" and "those textbooks with all sorts of things missing that kept us from getting a decent education" (64),[35] hence emphasizing scarcity on a cultural level.

Despite all, C. remembers those childhood and adolescent years "as a very happy time in my life" (64),[36] due in part to the refuge provided by literature, cinema, and other cultural products available during those years.[37] Ironically, the Franco-approved cultural products were used as an instrument to escape the limits imposed on women during the regime.[38] Therefore, in a period dominated by strict social and gender rules, for instance, the already mentioned actress Deanna Durbin and her movies were a symbol of freedom for women (59).[39] The female characters in Conchita Piquer's songs, moreover, provided the author's generation with alternative and transgressive models of women. They did not reflect the roles imposed on women by the regime, as they did not embody the myth of the respectable wives and mothers as "pillars of the Christian home and family"[40] preached by the Women's Section of the Fascist party (87).[41] Rather, these women were marginalized and, as the author states, "[t]hey were the rubble left by the war. They exposed to view that emptiness that lay all about, so hard to hide" (150).[42]

These women's lives testify to the desolation left by the War, this destruction that everybody pretended to ignore; in fact, in the author's words, "[n]obody wanted to speak of the cataclysm that had just torn the country apart, but the bandaged wounds still throbbed, though no moans and shots could be heard. It was an artificial silence, an emptiness that there was an urgent need to fill with anything whatsoever" (151).[43] The "artificial silence" revealed by the author signals the dimension of trauma of lost historical memory. The Post-war silence evoked by Conchita Piquer's songs continued through the first years of democracy when, according to Moreno-Nuño, the events of the Civil War became a myth as they were forced into a past with no relationship to the present (20). The silenced memories of the Civil War, however, are still "throbbing," thus confirming what Moreno-Nuño states about memory and trauma. She sees trauma as a "'wound in the memory,' when we consider the Civil War as a wound in the Spanish collective memory. This wound is provoked by the magnitude of the war and the suffering it caused" (19–20, translation is mine).[44]

Martín Gaite's denunciation of the atrocity of those years and her resistance to Franco's ideology is even more emphasized when she mentions Franco's daughter as a victim of her father's regime. Carmen shares with Franco's daughter, Carmencita, the same ideals of freedom and a pull towards the "reactionary" models of behaviors provided by the cultural products of the time. Both, in fact, as C. states, "[ha]ve been the victims of the same manners and mores, we've read the same magazines and seen the same movies. Our children may be different, but our dreams have surely been much the same" (133).[45] The shared ideals of freedom with Carmencita Franco not only exacerbates the criticism of Martín Gaite towards the regime, but also inserts the author's private memory into a collective context of shared memories.

The criticism of the regime illustrated through cultural products is evident throughout the novel. C., for instance, uses emblematic literary and religious figures to emphasize the paradox and hypocrisy surrounding the expectations towards women during that time. She notes that "staying put, conforming, and making the best of things was good; skipping out, escaping, running away were bad. Yet at the same time they were the heroic things to do, since Don Quixote, Christ, and Santa Teresa had fled, had abandoned home and family. That was where the contradiction lay, and the answer they gave us was that all of theirs was a noble madness" (121).[46] The author employs the regime-approved figures to undermine Franco's ideology and to demystify those narratives created around historical and literary characters used to legitimize his power and to silence women. For example, C. often mentions the historical figure of Queen Isabella the Catholic, who was considered the embodiment of all skills and qualities a young woman needed to acquire and aspire to. All young Spanish women were pressured to follow the teachings of the Social Service[47] to become the perfect wife and mother, "a worthy descendent of Queen Isabella" (36).[48] At the same time, Franco was portrayed as a timeless mythical figure, ruling over his people, uncontested, as we can infer from the narrator-protagonist's words:

> From the beginning it was clear that [Franco] was the one and only, that his power was *indisputable* and *omnipresent*, that he had managed to insinuate himself into all houses, schools, movie theatres, and cafés . . . his reign was *absolute*. If he was ill nobody knew it, *it seemed as though sickness and death could never touch him*. . . . The thought came to me that *Franco had paralyzed time*. (129–30, emphasis is mine)[49]

As Moreno-Nuño confirms, myth and politics are, in fact, inextricably linked during Franco's regime. She states that the "Francoist dictatorship was one that sought to legitimize its power through the manipulation—mythification—of the past. For this reason, the literature of democratic Spain establishes a complex dialogue with the mythic mode of representation, one in which the construction of myths . . . is followed by its deconstruction" (20, translation is mine).[50] As a matter of fact, with the objective of uncovering a lost history, Martín Gaite employs her novel (literature) and other mass cultural products to comment and deconstruct the mythical reality created during Franco's regime.[51]

In conclusion, the analysis of *El cuarto de atrás* shows the desire to recover those traumatic memories suppressed during Franco's regime, because they still affect, like specters, the author's present. The cultural products of the time—literature, romantic novels, movies, songs, and popular tales—contribute to the reappearance of those private memories, which the author shares with generations of Spaniards who, in one way or another, have been affected, directly or indirectly, by its silencing. In the last chapter of *El cuarto de atrás*, the narrator-protagonist finds "a large, neat pile of sheets of papers [the manuscript of the novel] with a paperweight on top" (205).[52] This same paperweight previously sat upon two objects associated with the recalling of past memories: the engraving *Luther's Discussion with the Devil* and a handwritten paper with a "conjuro" (incantation) quoted by Cervantes in his *Exemplary Novels* (94–95). Symbolically, at the end of the very novel that has originated in the revelation of the veiled past, instead of these two cultural products, the novel itself now appears under the paperweight that has facilitated the emergence of the narrator-protagonist's memories.

Ultimately, as shown by the quoted passages, in *El cuarto de atrás* literature constitutes a productive medium for the recovery of lost memories and, consequently, the retrieval of lost history. This dimension of literature reflects one of the issues Pierre Nora raises in his discussion of *lieux de mémoire*, when the historian bemoans the displacement of history (as an institution) by the contemporary emphasis on memory studies: "History has become the deep reference of a period that has been wrenched from its depth, a realistic novel in a period in which there are no real novels. Memory has been promoted to the center of history: such is the spectacular bereavement of literature" (24). Martín Gaite, however, has transcended the limitations of the monological official discourse of Francoist Spain precisely in the very space of literature, which unfolds as a site of memory through the act of narrating. Thus, to conclude with Martín Gaite's own words, "if one never *lost* anything, literature would have no reason for being . . . How fortunate, everything is *coming to light* little by little" (196, 198, emphasis is mine).[53] And through the writing of *El cuarto de atrás*, some of Spain's lost history "little by little" has reappeared.

## NOTES

1. When quoting and paraphrasing *El cuarto de atrás*, I will use the English translation by Helen R. Lane. In the "Notes" section I will provide the Spanish direct quotes from the original text by Carmen Martín Gaite.

2. See also the volume edited by Juan Ramón Resina on the topic of historical memory in the Spain of the transition to democracy. The articles composing the volume analyze the issue within the theoretical framework of cultural studies. In addition, see the 2005 book by José F. Colmeiro, *Memoria histórica e identidad cultural: De la postguerra a la postmodernidad*, where the author discusses the issue of historical memory for the period encompassing the post Civil War to democracy. The author analyzes an array of Spanish texts—novels, movies, poems, and songs—as sites for the recovery of the silenced past.

3. As the editor Jo Labanyi states, the compilation of this volume coincides with the debates surrounding the controversial Ley de Memoria Histórica (Law of Historical Memory) originally proposed by the PSOE government in 2004 and finally approved by Congress in 2007 (119). The Law, in fact, has been the object of discussion among several of the contributors to the volume. Stephanie Golob dedicates a section of her essay to the analysis of the Law of Historical Memory, which in spite of its approval in 2007 generated a political debate between left and right. The Law, Golob explains, "was met with muted applause on the left, and by indignant disbelief on the right" (136). The right wing party, Partido Popular (PP), especially reacted against the provision of the Law that demanded the review of all judicial sentences issued against Franco's opponents during his regime. Golob notes that "[t]he PP loudly accused the government of 're-opening the transition' and practicing the politics of revenge through these panels [of reviewers], even though they would not prosecute former regime officials" (136). On the other end, sectors of the left criticized those same panels of reviewers for not bringing to justice the perpetrators of illegal acts committed against the opponents of the regime (136). Golob concludes that although the Law does not meet the consensus among political constituencies, it has generated debates that have contributed to break the silence imposed over the past (138). On the political debates regarding the Law of Historical Memory, see also Marina Llorente ("La memoria") and Sören Brinkmann.

4. In his aforementioned 2005 book, José F. Colmeiro notes how, from the Spanish Civil War to contemporary society, generations of Spaniards have faced the specters of a silenced and ignored past: "La situación de ignorancia respecto al pasado común define varias generaciones de españoles nacidos después de la guerra civil y alcanza hasta nuestros propios días. . . . La desmemoria y el desencanto, la nostalgia y el olvido, son hoy por hoy claves dominantes de la cultura española contemporánea" (8).

5. On the different political perspectives on the Spanish transition to democracy, see, among others, Fernando León Solís.

6. To stress the importance of confronting the past to reach a true democracy, Golob uses the concept of *transitional justice culture* defined as "a set of beliefs and practices grounded in rejection of impunity, confrontation of the past, prioritizing state accountability and aiming towards a broader societal inclusion of past regime victims. . . . [T]he message from this set of cultural norms is that the moment of transition is the golden opportunity to forge a new, democratic social contract, and that the democratic future envisaged by that contract will be possible, and will last, only by using the law to confront and overcome the repressive and abusive past" (127–28). For a more detailed account of the Spanish contemporary political situation, see also Marina Llorente's contribution to this volume ("Exile and Erasure") and Alberto Reig Tapia's perspective on the importance of a strong democracy as a deterrent to the manipulation of the past.

7. Also in his 2001 article on *El cuarto de atrás*, José F. Colmeiro notes how the "silence pact" of the transition is still affecting contemporary Spain: "El gran tabú colectivo de la transición, y aquí vamos a transgredir la ley del silencio, es que la sociedad española todavía no ha reconocido su complicidad con el franquismo, su 'pecado de omisión,' según la acertada expresión metafórica de Ana María Matute, prefiriendo el simulacro de la amnesia colectiva" ("Memoria histórica" 155). Similarly, in his 1997 study, Manuel José Ramos Ortega states that "la guerra, la posguerra o como quiera llamársele, aún no ha terminado para algunos y que *el fantasma* de sus consecuencias sigue actuando para los herederos de ese episodio histórico y, lo que es más importante para nosotros, sigue revelándose como una fuente inagotable de argumentos novelescos que han marcado, sin duda ninguna, el panorama literario español de los últimos cincuenta años" ("Imagen" 66, emphasis is mine).

8. "Desde la actualidad de los setenta, muchos escritores empezaron a 'revisar' sus memorias y a tratar de contextualizar sus impresiones de la guerra y la posguerra" (33). See also the studies by Catherine G. Bellver, Mary T. Hartson, Manuel José Ramos Ortega ("Imagen" and "Discurso"), and Stephen Luis Vilaseca. Jean S. Chittenden, on the other hand, defines *El cuarto de atrás* as an autobiography rather than a memoir. Quoting Roy Pascal's theory on the difference between autobiography (focus on the self) and memoir (focus on others), Chittenden argues "*El cuarto* can be designated autobiography, since in the novel the narrator does not interact with other characters over a long period of time, nor does she include major characters or relationship on which to focus. Others are seen only as they relate to the protagonist's life— for example, her mother, her father, her childhood friend—but almost nothing is told of the relationship among them" (82). In addition, see the chapter Colmeiro dedicates to the analysis of *El cuarto de atrás* in his 2005 book (156–76). Using Derrida's essay "Plato's Pharmacy" as a point of departure for his analysis, Colmeiro interprets Martín Gaite's novel as "una forma simbólica de catarsis del trauma histórico personal y colectivo de la guerra civil y la postguerra, como proceso de cura y superación de los fantasmas del pasado a través del ejercicio de la palabra, la memoria y la escritura" (156).

9. The topic of private vs. collective memory constitutes a common interest among the contributions to the 2008 volume of the *Journal of Spanish Cultural Studies* edited by Jo Labanyi. In particular, the editor in her introduction to the volume mentions the interview with Emilio Silva, founder and president of the Asociación para la Recuperación de la Memoria Histórica, who emphasizes the limits of the Ley de Memoria Histórica (Law of Historical Memory): "[A] major problem in the Law of Historical Memory is its preamble which insists that memory is a private matter. This signally fails to acknowledge that 'historical memory' is a form of collective and not personal memory, quite apart from the fact that citizens have the right to express their personal memories in the public sphere. As Silva notes, this contentious relegation of memory to the private sphere allows the Law to duck the major question of the teaching of history in the education system. Indeed, the key issue at stake is that memory of the violence of the civil war and dictatorship has been forced to remain a private matter until very recently, thanks to the repression under the dictatorship and a lack of interested interlocutors at the time of the transition" (120). However, in spite of this flaw, according to Labanyi, the Law "was a major step in forcing the issue into the public sphere" (120).

10. "Un espacio cultural para la construcción de un *lieu de mémoire* o espacio de memoria sobre la Guerra Civil" (15). Pierre Nora defines *lieux de mémoire* as "remains, the ultimate embodiments of a memorial consciousness that has barely survived in a historical age that calls

out for memory because it has abandoned it" (12). As sites of memory, Nora mentions "[m]useums, archives, cemeteries, festivals, anniversaries, treaties, depositions, monuments, sanctuaries, [and] fraternal orders" (12).

11.  Using Maurice Halbwach's and Pierre Nora's theoretical frameworks in his reading of *El cuarto de atrás*, José F. Colmeiro studies the conflictive relationship between "memory and cultural identity," on the one hand, and "memory and oblivion," on the other, and how this relationship is affecting contemporary Spain. Colmeiro argues that "la construcción de la memoria histórica y la formación de la identidad cultural son procesos paralelos y mutuamente implicados, de igual manera que la memoria individual y la memoria histórica colectiva se construyen también recíprocamente" ("Memoria histórica" 151).

12.  "Hombre de negro" (49).

13.  " . . . estoy esperando a ver si se me ocurre una forma divertida de enhebrar los recuerdos" (111).

14.  "Como un pisapapeles provisional, sobre unos folios, que había junto a la máquina de escribir" (30).

15.  "Sus palabras hipnotizan como las de un cuento . . . puede sacar cualquier cosa de debajo del sombrero" (91).

16.  At the beginning of the novel, while trying to fall asleep, C. alternates memories of the past with present moments. She starts remembering the house of her childhood and its furniture. She also mentions the impact that the female characters in the sentimental novels she read as a child had in her dreams of freedom. She recalls the fantasy of receiving a letter from a barefoot man who would remember and long for her while gazing at the sea (6–7). The narrator wishes that the "Barefoot Man" were real and that she could have a conversation with him. This exchange would help her retain the past memories she was trying to recall: "I'd go on telling about them *aloud*, thus *rescuing from oblivion* all the things I've been *remembering* and heaven only knows how many more. There's no way of calculating how many ramifications a *story* will take on once one spies a gleam of attention in another's eyes. . . . [W]e would begin to exchange *memories* the way children exchange little colored cards. . . . An intriguing, rambling *story* would come out, a tissue of truths and lies, like all *stories*" (15, emphasis is mine). "al contarlas en voz alta, *salvaría del olvido* todas las cosas que he estado recordando y sabe Dios cuántas más, es incalculable lo que puede ramificarse un *relato* cuando se descubre una luz de atención en otros ojos. . . . [N]os pondríamos a cambiar *recuerdos* como los niños se cambian cromos y . . . saldría un *cuento* fresco e irregular, tejido de verdades y mentiras, como todos los *cuentos*" (22, emphasis is mine). The man in black will fulfill this need to retrieve and retain the memories of her past through a conversation with an interlocutor.

17.  "Ejemplo de moral y fortaleza, era una alegría loca inconveniente y egoísta, se basaba en que nos habían dejado solas" (97).

18.  "Se hablaba únicamente de ir a recoger los restos del coche, como de asistir a una ceremonia que tenía algo de funeral . . . la ciudad había perdido toda extravagancia. El cementerio de coches estaba en las afueras; era una especie de hangar muy extenso, donde se amontonaban muchos esqueletos de vehículos, carbonizados, agujerados o partidos por la mitad, yaciendo de cualquier manera, en la postura en que habían caído, como en un vertedero . . . tardaron en encontrarlo, porque la guerra lo había equivocado todo, nosotras les seguíamos a cierta distancia, sorteando los hierros, los neumáticos y los asientos destripados que poblaban aquel ámbito de chatarra, con esa especie de temor religioso que nos impide pisar las losas de las tumbas" (99).

19.  "Estaba inmóvil, frente al *cadáver* del Pontiac negro último modelo, casi se le habían saltado las lágrima" (100, emphasis is mine).

20.  "Unión entre una relectura de los hechos históricos de la España de los últimos cincuenta años y la experiencia del recuerdo colectivo de quienes los vivieron" (29).

21.  See also chapter 3 of David K. Herzberger's study (66–86), where he analyzes the relationship between history, myth, and memory using *El cuarto de atrás* as an example. The author legitimizes the historical value of Martín Gaite's novel, declaring that "[i]n contrast to the single-voiced discourse of myth that shapes social realism and Francoist historiography, and in contrast as well to the assertion of authority of this discourse over the real and the meaning of the real, the novel of memory offers a different claim upon history and its truths.

This claim is propositional rather than assertive because it recognizes that to know the historical is to mediate and to narrate it with the voice of a subject in the present who is positioned both within history and within discourse" (68).

22. "Al emprenderlos [los trabajos de investigación histórica], notaba que me estaba desviando, desertaba de los sueños para pactar con la historia, me esforzaba en ordenar las cosas, en entenderlas una por una, por miedo de naufragar" (51).

23. In her study Shirley Mangini highlights the dissatisfaction Martín Gaite felt towards official history. She states that Martín Gaite in *El cuarto de atrás* "encontró un modo de contar la *verdadera historia* según su imaginación y los recuerdos de la infancia" (40). According to Mangini, *El cuarto de atrás* is one of the best examples of "'novela de la memoria,' donde convergen una voluntad de romper con la mitología franquista y un deseo de embestirse con el temible olvido" (40).

24. "Ya es una peste, en el fondo, eso es lo que me ha venido desanimando, pensar que, si a mí me aburren las memorias de los demás, por qué no le van a aburrir a los demás las mías" (111).

25. "Un desafío a la lógica" (51).

26. "Un bloque homogéneo" (115).

27. " . . . son las versiones contradictorias, constituyen la base de la literatura, no somos un solo ser, sino muchos, de la misma manera que tampoco la historia es ésa que se escribe poniendo en orden las fechas y se nos presenta como inamovible" (145).

28. "Al principio me pasé varios meses yendo a la hemeroteca a consultar periódicos, luego comprendí que no era eso, que lo que yo quería rescatar era algo más inaprensible, eran las miguitas, no las piedrecitas blancas. Aquel verano releí también muchas novelas rosa, es muy importante el papel que jugaron las novelas rosa en la formación de las chicas de los años cuarenta. Bueno y las canciones, lo de las canciones me parece fundamental" (120).

29. "[D]e la necesidad de sobrevivir surge la inventiva" (155).

30. "Las riquezas se las puede uno inventar como hizo Robinson" (158).

31. "Amortizar, requisar, racionar, acaparar, camuflar y otros verbos semejantes . . . de la noche a la mañana, andaban en boca de todo el mundo y era imposible ignorarlos" (159).

32. "Reinaban el desorden y la libertad, se permitía cantar a voz en cuello, cambiar de sitio los muebles, . . . era un reino donde nada estaba prohibido" (161).

33. "Su esencia de aparador constituyó el primer pretexto invocado para la invasión. Cuando empezaron los acaparamientos de artículos de primera necesidad, mi madre desalojó dos estantes y empezó a meter en ellos paquetes de arroz, jabón y chocolate, que no le cabía en cocina. Y empezaron los conflictos, primero de ordenación para las cosas diversas . . . y luego de coacción de libertad, porque en el momento más inoportuno, podía entrar alguien. . . . Luego vinieron los embutidos colgados del techo, y la manteca y, a partir de entonces, hasta que dejamos de tener cuarto para jugar, porque los artículos de primera necesidad desplazaron y arrinconaron nuestra infancia, el juego y la subsistencia coexistieron en una convivencia agria, de olores incompatibles" (162–63).

34. "[C]omemos dinero" (160).

35. "Ignorancia y represión . . . aquellos deficientes libros de texto que bloquearon nuestra enseñanza" (63).

36. "A pesar de todo, como una época muy feliz" (63).

37. A different perspective is provided by Isolina Ballesteros in her article on the representation of the Civil War and Postwar from the perspective of childhood as represented in Spanish cinema from the 1980s and 1990s. She states that for that generation of directors "calificados por Marsha Kinder como los 'niños de Franco' a causa del papel obligado de 'testigos silenciosos' de una guerra trágica . . . [l]a concepción de la infancia . . . no responde al paraíso infantil mítico sino que, por el contrario, se presenta como un estado de terror nocturno, miedo a lo desconocido y soledad que coexisten con una curiosidad y una intensidad vitales pero, sobre todo, con una habilidad para fusionar memorias, alucinaciones y experiencias presentes" (232). However, the childhood perspective on the War and Postwar constitutes a subversive act towards the fascist ideology. In fact, Ballesteros says, "[r]epresentar la realidad de los años oscuros de la posguerra desde los ojos de una niña es un acto político, es renunciar a la mirada adulta hegemónica, al estado de dominación, al cuerpo político masculino, para dar autonomía

al cuerpo infantil, todavía sin órganos, símbolo del 'devenir-joven' de cada edad y concentrarse en el proceso del devenir mismo" (232–33).

38. Stephanie Sieburth analyzes the role of mass cultural products mentioned in *El cuarto de atrás* as means of "resistance" to the repression during Fascism. The author explains that for the young C., "mass culture constituted both a life-saving refuge and an invitation to rebellion" (230).

39. While discussing the novel *Love and the Professor*, in which the female protagonist "dared" to go to college and fall in love with her professor of Latin, C. recalls and comments on life for women during the regime. Women were discouraged from being well educated. She explains that "[r]hetoric in the post war era was devoted to discrediting the feminist stirrings that had begun in the years of the Republic, and stressed once again the unselfish heroism of wives and mothers, the importance of their silent and obscure labor as pillars of the Christian home and family" (87). "La retórica de la posguerra se aplicaba a desprestigiar los conatos de feminismo que tomaron auge en los años de la República y volvía a poner el acento en el heroísmo abnegado de madres y esposas, en la importancia de su silenciosa y oscura labor como pilares del hogar cristiano" (82).

40. "Pilares del hogar cristiano" (82).

41. As Inbal Ofer explains, the Women's Section of the Spanish Fascist party (Sección Femenina de la Falange) "was founded in Madrid in June 1934 as part of the Spanish Falange. Starting in April 1937 the SF [Sección Femenina] functioned as the sole secular women's organization of the Franco regime, employing a network of professional, provincial and local delegates throughout the country. . . . During the four decades of its existence, the SF managed to seize authority over most of the sectors and associations in Francoist Spain in which women operated" ("'New' Woman" 583). For more information regarding the Sección Femenina de la Falange, see also Matilde Peinado Rodríguez, Nino Kebadze, Inbal Ofer ("Historical Models"), Mercedes Carbayo-Abengózar, Luis Otero, and Luis Suárez Fernández.

42. "Escombros de la guerra, dejaban al descubierto aquel vacío en torno, tan difícil de disimular" (133).

43. "Nadie quería hablar del cataclismo que acababa de desgarrar al país, pero las heridas vendadas seguían latiendo, aunque no se oyeran gemidos ni disparos: era un silencio artificial, un hueco a llenar urgentemente de lo que fuera" (133).

44. "'Herida en la memoria,' entendiendo la Guerra Civil como una herida en la memoria colectiva española ocasionada por las dimensiones que alcanzó el conflicto bélico y la magnitud del sufrimiento que generó" (19–20).

45. "Hemos crecido y vivido en los mismos años, hemos sido víctimas de las mismas modas y costumbres, hemos leído las mismas revistas y visto el mismo cine, nuestros hijos puede que sean distintos, pero nuestros sueños seguro que han sido semejantes" (119).

46. "Quedarse, conformarse y aguantar era lo bueno; salir, escapar y fugarse era lo malo. Y sin embargo, también lo heroico, porque don Quijote y Cristo y Santa Teresa se habían fugado, habían abandonado casa y familia, ahí estaba la contradicción, nos contestaban que ellos lo hicieron en nombre de un alto ideal y que era la suya una locura noble" (109).

47. As Inbal Ofer clarifies, "[t]he Social Service was instituted during the Civil War as an alternative military service for women. It included six months of voluntary work for the state, as well as enforced daily religious and political classes. Completion of one's SS obligations was a precondition for receiving important documents, such as Passports, driver's licenses or work permits. Starting in 1939, the SS was overseen by the SF [Sección Femenina de la Falange]" ("'New' Woman" 603n).

48. "Descendiente de Isabel la Católica" (40).

49. "Desde el principio se notó que era unigénito, indiscutible y omnipresente, que había conseguido infiltrarse en todas las casas, escuelas y cafés . . . reinaba de modo absoluto, si estaba enfermo nadie lo sabía, parecía que la enfermedad y la muerte jamás podrían alcanzarlo . . . pensé que Franco había paralizado el tiempo" (115–116).

50. "El mito no es ajeno a la política, como bien mostrara una dictadura franquista que buscaba legitimar su poder mediante la manipulación—mitificación—del pasado. Por eso, la literatura de la democracia establece un complejo diálogo con el modo de representación mítico, donde la construcción de mitos . . . va acompañada de su deconstrucción" (20). In this

context, analyzing *El cuarto de atrás* together with *Si te dicen que caí* by Juan Marsé, Shirley Mangini notes that the two novels "aunque sean novelas autobiográficas en ciertos aspectos . . . ambas desarrollan una voz contestataria ante el mito fascista . . . Marsé y Martín Gaite . . . se apoderan de ese mundo mítico del franquismo, a veces subvirtiéndolo, otras contrastándolo con su versión de *la verdadera realidad* de los vencidos para revelar la historia moral de su país" (33–34).

51. On this topic, see also David K. Herzberger's study. He emphasizes the discourse of resistance and denunciation of novelists, such as Martín Gaite, who lived during Franco's regime. According to Herzberger, "within the fiction of many Spanish writers during the Franco years there frequently exists a compelling desire to confront Francoist Spain and to scrutinize the Spanish past. When novels of these writers are read within the context of Francoist historiography, it is possible to discern an opposing view of the past and of how the past ought to be written about" (x). Similarly, Shirley Mangini states that for the writers of memoirs during the seventies "era necesaria una compleja y diacrónica desmitificación del implacable franquismo. Había una voluntad de reformar y matizar, de deconstruir los mitos familiares" (33).

52. " . . . hay un montón de folios, grueso y bien ordenado con un pisapapeles encima" (177–78).

53. "[S]i no se perdiera nada, la literatura no tendría razón de ser . . . menos mal, todo acaba apareciendo" (168, 170, emphasis is mine).

# WORKS CITED

Ballesteros, Isolina. "Las niñas del cine español: La evasión infantil en *El espíritu de la colmena*, *El sur* y *Los años oscuros*." *Revista Hispánica Moderna* 49.2 (1996): 232–42.

Bellver, Catherine G. "War as Rite of Passage in *El cuarto de atrás*." *Letras Femeninas* 12.1–2 (1986): 69–77.

Brinkmann, Sören. "La recuperación de la 'memoria histórica': entre el incumplimento institucional y la instrumentalización política." *España: Del consenso a la polarización. Cambios en la democracia española*. Eds. Walther L. Bernecker and Günter Maihold. Madrid: Iberoamericana; Vervuert, 2007. 203–17.

Carbayo-Abengózar, Mercedes. "Shaping Women: National Identity through the Use of Language in Franco's Spain." *Nations & Nationalism* 7.1 (2001): 75–92.

Chittenden, Jean S. "*El cuarto de atrás* as Autobiography." *Letras Femeninas* 12.1–2 (1986): 78–84.

Colmeiro, José F. *Memoria histórica e identidad cultural: De la postguerra a la postmodernidad*. Barcelona: Anthropos, 2005.

———. "Memoria histórica e identidad cultural: Del cuarto de atrás a la primera plana." *Revista de Estudios Hispánicos* 35.1 (2001): 151–63.

Dupláa, Christina. "Memoria colectiva y *lieux de mémoire* en la España de la Transición." *Disremembering the Dictatorship: The Politics of Memory in the Spanish Transition to Democracy*. Ed. Joan Ramón Resina. Atlanta: Rodopi, 2000. 29–42.

Golob, Stephany R. "*Volver*: The Return of/to Transitional Justice Politics in Spain." *Journal of Spanish Cultural Studies* 9.2 (2008): 127–41.

Hartson, Mary T. "The False-Bottomed Suitcase: Historical Memory and Textual Masochism in Carmen Martín Gaite's *El cuarto de atrás*." *Romance Notes* 48.1 (2007): 35–47.

Hertzberger, David K. *Narrating the Past: Fiction and Historiography in Postwar Spain*. Durham, NC: Duke University Press, 1995.

Kebadze, Nino. "The Right To Be Selfless and Other Prerogatives of the Weak in the Rhetoric of Sección Femenina." *Romance Quarterly* 55.2 (2008): 109–27.

Labanyi, Jo. "The Politics of Memory in Contemporary Spain." *Journal of Spanish Cultural Studies* 9.2 (2008): 119–25.

Llorente, Marina. "Exile and Erasure: A Poetic Reconstruction of the Spanish Past in Antonio Crespo Massieu's *Elegía en Portbou*." *Sites of Memory in Spain and Latin America*. Ed.

Aída Díaz de León, Marina Llorente, and Marcella Salvi. Lanham, MD: Lexington Books, 2015.

———. "La memoria histórica en la poesía de Isabel Pérez Montalbán y David González." *Hispanic Review* 81.2 (2013): 181–200.

Mangini, Shirley. "Infancia, memoria y mito en *Si te dicen que caí* y *El cuarto de atrás.*" *Cuadernos Hispanoamericanos* 617 (2001): 31–40.

Martín Gaite, Carmen. *El cuarto de atrás.* [1978] Barcelona: Destino, 2000.

———. *The Back Room.* Trans. Helen R. Lane. New York: Columbia University Press, 1983.

Moreno-Nuño, Carmen. *Las huellas de la Guerra Civil: Mito y trauma en la narrativa de la España democrática.* Madrid: Libertarias, 2006.

Nora, Pierre. "Between Memory and History: *Les Lieux de Mémoire.*" *Representations* 26 (1989): 7–24.

Ofer, Inbal. "A 'New' Woman for a 'New' Spain: The Sección Femenina de La Falange and the Image of the National Syndicalist Woman." *European History Quarterly* 39.4 (2009): 583–605.

———. "Historical Models—Contemporary Identities: The Sección Femenina of the Spanish Falange and its Redefinition of the Term 'Femininity.'" *Journal of Contemporary History* 40.4 (2005): 663–74.

Otero, Luis. *La Sección Femenina.* Madrid: Edaf, 1999.

Pascal, Roy. *Design and Truth in Autobiography.* Cambridge: Harvard University Press, 1960.

Peinado Rodríguez, Matilde. *Enseñando a señoritas y sirvientas: Formación femenina y clasismo en el franquismo.* Madrid: Los Libros de la Catarata, 2012.

Ramos Ortega, Manuel José. "Imagen de un tiempo de derrota y esperanza: La posguerra según Martín Gaite." *Historicidad en la novela española contemporánea* (1997): 63–79.

———. "Discurso e historia en la novela española de Posguerra." *Signa: Revista de la Asociación Española de Semiótica* 5 (1996): 289–305.

Reig Tapia, Alberto. "El debate sobre el pasado y su importancia para el presente." *España: Del consenso a la polarización. Cambios en la democracia española.* Ed. Walther L. Bernecker and Günter Maihold. Madrid: Iberoamericana; Vervuert, 2007. 167–202.

Resina, Joan Ramón, ed. *Disremembering the Dictatorship: The Politics of Memory in the Spanish Transition to Democracy.* Amsterdam; Atlanta, GA: Rodopi, 2000.

Sieburth, Stephanie. "The Conversation I Never Had with Carmen Martín Gaite." *Revista de Estudios Hispánicos* 36.1 (2002): 227–39.

Solís, Fernando León. "The Transition(s) to Democracy and Discourses of Memory." *International Journal of Iberian Studies* 16.1 (2003): 49–63.

Suárez Fernández, Luis. *Crónica de la sección femenina y su tiempo.* 2nd ed. Madrid: Asociación "Nueva Andadura," 1993.

Vilaseca, Stephen Luis. "From Spaces of Intimacy to Transferential Space: The Structure of Memory and the Reconciliation with Strangeness in *El cuarto de atrás.*" *Bulletin of Hispanic Studies* 83.3 (2006): 181–92.

## Chapter Four

# Exile and Erasure

## A Poetic Reconstruction of the Spanish Past in Antonio Crespo Massieu's Elegía en Portbou

### Marina Llorente

In one of the best and more insightful articles about Walter Benjamin, John Collins[1] describes the last hours of the German thinker and the grave where he now rests: "For those who know the story of Walter Benjamin's flight out of Nazi occupied Paris, the monument located in the small Catalan town of Portbou promises to haunt forever" (67). I have chosen to start with this quote because it depicts the spectral quality of the monument and the figure of Benjamin himself, which are both important elements of my analysis. Benjamin died in September 1940 at the Franco-Spanish border. He was hoping to pass through Spain on his way to the United States, but was denied entrance and allowed to spend the night at the Hotel de Francia in Portbou, where he was found dead in the morning after apparently taking a lethal dose of morphine. "Passages" is the name of the monument to Benjamin in Portbou, a monument that Collins describes as follows: "Entering the staircase, one is gripped with a sense of unease bordering on panic. The enclosed passageway leads straight down over the cliff and appears to open directly into the bay below. It is as if the artist wished to construct a three-dimensional photograph of the final image a suicidal person sees before jumping into the abyss" (67). Unfortunately, I haven't had the chance to visit Portbou or the monument, but this description helped me when I started analyzing the 2011 book of poems *Elegía en Portbou* (*Elegy in Portbou*), by Antonio Crespo Massieu.[2] For the purposes of my analysis, "Passages" can also be seen as an example of what Pierre Nora calls a "site of memory (*lieu de mémoire*)."[3] According to Nora, these sites preserve the historical memory of a particular society. The word *lieu*, or site, represents not only places, like cathedrals or monuments, but also artifacts; for instance, sacred texts, and events such as rituals or historical ceremonies. An important element in the creation of a *lieu de mémoire* is the desire to remember. As Nora explains, "[w]ithout the intention to remember, *lieux de mémoire* would be indistinguishable from *lieux de histoire*" (19).

This desire of remembering permeates Crespo Massieu's *Elegía en Portbou,* a book whose cover art includes a photograph of "Passages," the monument to Benjamin in the cemetery of Portbou. The book comprises ten songs, which are divided into three sections: *Libro de los pasajes* (*Book of Passages*), *Libro de la frontera* (*Book of the Border*), and *Libro del descenso* (*Book of Descent*). Nevertheless, this collection of poems does display "a thematic and emotional unity that makes it a lengthy and intense elegiac poem" (Martínez 116) with biblical and testimonial resonances. For example, the titles of the three sections allude to the organization of the Bible by *books*. Some of the poem titles, such as the last one, "Zarza ardiente de la piedad y la restitución" ("Burning Bush of Compassion and Restitution"), which I analyze later on, also reinforce this biblical tone. The poetic voice in the first person, moreover, reconstructs along testimonial lines the long journey of the people who had to be exiled in order to survive the devastation caused by the wars of the third and fourth decades of the last century. Thus, *Elegía en Portbou* is dedicated to all the dreams that were lost with the deaths of millions of people who fought for social justice, as Benjamin did, during the twentieth century. Specifically, the Spanish Civil War is the backdrop of this dense and heartbreaking book of poems, which foregrounds the cemetery of Portbou as representative of many other cemeteries, such as the cemetery of Collioure or the one referred to as *de los españoles* (the Spanish cemetery) in the internment camp of Argelès-sur-Mer in the south of France. These cemeteries were the final destination for many of the approximately 500,000 Republican men and women who, in the winter of 1939, crossed the Franco-Spanish border by land or by sea to escape fascism.[4] By choosing Portbou and not any of the other French cemeteries, Crespo Massieu connects the antifascist fight of Benjamin with that of the Spanish Republicans, thereby establishing the link between the Jewish genocide perpetrated by German fascism and the thousands of deaths produced by the Spanish Civil War, the later exile of Spanish Republicans, and the terrible postwar period during the fascist dictatorship known as *el franquismo*, or the Francoist years. The poem titled "¿A partir de cuándo?" ("Since when?") opens the book with the following verses that allude to the almost seventy years of silence in Spanish society regarding the experiences of the Spaniards who died far from their motherland: "since when the silence and its shadows, / since what time without time pierces renunciations, / enumerates betrayals, oblivion, when?" (11).[5] After this poem, we encounter the first section called

*Libro de los pasajes* (*Book of Passages*), which is prefaced by an illuminat-
ing quote from Benjamin: "The chronicler who narrates events without dis-
tinguishing between large and small ones, recounts a truth: nothing that has
ever occurred should be assumed lost for history" (13).[6] And so, the poetic
voice describes the Republicans who left Spain in 1939 in the following
manner:

> The women, the distressed, the old, the mothers
> the ones who left the rifle at the border,
> the children of tomorrow with neither passport nor homesickness,
> the ones who cried, the ones stiffened by the cold, the defiant ones
> the ones who drag their suitcase as if it were still origin
> or embers, persistence or tremor of a lost home,
> and the ones who still play or hold the hand that is taking them
> to uncertainty, the ones who now appear unexpectedly as an absurd specter
> in this darkness, this tunnel, this black hell. (104)[7]

The description refers to the pictures of the Spanish Republican exodus that
we have seen in museums or documentaries; for example, the well-known
photograph of a little girl of perhaps twelve years of age, holding on to her
father's hand and looking at the camera, or the picture of several boys drag-
ging small suitcases.

The poetic voice's position is not of total presence because it is not
recalling episodes from direct personal experience. This voice is a mediated
memory, a prosthetic memory, as Alison Landsberg has called it, a collection
of accounts based on someone else's recollections (26).[8] As Maurice Halbwachs suggests, individual memory is constructed naturally and depends on
collective recollection for its emergence (23). The memories of these Republican exiles still survive because of collective memory, and thus can be
reconstructed. In this manner, *Elegía en Portbou* begins the work of reconstruction of the last moments of those thousands of Spanish exiles who were
silenced during the forty-year dictatorship because they lost the civil war and
whose experiences were erased from Spanish history. Later on, these women
and men who died in exile would fall into an even more painful oblivion
during the transition from dictatorship to democracy, a transition that began
with the death of the dictator Francisco Franco in 1975. That period would
have been the proper moment to reconstruct and recognize those experiences,
but it did not happen.

In the context of Spanish history, neither the death of the dictator nor the
political transition produced an authentic reconciliation after the long dictatorship. Instead, the country chose the so-called *cambio sin ruptura* ("change
without rupture") and the *pacto de silencio* ("pact of silence"), taking the
train to democracy and European integration and failing to confront fully the
meaning of the civil war and the forty years of Francoism. In fact, a process
of national reconciliation that would have represented a real confrontation

with the past was never carried out. In this sense, the civil war itself could be viewed as unfinished, especially given the fact that it was erased from the national imaginary during the transition through a rhetoric claiming that revisiting the country's violent past would only provoke divisions and that it was better to look to the future. The 1977 Amnesty Law, which freed all political prisoners of the dictatorship while also erasing all political crimes committed by the dictatorship and its supporters, encouraged this collective amnesia.

Until very recently, the norm in Spain was to refer to the transition as a model process in which no blood was shed. Nonetheless, there are historians and political scientists who have offered critiques of this idealized picture. For example, Juan Carlos Monedero, Paloma Aguilar, and Víctor Pérez Díaz[9] have noted that even before Franco's death, the Left itself helped ensure that the transition would take place in the way that it did.[10] On the cultural level, a thick veil was thrown over the memories of the Second Republic, the civil war and the Francoist years; and the 130,000 Spaniards buried in mass graves throughout the country were forgotten as well as the Spanish Republicans who died in exile. The transition itself was presented as a division between conservatives and reformers, meaning of course that because the Left didn't want to be accused of being reactionary, it had no choice but to accept the rules of the game introduced by the young socialists and the inheritors of Francoism who were presenting themselves as liberal centrists.

The amnesia imposed on the Spanish social fabric masked the trauma of the civil war, preventing a process of national reconciliation and also erasing the class struggle by presenting it as something obsolete and anachronistic. There was no room for Marxist paradigms because, of course, in the Spain that was being born, there would be no working classes because all would be "modern" and "European," belonging to an immense and powerful middle class. This rhetoric was quite successful: the majority of Spaniards accepted the "pact of silence" and took the euphoric European train, leaving behind a past of which they had become ashamed or which they viewed as an obstacle. Today, however, many Spaniards recognize that the transition from dictatorship to democracy remains incomplete and that a process of national reconciliation is still needed along with a dismantling of the Francoist traces in public institutions and society in general. Poetry echoes these necessities and critiques the entire process. *Elegía en Portbou*, for example, symbolizes how, in spite of this official oblivion, the memories of the Republicans were kept alive not only by their families but also by art in general and literary works, documentaries, and feature films, in particular.

Crespo Massieu (2011) notes on page 179 that *Elegía en Portbou* was written during the first decade of the twenty-first century, at a time when the grassroots movements for the recovery of the historical memory were gaining strength. Beginning in 2002, the Association for the Recovery of the Historical Memory (Asociación por la Recuperación de la Memoria Histórica [ARMH]), the pioneer group in this movement, established associations in cities throughout Spain.[11] The opposition Socialist Party (Partido Socialista Obrero Español [PSOE]) and United Left (Izquierda Unida) joined this grass-roots movement by presenting parliamentary proposals that condemned Francoism and honored its victims, after twenty years of inactivity on this subject. The ruling People's Party (Partido Popular [PP]), nevertheless, de-fended its argument of not wanting to reopen old wounds and revisit old resentments, insisting that national reconciliation had already been reached with the democratic Constitution of 1978. While the PP government was able to defeat most of the proposals, many Spaniards have continued to demand a revisiting of the civil war and the dictatorship.[12] When it took power in 2006, the PSOE listened to this desire to remember the past and presented a "[d]raft Bill to recognize, increase the rights of, and establish measures in favor of those who suffered persecution or violence during the civil war and the dictatorship."[13] The preamble of the Law of Historical Memory emphasizes the following:

> The beliefs that guided the transition—the spirit of reconciliation and harmo-ny, and of respect for pluralism and the peaceful defense of ideas of all kinds—allowed us to formulate a Constitution in 1978, one that translated into legal terms the Spaniards' will to come together again and that articulated, with a clearly integrative intent, a social and democratic nation under the rule of law. Understood in this way, the spirit of the transition created the most effective constitutional model of coexistence that Spaniards have ever en-joyed. And it is this same spirit that explains also the different measures and rights that have been recognized, from the origin of the democratic period, in favor of the people who in the decades previous to the Constitution suffered the consequences of the civil war and the dictatorial régime that came after. In spite of this legislative effort, we have pending initiatives to adopt to respond definitively to the demands of these citizens, demands that have been posed in the parliamentary context, as well as by different civic associations. We are dealing here with legitimate and fair petitions that our democracy—in light of its core spirit of harmony and in the framework of the Constitution—cannot dismiss. (*Boletín Oficial del Estado* 543100)[14]

In spite of the opposition who fought to stop the process, the Law of Histori-cal Memory was finally approved in congress on November 6, 2007, and took effect on December 27 of that same year. Nevertheless, this law did not satisfy everyone: supporters of reconstruction of the historical memory be-lieved the law was too weak on the Francoist regime, while others, such as former President José María Aznar,[15] insisted that it was better to look to the future than to revisit the past and "disturb bones." In fact, the law was paralyzed when the PP returned to power after winning the elections in

November 2011. Without a national reconciliation with the war that divided Spain into winners and losers during a long dictatorship, it will be very difficult to move forward as a truly democratic society.

The body of Spanish and foreign artistic production about the civil war and the Francoist years is ample and has been disseminated widely both within and beyond the country. Historical studies, articles, essays, literary criticism, films, plays, songs, and novels have proliferated since 1975, but their production has grown significantly during the last decade. Within this huge thematic corpus, there are several key studies that explain thoroughly the concept of the so-called "recuperation of historical memory."[16] For example, Carmen Moreno-Nuño devoted the introduction of her book *Las huellas de la Guerra Civil* (*Traces of the Civil War*) to the critical literature about this topic, based also on the theory of Pierre Nora (1989) concerning sites of memory (*lieux de mémoire*). According to Moreno, the post-Francoist literature—and I would add art in general—has produced literary works that have become sites of memory of the civil war. Her analysis focused on how the war is represented in key novels of the transition and of the subsequent period of the consolidation of the democracy. In 2008, Jo Labanyi edited a special issue of the *Journal of Spanish Cultural Studies* devoted to this topic under the cultural studies framework. The nine articles of the volume, titled "The Politics of Memory in Contemporary Spain," are written by researchers from different disciplines, such as comparative literature, anthropology, political science, literary and film studies, gender studies and art. Each essay addresses the different discourses in favor of and against the reconstruction of historical memory, which have materialized in the democratic Spain of recent years. For Stephanie R. Golob, author of one of these essays, this return to the past in Spain has its origins as much in the national as in the international context:

> This is a process of cultural as well as political change, channeled by the institutions constructed and the deals made in transition and as part of consolidation. What we are now witnessing in Spain is the convergence of two propitious moments for cultural change, one international and one domestic, that have resulted in key transformations in the political arena and in the range of policy options deemed legitimate for confronting the past. (128)

Golob's hypothesis then explains the need to confront the past of the democratic society that Spain has become. On one hand, this sociopolitical process of revisiting the traumatic past is a search for national reconciliation; on the other hand, it is part of an international trend, because similar movements have been developing in other countries, such as Chile, where a detention order against General Augusto Pinochet was carried out through the work of Spanish judge Baltasar Garzón.[17]

In the middle of all these discourses, art in general, and literature and cinema in particular, record densely this need to recover historical memory. Literary critics have been analyzing in-depth how this topic is presented in novels and films, but there is relatively little work on how poetry records this confrontation with the past in Spain. For that reason *Elegía en Portbou* is unique because these poems recover the memory of the Republicans' experience on their way to exile. Crespo Massieu's work, moreover, becomes a site of memory, in Nora's terms, by clearly and directly calling attention to the necessity to revisit a past that is still not completely known. But the most interesting aspect of the literary works that have reexamined the Spanish past is the spectral quality that such memories often display. This quality is linked with the spectrality that is identified in *Elegía en Portbou*, where the figures of Walter Benjamin and the Spanish Republican poet Antonio Machado, who died in exile in Collioure in 1939, appear and disappear unexpectedly throughout the book.[18] In his article "A Nation of Ghosts?: Haunting, Historical Memory and Forgetting in Post-Franco Spain," José Colmeiro highlights the resurgence of public interest in memory in Spain in recent years, after several decades of diagnosed "collective amnesia," and examines how Spanish literature and cinema are dealing with the past. He sees two trends: one presents the "transparent mimetic representation of the past using traditional linear structures"; the second trend comprises works that "have recurred to other non-realistic modes, in an effort to better capture the work of memory, the experiences of trauma, the silences and the voids of the past, the historical discontinuities, and the elusive nature of historical narrativization" (29–30). Colmeiro explains how

> one recurring element used in these works has been the trope of haunting, which underlies the ghostly nature of the past in its ever-returning nature, projecting its shadow towards the present and the future. These haunting narratives thus make visible the disappearances and absences silenced in normative historical accounts, and replicate the process of confronting a difficult past that still needs to be dealt with in the present. (30)

*Elegía en Portbou* is a good example of how the trope of haunting works: Benjamin and Machado are specters who wander in the verses cited below, walking with the thousands of Spanish Republicans who headed for a forced exile, crossed the French border and ended up populating nearby cemeteries such as the one in Portbou. Crespo Massieu decided to honor some of these Republicans with names, as when he describes the monument to Benjamin in the section *Libro de frontera* (*Book of the Border*) with these verses:

> Now to feel this blue as demand or debt
> Mistaking the names: Antonio, Paca, María,
> Teresa, Walter, Ana, José, Matea and the paintings:
> the angel with broken wings, the view of the bay,

the girl who was holding on to her father's hand, to mingle
the small stories of history, landscapes,
. . . . . . . . . . . . . . . . . . . . . . . . . . . . . . . . . . . . . .
At the end, alas!, this is the same blue,
the same painting, the same beauty,
the same pain, identical traces of absence,
here in Portbou,
on the border of light and history. (74)[19]

Crespo Massieu locates on the same level as Walter Benjamin and Antonio Machado the Republican people Paca, María, Teresa, Ana, José, and Mate, as representatives of many others who shared the same political ideals. While Benjamin and Machado are well recognized as part of literary and cultural history, the political aspect of their work is crucial to understand the way that they died and where they died. What is the common denominator of the people that Crespo Massieu names in this section? Exile and erasure. The poet is honoring the memory of the Republicans, and by naming them he is humanizing them, dignifying them, and unearthing them from multiple layers of institutional oblivion. We see them crossing the border and arriving in France defeated, exhausted, exiled, helpless, and finally forgotten. Nevertheless, a recurrent element in this poetic composition is the trope of haunting, which depicts the ghostly nature of the past, projecting its shadow towards the present and the future as conveyed in the description by Benjamin of Paul Klee's painting *Angelus Novus*, which appears in the verses just quoted and in the book's last lines. It is an angel of "broken wings" who is joining "the incessant dialogue with the dispossessed / its irrepressible dignity" (125).[20]

In *Elegía en Portbou*, the experiences of these specters of men, women, and children are recovered in order that they might receive the well-deserved recognition in the present, which is given in the last section titled *Libro del descenso* (*Book of Descent*). This closing section contains two long poems whose titles speak for themselves: "Zarza ardiente de la piedad y la restitución"[21] ("Burning Bush of Compassion and Restitution") (117) and "Mira, descansa, descansad al fin hemos llegado" ("Look, Rest, Rest, Everyone, We Have Finally Arrived") (138). The theme of restitution and the figure of Benjamin fill the verses. Once again, a quote from Benjamin prefaces this last section, which closes the circle started by Crespo Massieu in the first pages. Here he mentions how the dead will not be safe in the presence of the victorious enemy and how this "enemy has not stopped winning"[22] (115). The "defeated generation"[23] (117) that Crespo Massieu is describing from the present was betrayed twice, and it is still being betrayed because, as Benjamin said, the fascists are still keeping all those memories in oblivion. These voices and specters did not disappear during all these years but were in stagnation: "They, the ones who were never forgotten, / illuminated memory of a people condemned to oblivion / who never forgot" (146), because they have always been present in spite of the transition and the democracy that have not facilitated the creation of specific sites for them to reappear.[24] And yet, poetry has the power of enacting the very space where memory can materialize. The poem, therefore, transcends the immateriality of the specter by "overfilling the memory of hollows"; in this manner, the poetic space allows for the joining of "pieces, fringes, / to reconstruct world, fragments, voices" (119).[25] The testimonial aspect of the book can be found in these final verses. As Tzvetan Todorov explains in *Los abusos de la memoria* (2000 [1995]), the point of recovering memories is not only to go back to the past but to inscribe stories in the present in order to actualize them and make some sense of the past. In this way, recovering memories is a political act that creates empathic bonds with potential victims of new abuses and at the same time gives voice to the erased experiences. Moving towards closure, the poetic voice of *Elegía en Portbou* ends with the following verses: "the interior courtyards are passages, time / standing still in life, fragments, interstices, / open ribs of the fan of memory / which unfolds, closes, turns, sounds before the sea / where everything shines, becomes light, descent, arrives" (167–68).[26] Crespo Massieu's verses reveal to us the unequivocal certainty that memory is an indispensable tool for the future; memory is vital to construct identity and to prevent the repetition of past mistakes. *Elegía en Portbou* is, in this manner, a site of memory; it is clearly and directly calling for a process of revisiting a past that we still don't know completely.

## NOTES

1. In "From Portbou to Palestine, and Back," John Collins describes the monument where Walter Benjamin is buried and offers an insightful and powerful analysis of the Israeli/Palestinian conflict. Collins notes that near the monument are an olive tree, symbol of the Palestinian people, and a prickly pear cactus, symbol of the Israeli people. These two plants "appear to mingle quite freely and patiently, partaking of the same soil and often growing of the same rock. At the other end of the Mediterranean from the conflict of Israel/Palestine, both keep watch over to the memorial of the man who refused to become a Zionist" (71).

2. Antonio Crespo Massieu (Madrid, 1951) belongs to the group of Spanish poets of the critical conscience. He has published two other poetry books: *En este lugar* (2004) and *Orilla del tiempo* (2005). For more information about Crespo Massieu and the group of the critical conscience, see Alberto García-Teresa's *Poesía de la conciencia crítica (1987–2011)* and Marina Llorente's "Poemas críticos en la España contemporánea" and *Poesía en acción* (2014).

3. The multivolume project *Lieux de Mémoire*, by Pierre Nora, is considered an important theoretical development in memory studies research. Nora's introduction to this collective work was first translated into English and published as an article titled "Between Memory and History: Les Lieux de Mémoire," in the academic journal *Representations* in 1989. For more information about the use of Nora's concept of site of memory in the Spanish context, see Christina Dupláa, "Memoria Colectiva y *Lieux de Mémoire* en la España de la Transición."

4. For more information about the crossing of the Franco-Spanish border by Republicans in 1939 and their life in the south of France afterward, see Patricia Fernández's *Points of Departure (Between Spain and France)* exhibition, and Jean-François Berdah's "The Devil in France. The Tragedy of Spanish Republicans and French Policy after the Civil War (1936–1945)."

72 Marina Llorente

5. "A partir de cuándo el silencio y sus sombras, / desde que tiempo sin tiempo horada renuncias, / enumera traiciones, olvidos, cuándo" (11).
6. "El cronista que narra los acontecimientos sin distinguir entre los grandes y los pequeños, da cuenta de una verdad: que nada de lo que una vez haya acontecido ha de darse por perdido para la historia."
7. Ellas, los doloridos, los viejos, las madres
   los que dejaron el fusil en la frontera,
   los hijos del mañana sin pasaporte ni nostalgia,
   los que lloraban, los ateridos de frío, los desafiantes,
   los que arrastran la maleta como si aún fuera origen
   o rescoldo, persistencia o temblor de casa perdida,
   y los que aún juegan o agarran la mano que a lo incierto
   les lleva, los que ahora surgen como absurda aparición
   en esta tiniebla, este túnel, este negro infierno. (104)

8. According to Landsberg: "*Prosthetic Memory* theorizes the production and dissemination of memories that have no direct connection to a person's lived past and yet are essential to the production and articulation of subjectivity" (20). Landsberg refers to these memories as "prosthetic memories" for four reasons. First, they are derived from engagement with a mediated representation, like seeing a film. Second, they are memories produced by an experience of mass-mediated representation. Third, these forms of memory "underscore their commodified form"; and fourth, they "underscore their usefulness" (20–21).
9. For more information, see Vicenc Navarro, *Bienestar insuficiente, democracia incompleta: Sobre lo que no se habla en nuestro país* (2002); J. Trullén, *Fundamentos económicos de la transición política española: La política económica de los acuerdos de la Moncloa* (1993); J. Tusell, *Historia de España en el siglo xx: La transición democrática y el gobierno socialista* (1999); and J. Tusell and Á. Soto, *Historia de la transición (1975–1986)* (1996).
10. In *La transición contada a nuestros padres. Nocturno de la democracia española*, Monedero underscores the fact that in its famous 13th Congress, which was held in exile near Paris in 1974, the Spanish Socialist Party began a process of reform that sparked a major ideological change in the party. It was there that a group of young Socialists led by Felipe González proposed a shift away from Marxism and toward European-style social democracy. The young wing of the party captured the pulse of the traditional leaders and managed to get González elected as Secretary-General of the party. This moment would shape the country's political future and the development of the transition.
11. For more information, see "La recuperación de la 'memoria histórica': entre el incumplimiento institucional y la instrumentalización política," by Sören Brinkmann.
12. For more information, see "El debate sobre el pasado y su importancia para el presente," by Alberto Reig Tapia.
13. "Anteproyecto de ley por la que se reconocen y amplían derechos y se establecen medidas a favor de quienes padecieron persecución o violencia durante la Guerra Civil y la dictadura" (*Boletín Oficial del Estado* 543100).
14. "El espíritu de reconciliación y concordia, y de respeto al pluralismo y a la defensa pacífica de todas las ideas, que guio la Transición, nos permitió dotarnos de una Constitución, la de 1978, que tradujo jurídicamente esa voluntad de reencuentro de los españoles, articulando un Estado social y democrático de derecho con clara vocación integradora. El espíritu de la Transición da sentido al modelo constitucional de convivencia más fecundo que hayamos disfrutado nunca y explica las diversas medidas y derechos que se han ido reconociendo, desde el origen mismo de todo el período democrático, en favor de las personas que, durante los decenios anteriores a la Constitución, sufrieron las consecuencias de la guerra civil y del régimen dictatorial que la sucedió. Pese a ese esfuerzo legislativo, quedan aún iniciativas por adoptar para dar cumplida y definitiva respuesta a las demandas de esos ciudadanos, planteadas tanto en el ámbito parlamentario como por distintas asociaciones cívicas. Se trata de peticiones legítimas y justas, que nuestra democracia, apelando de nuevo a su espíritu fundacional de concordia, y en el marco de la Constitución, no puede dejar de atender" (*Boletín Oficial del Estado* 543100).

15. José María Aznar, member of the PP (People's Party) and former president of Spain (1996–2004), stated the following: "España no necesita mirar hacia atrás ni remover huesos, ni tumbas, ni hablar de guerras civiles. España lo que necesita es mirar más que nunca al futuro y tender puentes pero no volver a etapas absurdas de divisiones y de confrontaciones." ("Spain does not need to look back; it is does not need to disturb bones or graves, or to talk about civil wars. What Spain needs more than ever is to look toward the future and build bridges, but it does not need to revisit absurd periods of divisions and confrontations.") For more information, see "Aznar ataca al Gobierno."

16. Memory studies have been developing extensively in the last decades. Regarding the case of Spain and studies of literary criticism, see the following for more information: *Disremembering the Dictatorship: The Politics of Memory in the Spanish Transition to Democracy* (2000), edited by Joan Ramón Resina; *Memoria histórica e identidad cultural. De la posguerra a la postmodernidad* (2005), by José F. Colmeiro; *La memoria novelada: Hibridación de géneros y metaficción en la novela española sobre la guerra civil y el franquismo* (2011), edited by Hans Lauge Hansen and Juan Carlos Cruz Suárez; *La memoria novelada II. Ficcionalización, documentalismo y lugares de memoria en la narrativa memorialista española* (2013), edited by Martín Diana González and Juan Carlos Cruz Suárez; and "La memoria histórica en la poesía de Isabel Peréz Montalbán y David Gonzalez" and *Poesía en acción. Poemas críticos en la España contemporánea* by Marina Llorente.

17. Nevertheless, Garzón was unable to finish his investigation of "the killings of 114,000 people at the hands of Franco's supporters during the 1936–1939 Civil War and the dictatorship that followed and the exhumation of at least 19 mass graves. He accused Franco and 34 former generals and ministers of crimes against humanity. In 2012 the Supreme Court of Spain considered three charges against Garzón. They found against him in relation to one of the charges, that relating to his investigation of the corrupt, money-laundering "Gurtel" network. On 9 February 2012 the Supreme Court convicted him of illegally wiretapping conversations between suspects (on remand in connection with inquiries into "Gurtel") and their lawyers who were believed to be moving their money beyond the reach of the court. The trial judge described this act as appropriate to a dictatorship and sentenced him to eleven years disqualification from judicial activity. The Court did not find against him in the other two cases: On 12 February, a charge against Garzón relating to his relationship with a bank was abandoned on a technicality. On 27 February 2012 he was cleared of abusing his powers in investigating the crimes of the Francoist era (the charge which had resulted in his first suspension in 2010)" (Guarino 63). For more information, see *Shoot the Messenger?: Spanish Democracy and the Crimes of Francoism from the Pact of Silence to the Trial of Baltasar Garzón* (2013), by Francisco Espinosa Maestre.

18. Antonio Machado (1875–1939), a Republican poet who crossed the Franco-Spanish border at the end of Spanish Civil War, died on February 22 of 1939 and is buried in the cemetery of Collioure, France. He was one of the leading poets of the Generation of 1898 group of writers. He wrote *Soledades* (1903), *Soledades, galerías y otros poemas* (1907), *Campos de Castilla* (1912), *Nuevas canciones* (1924) and *Juan de Mairena* (1936).

19. Ahora sentir ese azul como exigencia o deuda
    Confundir los nombres: Antonio, Paca, María,
    Teresa, Walter, Ana, José, Matea y los cuadros:
    el ángel de alas rotas, la vista sobre la bahía,
    la niña que iba de la mano del padre, confundir
    historias pequeñas de la historia, paisajes,
    la mirada del joven, la piedad que vio en Giotto,
    el dolor de Mantegna, la desmesura de Miguel Ángel,
    la belleza de Botticelli, el insinuado misterio
    de Leonardo, toda la luz, la forma, el ritmo.
    Pues al fin este es el mismo azul,
    el mismo cuadro, la misma belleza,
    el mismo dolor, idénticas huellas de ausencia,
    aquí en Portbou,
    en la frontera de la luz y la historia.

20. "Angel de alas rotas," "El incesante coloquio con los desposeídos / su irreductible dignidad" (125).
21. In the book of Exodus, Yahweh first speaks to Moses by luring him to the "burning bush that does not waste by burning" (*The Knox Bible,* Exod. 3.3). Once Moses approaches the miraculous burning bush, Yahweh identifies himself to entrust Moses with the tasks of liberating the Jewish people from their Egyptian captors and leading them to the promised land. For the refugees who left Spain in 1939, the movement was, sadly, in the opposite direction: they were leaving the beloved República only to enter the land of suffering, loss, and exile.
22. "Y este enemigo no ha dejado de vencer" (115).
23. "Generación vencida" (117).
24. "Ellos, los nunca olvidados, / encendida memoria de un pueblo condenado al olvido / que nunca olvidó" (146).
25. "Colmando la memoria de huecos / alzados contra el olvido, guardados como testigos / de un tiempo herido, hecho ausencia, daguerrotipo, / memoria ajena, penumbra. / Y unir así trozos, flecos, / reconstruir mundo, fragmentos, voces" (119).
26. "Los patios interiores son pasajes, tiempo / detenido en vida, fragmentos, intersticios, / varillas abiertas del abanico de la memoria / que se despliega, se cierra, gira, suena frente al mar / donde todo resplandece, se hace luz, descenso, llega" (167–168).

## WORKS CITED

Aguilar, Paloma. *Memory and Amnesia. The Role of the Spanish Civil War in the Transition to Democracy.* New York: Berghahn Books, 2002.
———. *Políticas de la memoria y memorias de la política. El caso español en perspectiva comparada.* Madrid: Alianza, 2008.
Aznar, José María. "Aznar ataca al Gobierno." El País.com 23 mayo 2007. Web. 12 Jan. 2011. http://www.elpais.com/videos/espana/Aznar/ataca/Gobierno/elpvidnac/20070523elpepunac_6/Ves/.
Berdah, Jean-François. "The Devil in France. The Tragedy of Spanish Republicans and French Policy after the Civil War (1936–1945)." *Discrimination and Tolerance in Historical Perspective.* Ed. Guomundur Hálfdanarson. Pisa: Edizioni Plus, 2008. 301–318.
*Boletín Oficial del Estado* 310 (27 de diciembre del 2007): 54310–16. Web. 10 Oct. 2014. http://www.boe.es/buscar/doc.php?id=BOE-A-2007-22296.
Brinkmann, Sören. "La recuperación de la 'memoria histórica': entre el incumplimiento institucional y la instrumentalización política." *España: Del consenso a la polarización: Cambios en la democracia española.* Ed. Walther L. Bernecker and Günther Maihold. Madrid: Iberoamericana; Vervuert, 2007. 203–17.
Collins, John. "From Portbou to Palestine, and Back" *Social Text* 24.4 (Winter 2006): 66–85.
Colmeiro, José. "A Nation of Ghosts?: Haunting, Historical Memory and Forgetting in Post-Franco Spain" *452 F Electronic Journal of Theory of Literature and Comparative Literature* 4 (2011): 17–34. Web. 15 Mar. 2014. http://www.452f.com/pdf/numero04/colmeiro/04_452f_mono_colmeiro_indiv.pdf.
———. *Memoria histórica e identidad cultural. De la posguerra a la postmodernidad.* Anthropos: Barcelona, 2005.
Crespo Massieu, Antonio. *Elegía en Portbou.* Madrid: Bartleby, 2011.
———. *En este lugar.* San Sebastián: Fundación Kutxa, 2004.
———. *Orilla del tiempo.* Alzira: Germanía, 2005.
Dupláa, Christina. "Memoria colectiva y *lieux de mémoire* en la España de la Transición." *Disremembering the Dictatorship: The Politics of Memory in the Spanish Transition to Democracy.* Ed. Joan Ramón Resina. Atlanta: Rodopi, 2000. 29–42.
Espinosa Maestre, Francisco. *Shoot the Messenger?: Spanish Democracy and the Crimes of Francoism from the Pact of Silence to the Trial of Baltasar Garzón.* East Sussex: Sussex Academic Press, 2013.

Fernández, Patricia. *Points of Departure (Between Spain and France)*. 18th Street Arts Center, Santa Monica, CA. Web. 8 Sept. 2014. http://18thstreet.org/events/exhibition-patricia-fernandez.

García-Teresa, Alberto. *Poesía de la conciencia crítica (1987–2011)*. Madrid: Tierradenadie, 2013.

Garzón, Baltasar. Texto íntegro del juez Garzón solicitando la prisión provisional incondicional de Pinochet. Web. 12 Oct. 2014. http://web.ua.es/up/pinochet/documentos/auto-18-10-98.html.

Golob, Stephanie R. "*Volver*: The Return Of/To Transitional Justice Politics in Spain." *Journal of Spanish Cultural Studies* 9.2 (2008): 127–41.

González, Martín Diana, and Juan Carlos Cruz Suárez. *La memoria novelada II. Ficcionalización, documentalismo y lugares de memoria en la narrativa memorialista española*. New York: Peter Lang, 2013.

Guarino, Angela M. "Chasings Ghosts: Pursuing Retroactive Justice for Franco-Era Crimes against Humanity." *Boston College International and Comparative Law Review* 33. 1 (2010): 61–85. Web. 15 Oct. 2014. http://lawdigitalcommons.bc.edu/cgi/viewcontent.cgi?article=1003&context=iclr.

Halbwachs, Maurice. *The Collective Memory*. Trans. Francis J. Ditter and Vida Yazdi Ditter. New York: Harper, 1980.

Hansen, Hans Lauge, and Juan Carlos Cruz Suárez. *Hibridación de géneros y metaficción en la novela española sobre la guerra civil y el franquismo*. New York: Peter Lang, 2011.

*The Knox Bible*. Web. 18 Dec. 2014. http://www.newadvent.org/bible/exo003.htm.

Labanyi, Jo. "The Politics of Memory in Contemporary Spain." *Journal of Spanish Cultural Studies* 9.2 (2008): 119–25.

Landsberg, Alison. *Prosthetic Memory: The Transformation of American Remembrance in the Age of Mass Culture*. New York: Columbia University Press, 2004.

Llorente, Marina. "La memoria histórica en la poesía de Isabel Pérez Montalbán y David González" *Hispanic Review* 81.2 (2013): 181–200.

———. "Poemas críticos en la España contemporánea." *Hispania* 91.3 (2008): 579–89.

———. *Poesía en acción. Poemas críticos en la España contemporánea*. Tenerife: Baile del Sol, 2014.

Martínez i Ferrer Antonio. "Una lectura vivida de Elegía en Portbou." *YouKali*, 115–20 Web., 19 June 2014. http://www.youkali.net/youkali12-4aResena1.pdf.

Monedero, Juan Carlos. *La transición contada a nuestros padres. Nocturno de la democracia española*. Madrid: Catarata, 2011.

Moreno-Nuño, Carmen. *Las huellas de la Guerra Civil. Mito y trauma en la narrativa de la España democrática*. Madrid: Libertarias, 2006.

Navarro, Vicenc. *Bienestar insuficiente, democracia incompleta: Sobre lo que no se habla en nuestro país*. Barcelona: Anagrama, 2002.

Nora, Pierre. "Between Memory and History: *Les Lieux de Mémoire*." Trans. Marc Roudebush. *Representations* 26 (1989): 7–24.

Pérez Díaz, Víctor. *La primacía de la sociedad civil: El proceso de formación de la España democrática*. Madrid: Alianza Editorial, 1994.

Reig Tapia, Alberto. "El debate sobre el pasado y su importancia para el presente." *España: Del consenso a la polarización: Cambios en la democracia española*. Ed. Walther L. Bernecker and Günther Maihold. Madrid: Iberoamericana; Vervuert, 2007. 167–202.

Resina, Joan Ramón. "Short of Memory: The Reclamation of the Past Since the Spanish Transition to Democracy." *Disremembering the Dictatorship: The Politics of Memory in the Spanish Transition to Democracy*. Ed. Joan Ramón Resina. Atlanta: Rodopi, 2000. 83–126.

Todorov, Tzvetan. *Los abusos de la memoria*. Barcelona: Paidos Ibérica, 2008.

Trullén, J. *Fundamentos económicos de la transición política española: La política económica de los acuerdos de la Moncloa*. Madrid: Ministerio de Trabajo, 1993.

Tusell, J. *Historia de España en el siglo xx: La transición democrática y el gobierno socialista*. Madrid: Taurus, 1999.

Tusell, J., and Á. Soto. *Historia de la transición (1975–1986)*. Madrid: Alianza Editorial, 1996.

*Chapter Five*

# Translation as a Means of Preserving Historical Memory in Spain, Nicaragua, and Chile

## Steven F. White

According to Katherine Hite, Spain's Law of Historical Memory, passed by congress in 2007, is

> a comprehensive piece of legislation that includes exhuming and reburying the remains of thousands of Republicans killed during the Spanish Civil War; ridding the country of monuments to Franco, as well as to either side of the civil war; compensating all validated legal claims of major human rights abuse during the war and the dictatorship; [and] granting citizenship to children and grandchildren of Republican exiles. (23)

In attempting to define historical memory, Spaniard José María Pedreño speaks of the processes involved in the recovery of what has been lost, repressed and forgotten that include an initial stage of historical and scientific research (seminars, documentaries, debates) followed by the production of aesthetic works (novels, films, theater, poetry, songs, painting, and sculpture)—a sequence that, significantly, was reversed in Spain. For Pedreño, a people "that does not know its history does not understand its present," and this results in a "profound democratic deficit that increases day by day in a depoliticized, non-participatory society" (11). Spain's attempt to deal with a specific (and increasingly remote) period of its history has been an extraordinarily long and painful process, especially in comparison to certain Hispanic American countries such as Argentina, Chile, Uruguay, Nicaragua, and El Salvador, where the emergence from repressive dictatorships and a return to democracy brought a relatively more rapid period of reflection on historical memory, even if this is, perforce, an ongoing social project. Few people are as acutely aware of the social and psychological ramifications of this process as Spanish magistrate Baltasar Garzón (the same official responsible for having Chilean dictator Augusto Pinochet arrested in London in 1998), who said in a recent interview:

> One comes to the very clear conclusion that Francoism is inoculated in our genes, that it's alive and well. Spain is the only European country that has not thoroughly examined its past. There is a culture of denial, and before us, more than 150,000 victims who await reparation. It's a matter of respecting the dignity of the defeated. Given the time that has passed, they have the right to know the truth and receive reparation. (Ruiz Mantilla 32–33)

If poems, then, as Pedreño suggests, can be considered potential sites or repositories of historical memory, literary translation may be understood as an important, though not entirely unproblematic, related dynamic. Over the last thirty-five years, I have been an active translator of poetry from Spain and Hispanic America, often in situ and sometimes during tumultuous periods of history such as the insurrection in Nicaragua in 1979 and two years of the Pinochet dictatorship in 1978 and 1983. In 1988, the year that I published the translation I did with Greg Simon of Federico García Lorca's *Poet in New York*, I traveled to Spain for the first time as director of the St. Lawrence University Program Abroad in Spain and finally had a fuller chance, over a year's time, to reflect on the tragic magnitude of Lorca's death: remembering when I had seen Picasso's *Guernica* at the Museum of Modern Art in New York as a college student more than a decade before as I stood before the painting at the Casón del Buen Retiro in Madrid; visiting Lorca's magnificent city of Granada; traveling with the last remaining survivors of the Abraham Lincoln Battalion on a bus ride that took us to the site of the Battle of Jarama (where I cut a twig and leaf of an olive tree to send to the poet Philip Levine, who has written such admirable poems about the Spanish Civil War); and entering the truly macabre subterranean space of the Valle de los Caídos, which overwhelmed me with sadness in the phantasmal presence of those who murdered a century's greatest poet.

Initially, I am sure that I considered my work as a translator as something that was helping to break linguistic barriers so that English-speaking readers might understand how poets in Latin America and Spain perceive their world and also the United States, especially when the texts more explicitly addressed the historical moment in which they were composed. However, with the passage of time and as someone who teaches translation theory, I now tend to agree with Lawrence Venuti when he maintains that:

> Translation never communicates in an untroubled fashion because the translator negotiates the linguistic and cultural differences of the foreign text by

reducing them and supplying another set of differences, basically domestic, drawn from the receiving language and culture to enable the foreign to be received there. The foreign text, then, is not so much communicated as inscribed with domestic intelligibilities and interests. The inscription begins with the very choice of a text for translation, always a very selective, densely motivated choice, and continues in the development of discursive strategies to translate it, always a choice of certain domestic discourses over others. (468)

"Seen as domestic inscription," then, according to Venuti, translation is "never quite cross-cultural communication" (469). Too, there is an ethical dimension to the act of translation, directly linked, in my mind as a translator, to the preservation of historical memory, an attitude that Venuti views as "simultaneous with a political agenda: the domestic terms of the inscription become the focus of rewriting in the translation, discursive strategies where the hierarchies that rank the values in the domestic culture are disarranged to set going processes of defamiliarization, canon reformation, ideological critique, and institutional change" (469). If poems, like many aesthetic works, store historical memory, so do their translations, and my English versions of poems written in Spain and in Hispanic America also serve the same function with the added layer that they are also places that house my domesticating energies as a translator as I metabolize my own history and memories, which are inseparable, though not always as visible, as those of the authors whose work I render in my first language. Because the terminology "historical memory" is most closely linked with relatively recent Spanish legislation, perhaps it is most appropriate to begin with a highly representative poet from Spain. The same political and sexual ideals that Lorca expresses in *Poet in New York* also made him a threat to the fascist, Catholic Spain of the Falangists who silenced him in Viznar. Any poem by Lorca, such as "The King of Harlem," in any of the many languages into which his poetry has been translated, as well as any poem dedicated to Lorca's memory (such as "F. G. L" by Gastón Baquero, a Cuban poet who lived for decades in Spain, and Neruda's "Ode to Federico García Lorca") are effective and affective sites of perpetuating the poet's legacy against oblivion and resisting the repressive political apparatus designed precisely for cultural erasure:

> The King of Harlem (fragment)
>
> Ay, Harlem! Ay, Harlem! Ay, Harlem!
> There is no anguish like that of your oppressed reds,
> or your blood shuddering with rage inside the dark eclipse,
> or your garnet violence, deaf and dumb in the penumbra,
> or your grand king a prisoner in the uniform of a doorman.
> [. . .]
> Through the all-knowing silence,
> waiters, cooks, and those whose tongues lick clean
> the wounds of millionaires

seek the king in the streets or on the sharp angles of
saltpeter.
A wooden wind from the south, slanting through the black
mire,
spits on the broken boats and drives tacks into shoulders.
A south wind that carries
tusks, sunflowers, alphabets,
and a battery with drowned wasps.
[. . .]
Ay, Harlem in disguise!
Ay, Harlem, threatened by a mob of headless suits!
I hear your murmur,
I hear it moving through tree trunks and elevator shafts,
through gray sheets
where your cars float covered with teeth,
through dead horses and petty crimes,
through your grand, despairing king
whose beard reaches the sea. [1]
(García Lorca 27, 31, 33)

   F.G.L.

Peace. Now it's death that has landed
on the steel bands around his chest.
Today the dawn unmakes his bed,
and his dreams play on in the mirror.
A whole life has been summoned into
a limitless field, space still empty
of his being. He decides to go,
to hear his luminous silence spill.
He will need to drink the fragrance
of the snow he shelters, of the sands
that could open and swallow a bull.
Dream of him as our gift to God, bursting
with laughter, verse, passion. Dream of him—
sweet fires on unseen shores start to sing. (Baquero 91)

   Ode to Federico García Lorca (fragment)

If only in the night of being, so lost and alone,
I could gather oblivion, shadow and smoke
from trains and ocean liners,
with a black funnel,
with ashes in my teeth,
I'd do it for the tree in which you grow,
for the nests of golden water you've gathered,
and for the vine that covers your bones,
revealing to you the secret of the night. (Neruda 120)

The final image of the vine in Neruda's famous homage to Lorca recalls
Walter Benjamin's biomimetic approach to translation in "The Task of the

Translator," in which he describes translations in the following way: "In them, the life of the originals attains its latest, continually renewed, and most complete unfolding" (255). This transtemporal flowering of a work of art by means of the translation process, says Benjamin, implies an ongoing vitality: "For in its afterlife—which could not be called that if it were not a transformation and a renewal of something living—the original undergoes a change" (256). And it is precisely in this way that translation is linked to the dynamic processes of life and the creation of organic, symbiotic sites that evolve over time.

Lorca's continuing presence in other languages as well as in his own is also a means of fortifying and protecting democracy over time in Spain and, no doubt, elsewhere as well. An example of this is when the Spanish poet José Hierro was awarded the Príncipe de Asturias Prize on October 3, 1981, just a few months after the coup d'état attempt in Spain. Prince Phillip, now King, who awarded the prize in his first public act, was thirteen years old at the time. During the ceremony, Hierro declared, "Dictatorships place culture—a single culture, their own—at the service of their politics. Democracies place themselves at the service of culture, accepting it as it is. Ultimately, it is intelligently political work" (Cruz 15). Hierro added that the poet might appear to resemble something that adorns the pinnacle of a building: "But that object considered something merely decorative can cause enormous damage when it is cruelly broken and sent falling. If one gives the name Federico García Lorca to the scroll at the top of the column, from the public's point of view, we know how damaging it can be when it is toppled" (Cruz 15).

Lorca collaborated with Neruda in 1934 to produce their well-known homage to Darío in alternating voices "Discurso al alimón a Rubén Darío." Using this text as a model, Greg Simon and I wrote our own letter addressed to the poet on the occasion of the presentation in Managua and León in 2005 of the translations we did for his *Selected Writings* published by Penguin. When I read this passage before two large audiences, I was confirming in public how thoroughly Nicaragua had transformed my life through the translation of its poets:

> Rubén, we understand your fear of the cruel barbarian invaders as you said it in your famous line: *Is it our fate that millions of us will speak in English?* But we hope that the country where the cult of Hercules is joined to the cult of Mammon will grow more bilingual each and every day. As we arrive in your homeland now, Rubén, we wonder what the customs officials will think of *us* when they open the suitcases and see books of *dariana* coming back into their country. Invading *filibusters* with past and future bullets? No. On the pages of this book that we are launching and celebrating tonight are your bittersweet words, Rubén, because your work will live on as long as there are poets in the

world who are born in Nicaragua, or who are born and come to Nicaragua, or who come to Nicaragua and are born. (Simon and White n.p.)

Even if this were true, and I think it is, the real beginning for me occurred when I was a student at Williams College in 1976 and my Nicaraguan friend Marcel Pallais (whose murder in Managua on October 4, 1979, some three months after the Sandinista triumph, remains unsolved) recited Darío's "Lo fatal" at a small party and deeply, irrevocably impressed everyone, including me. Marcel left the invitation to his home, his country and his country's poets open, and I arrived in Managua in January 1979 to begin the work on what would be my first published book, the bilingual anthology *Poets of Nicaragua*.

Over the years, my familiarity with Nicaraguan history that is character-ized by successive U.S. invasions of Nicaragua, the U.S.-backed dictatorship of the Somoza family for nearly half a century and an unconstitutional U.S.-funded Contra war, has made it clear to me now how valid Venuti's defini-tions of translation are in terms of developing, as a translator, a keener sense of positionality, identity, and, ultimately, of *solidarity*: "Translating is always ideological because it releases a domestic remainder, an inscription of values, beliefs, and representations linked to historical moments and social positions in the domestic culture" (485). One of the texts I translated for *Poets of Nicaragua* (1982), for example, was Ernesto Cardenal's indigenous-themed persona poem "Tahirasawichi in Washington," which, for me, became a way of "talking back" across time to the Reagan administration. At any rate, it was easier for me to understand the United States and its unethical foreign policy when I was outside my country and able to return to it inside words originally written by a Nicaraguan poet that I had translated into English, such as Darío's "To Roosevelt," "Poem to the Foreigners' Moment in Our Jungle"[2] by Pablo Antonio Cuadra (1912–2002), and Gioconda Belli's "Nic-aragua Water Fire" (published by the ferociously progressive Curbstone Press founded by Sandy Taylor and Judith Ayer Doyle):

> To Roosevelt (fragement)
>
> You will be a future invader
> of naive America, the one with Indian blood,
> that still prays to Jesus Christ and still speaks the Spanish tongue [. . .]
> You think that life is one big fire,
> that progress is just eruption,
> that wherever you put bullets,
> you put the future, too.
> No.
> The U.S. is a country that is powerful and strong.
> When the giant yawns and stretches, the earth feels a tremor
> rippling through the enormous vertebrae of the Andes. (Darío 119)

Poem to the Foreigners' Moment in Our Jungle (fragment)

In the heart of our mountains, where the old jungle
devours roads the way the *guás* eats snakes,
where Nicaragua raises its flag of blazing rivers among torrential drums . . .
There, long before my song,
even before I existed, I invent the stone called flint
and I ignite the sordid green of *heliconias*,
the mangroves' boiling silence,
and I set fire to the orchid in the boa constrictor's night.
I cry out. Scream. Star! Who just opened the night's doors?
I must make something from the mud of history,
dig down in the swamp and unearth the moons
of my forefathers. Oh, unleash
your dark rage, magnetic snake,
sharpen your obsidian claws, black tiger, stare
with your phosphorescent eyes, there!
In the heart of the jungle,
500 North Americans!
They're marching,
singing among the *sotocaballos* and the *ñámbaros*,
singing to the rhythm of their marching feet.
And Nicaragua's last moons plummet from treetops.
(Red macaws chatter in crazy tongues.)
In the heart of our mountains, 500 Marines with machine-guns make their way.
I hear voices.
(Cuadra, *The Birth of the Sun* 15)

Nicaragua Water Fire (fragment)

borders of a day that must be fought
there's no other way no alternative but the struggle
Behind curtains of water
I write fingers on triggers
great wars
suffering the size of mothers' eyes
dripping uncontainable cloudbursts
here come the small cold corpses
*los muchachos* come down from the mountains
with hammocks they recovered from the contras
we don't eat much there isn't much we all want to eat
big white hands want to kill us
but we made hospitals beds
where women scream births
all day we beat like hearts
*tum tum tam tam*
Indians' veins repeat history:
We don't want children who will be slaves
flowers blossom from coffins
no one dies in Nicaragua

> Nicaragua my love my raped child
> getting up straightening her skirt
> walking behind the murderer following him
> down the mountain up the mountain
> they will not pass say the birds
> they will not pass say the couples who make love
> who make children who make bread who make trenches
> (Belli 87)

Elsewhere, I have written about how two other Nicaraguan poets synthesized crucial moments of history in their poetry: Salomón de la Selva (1893–1958) provides first person testimony of his experiences as a combatant in World War I in *El soldado desconocido* (*The Unknown Soldier*) (1922), and Joaquín Pasos (1914–1947), in his epic masterpiece "The Warsong of the Things," describes the future extinction of the human race in the postnuclear world of World War II.[3] Especially compelling in terms of defining how a poem can become a repository for historical memory, even in the case of conflict viewed from afar, is this fragment from Pasos's long poem:

> Finally, Lord of the Armies, here is the supreme pain.
> Here, without pity, without subterfuge, without verses,
> is the true pain.
> At last, Lord, before us all is the pain stopped cold.
> It is not pain felt for the wounded or the dead,
> nor for the blood that was shed, nor for the earth filled with laments,
> nor for the cities empty of houses, nor for the fields filled with orphans.
> It is the whole pain.
> There can be no tears, no sorrow,
> no words, no memories.
> Nothing fits now inside the chest.
> All the noises of the world form one great silence.
> All the men of the world form a single specter.
> In the middle of this pain, soldier!, your post remains,
> empty or filled.
> The lives of those who are left have hollows—
> complete voids—
> as if they had taken mouthfuls of flesh from their bodies.
> Look into this gap, the one I have here in my chest,
> so you can see heavens and hells.
> Look at my head. It has thousands of holes:
> through it shines a white sun, through it a black star.
> Touch my hand, this hand that yesterday bore steel:
> you can pass your fingers through it in the air!
> Flight of flesh, fear,
> days, things, souls, fire.
> Everything remained in time. Everything burned over there, far away. (277–278)

Perhaps the most important literary connection between Nicaragua and Chile was when Rubén Darío traveled to Valparaíso and published his groundbreaking first book *Azul . . .* there in 1888. These are the countries where I have spent the most time as a translator, and I cannot think of two places in Latin America with a greater appreciation for the outstanding poetry that is an integral part of their cultural identities. In 1983, with the support of a Fulbright grant, I began editing and translating *Poets of Chile: 1965–1985*, comprised of poetry by two generations of writers who published their work over two decades and who were divided by the 1973 military coup, which resulted in the imprisonment, torture, death, and exile of so many Chileans. As I write these words, in León, Nicaragua, I am reading in the newspapers that, even though it took more than forty years, the people responsible for the murder of Víctor Jara are finally being brought to trial in Chile. Nineteen eighty-three was the tenth anniversary of the violation of Chile's democratic tradition and also the year that the general population decided enough was enough and took to the streets massively to protest the Pinochet regime. A key safe place at that time in Santiago to do research and meet with writers was the Referencias Críticas section of the Biblioteca Nacional de Chile, which was run by the truly admirable Justo Alarcón and Juan Camilo-Lorca. I would stop by at least several times a week, if only to leave with Juan (to share with others) the month's supply of *Ventana* published by the Frente Sandinista's newspaper *Barricada*. The revolutionary cultural supplement published in Nicaragua had taken the Pacific coast scenic route to Chile via the University of Oregon, where my mail was forwarded to me in Santiago. I remembered another Chile-Nicaragua connection that I had almost forgotten when I recently met Sergio Marras, former director of Chile's *Revista APSI*, at a dinner at Niall Binns' home in Madrid. This magazine, a stellar example of journalism of resistance during the worst years of the Pinochet dictator-ship, published an interview I did with Nicaraguan novelist and former Vice President Sergio Ramírez in 1984. The English translation of this interview formed part of my book *Culture & Politics in Nicaragua: Testimonies of Poets and Writers* (1986).

My travels in Chile have taken me from Arica in the north to Punta Arenas on the Straits of Magellan in the south. I feel privileged to have met and worked with poets as astonishingly accomplished as Nicanor Parra, Gon-zalo Rojas (whom I interviewed in 1983 at his Torreón del Renegado), En-rique Lihn, Jorge Teillier, Óscar Hahn, Juan Luis Martínez, and Raúl Zurita.[4]

The person with whom I worked most closely in 1983 in Chile, however, was Aristóteles España (1955–2011). When I met him at the very end of 1982 in Santiago, I bought a copy of *Equilibrios e incomunicaciones*, a typed, photocopied text bound by a metal bar. This was the clandestine edition of the testimonial poems he wrote as a prisoner in the remote and isolated Dawson Island concentration camp, where he was sent to be interro-gated and tortured as a seventeen-year old student leader from the relatively nearby city in Chile's extreme south, Punta Arenas, along with the most important political prisoners from the Popular Unity government of Salvador Allende, including José Tohá and Orlando Letelier.[5] My translations of these poems that describe the cycle of Aristóteles España's Season in Hell and originally were written on toilet paper smuggled from the infamous prison, first appeared early in 1984 in the Los Angeles-based cultural magazine *Third Rail*, edited by Uri Hertz, in a section that also included previously unpublished photographs of the concentration camp: in one, there is the unmistakable forlorn adolescent face of Aristóteles, who was wearing a hat and a heavy coat against the Patagonian cold. Published in subsequent editions as, simply, *Dawson*, these poems earned the poet the Rubén Darío Latin American Prize given by Nicaragua's Sandinista Ministry of Culture in 1985. One of the most chilling poems from *Dawson* is "The Blindfold":

> The blindfold is a slice of darkness
> that oppresses,
> a black beam of light striking shadows,
> the intimate moaning of the mind.
> It penetrates like an insane needle:
> the blindfold.
> In the hard seasons of anger
> and fear
> it wounds and bewilders.
> Images get bigger.
> Sounds are bells
> tolling and tolling.
> The blindfold
> is a wall covered with mirrors and moss,
> a room where no one lives,
> a stairway to the unknown.
> The blindfold
> fills the air with phantoms
> and helps blast open the way
> to the hurricaned corridors
> of meditation and panic. (213)

The last time I saw Aristóteles was in Santiago in June 2007. As we drank wine in our favorite place (the celebrated bar Unión Chica, which has a plaque to commemorate Teillier), he calmly said, as if it were an indisputable scientific fact: "People like me never reach old age."

For Aristóteles, as well as so many other victims of dictatorial regimes, this turned out to be the case, precisely because the human body is unable to withstand the cumulative effects of assimilated extreme violence. In the late 1970s, when Aristóteles was struggling to find employment in Santiago and trying overcome the trauma of his imprisonment on Dawson Island, the doors of the metro opened at the stop below La Moneda (the presidential palace where Allende died during the 1973 military coup) and in walked the man who had tortured him in the concentration camp. They both recognized each other. What does it mean to a society and its social fabric when the torturers live freely among the general population? From 1986–1993, Aristóteles lived in Argentina, where he studied screenplay writing at the University of Buenos Aires and received a degree in Human Rights at the Instituto Argentino por los Derechos del Hombre. When I visited him in Buenos Aires in 1992, he and his wife, Georgina García, and I took the train to Santos Lugares so that we could speak with Ernesto Sábato (1911–2011) and ask him about his work as president of the National Commission on the Disappearance of Persons (CONADEP, in Spanish). Sábato spoke to us of his investigation into the repression carried out by the military regime in Argentina that resulted in the *Informe Sábato*, the constant death threats he received and the severe psychological toll that this work exacted on him and especially on his wife, who was sitting next to her husband as we talked, quietly weeping.

In the chilling study "Violencia extrema," Sergio González Rodríguez affirms the following:

> Extreme violence is linked to the predatory instinct of human beings and the way it is registered in literature as well as in art will be expressed in the tension of showing the results of such violence and the desire to be a witness to them, in broad daylight or in in an explicit way. Throughout history, the understanding of violence has oscillated between one and the other conduct. This movement indicates the rational contrasts between morality and aesthetics that has its point of balance between the ethical stance that each writer, artist or persona in general practices when faced with the facts of the compendium of violent images. (50)

The author goes on to link the anesthetizing effect of exposure to violent imagery that leads to forgetting and contrasts this to an active, rational process of formulating questions, conjectures regarding victims and those who perpetrated the violence against them in a particular historical context and in a specific "space of the cruel act" (52). The spatial and temporal context of "The Blindfold," for example, is inevitably domesticated in the translation process, adapting itself to the culture that defines the language into which it has been translated. Presenting this text in a university classroom, I try to take this into account as I attempt to read the faces of my own students (who are the same age or even a little older than the author when he wrote the poem). Ultimately, both the original text and the translation "help elaborate a critical vision: neither insensitivity, nor forgetfulness, nor annihilation, nor pleasure": what remains instead, suggests González Rodríguez, is a "wise lucidness that allows the wound to be present in which the decision between instinct and reasoning covers a re-encounter with pain" (52).

I traveled from Chicago to Ottawa in the late fall of 1978 expressly to meet exiled Chilean poet Gonzalo Millán (1947–2006), who was finishing his pioneering, austere, anti-lyrical book *La ciudad*, the blue cover of which was a montage (done by Millán himself) of a military figure mounted on a horse superimposed on a monstrous humanoid that straddles two tall buildings. My English version of Millán's "Tiempo atrás" (which became "Poema 48" in this book) was called "Some Time Ago: Backwards," one of the first translations I ever published, and appeared in the Chilean literature issue of *Review: Latin American Literature & Arts* 27 (1980). As luck would have it, I was in Madrid for the spring 2014 presentation by Universidad Complutense professor Niall Binns and Spanish poet Juan Carlos Mestre of a new edition of *La ciudad* published by Amargord/Colección Transatlántica, an event that concluded with an *al alimón* reading of the remarkable "Poema 48," which brought down the house at the Casa de América:

> The river reverses its flow.
> Waterfalls rise.
> People begin to recede.
> Horses trot backwards.
> Soldiers break ranks.
> Bullets leave the flesh.
> Bullets enter the gun barrels.
> Officers put away their pistols.
> The current flows out through the cords.
> The current penetrates the outlets.
> Those who were being tortured stop shaking.
> Those who were being tortured close their mouths.
> The concentration camps are emptied.
> Those who were missing appear.
> The dead rise from their graves.
> The planes fly backwards.
> The rockets climb toward the planes.
> Allende fires his gun.
> The flames die down.
> He takes off his helmet.
> La Moneda makes itself whole again.
> His skull mends itself.
> He steps onto a balcony.
> Allende goes back to Tomás Moro Street.
> Those who were arrested leave the stadiums backwards.
> September 11.
> Planes full of refugees return.
> Chile is a democratic country.
> The armed forces respect the constitution.
> The soldiers return to their barracks.
> Neruda is reborn.
> He returns to Isla Negra by ambulance.
> His prostate is painful. He writes.
> Víctor Jara plays the guitar. He sings.

Speeches enter mouths.
The tyrant embraces Prat.
He disappears. Prat lives again.
The unemployed are rehired.
The workers are marching, singing
*Venceremos*! (115)

This poem that echoes as filmic literature the legendary epic documentary film by Patricio Guzmán *La batalla de Chile* (*The Battle of Chile*) is a willed reencounter with that painful past, a wound that remains open in song. Writing in "Fosa común" ("Mass Grave"), Miguel Ángel López maintains that

> the return of democracy in several of these countries did not solve, but rather made more complex the problem of memory, which, as the critic Nelly Richard maintains, in many cases is anchored in a false dispute between the possibility of "forgetting (burying the past of the bodies that remain unburied: a re-covering) and remembering (exhuming what covers—veils—that past: a discovering." (57)

Writing and translating these remembrances, reliving them, or, making them live again, is a way to preserve, as we have seen, the analogous episodes of historical memory and the search for social justice that reverberate throughout the Hispanic world. At breakfast, my wife, Esthela Calderón, reminds me what day it is today and starts singing "Yo pisaré las calles nuevamente" ("I Will Walk the Streets Again") by Pablo Milanés.

*September 11, 2014*

## NOTES

1. All translations of poems are mine or work done in conjunction with Greg Simon, as indicated. The original Spanish of this poem and all others cited in this chapter can be found by means of the references for the English since all the translations were originally published in a bilingual *en face* format.

2. Pablo Antonio Cuadra and I presented this dramatic long poem, which he wrote in the 1930s and revised extensively in the 1960s, in alternating voices at readings at the University of Oregon and St. Lawrence University in 1987 and 1988.

3. See White, *La poesía de Nicaragua*, 117–148 and 151–188, as well as White, *Arando el aire*, 153–73 and 231–69.

4. In 1978, Zurita made me a book I still have of his *Desierto de Atacama* poems at the Olivetti typewriter company where he worked. The copyright page says Edición de un Ejemplar, Ejemplar No. 1—Edition of One Copy, Copy No. 1. Zurita and Diego Maquieira brought it to the house on the calle Merced in downtown Santiago where I spent three months in bed recovering from hepatitis that I contracted in the fishing village of Horcón.

5. According to Aristóteles España, it was Letelier who translated the uplifting message of solidarity sent by Ted Kennedy to the prisoners at Dawson Island via the International Red Cross some weeks after the 1973 military coup. Letelier was later murdered on Embassy Row in Washington, DC by the Chilean secret police in conjunction with American Michael Townley and right-wing Cuban exiles.

# WORKS CITED

Baquero, Gastón. "F. G. L." *The Angel of Rain*. Trans. Greg Simon and Steven F. White. Spokane: Eastern Washington University Press, 2006. 91.

Belli, Gioconda. "Nicaragua Water Fire." *From Eve's Rib*. Comp. and trans. Steven F. White. Willimantic, CT: Curbstone Press, 1989. 86–91.

Benjamin, Walter. "The Task of the Translator." *Selected Writings, Volume 1, 1913–1926*. Ed. Marcus Bullock and Michael W. Jennings. Cambridge and London: Harvard University Press 1996. 253–63.

Cruz, Juan. "Lo que el poeta le dijo al Príncipe." *El País* 6 de junio 2014: 15.

Cuadra, Pablo Antonio. "Poem of the Foreigners' Moment in Our Jungle." *The Birth of the Sun: Selected Poems of Pablo Antonio Cuadra (1935–1985)*. Ed. and trans. Steven F. White. Greensboro, NC: Unicorn Press, 1988. 14–19.

Darío, Rubén. "To Roosevelt." *Rubén Darío: Selected Writings*. Poem trans. by Greg Simon and Steven F. White. New York: Penguin, 2005. 118–21.

España, Aristóteles. "The Blindfold." *Poets of Chile: A Bilingual Anthology, 1965–1985*. Ed. and trans. Steven F. White. Greensboro, NC: Unicorn Press, 1986. 212–13.

García Lorca, Federico. "The King of Harlem." *Poet in New York*. Trans. Greg Simon and Steven F. White. New York: Farrar, Straus & Giroux, 1988.

García Lorca, Federico and Pablo Neruda. "Discurso al alimón sobre Rubén Darío" (1934). http://www.neruda.uchile.cl/discursoalimon.htm.

González Rodríguez, Sergio. "Violencia extrema." *Carta* 4 (primavera–verano 2013): 50–53.

Hite, Katherine. *Politics and the Art of Commemoration: Memorials to Struggle in Latin America and Spain*. London: Routledge, 2011.

López, Miguel Angel. "Fosa común." *Carta* (Primavera–Verano 2013) 4: 56–58.

Millán, Gonzalo. "Poem 48." *Poets of Chile: A Bilingual Anthology, 1965–1985*. Ed. and trans. Steven F. White. Greensboro, NC: Unicorn Press, 1986. 114–15.

Neruda, Pablo. "Ode to Federico García Lorca." *The Poetry of Pablo Neruda*. Ed. Ilán Stavans. Poem trans. by Greg Simon and Steven F. White. New York: Farrar, Straus & Giroux, 2003. 120–23.

Pasos, Joaquín. "Warsong of the Things." Fragment trans. by Steven F. White. *The Oxford Book of Latin American Poetry*. Ed. Cecilia Vicuña and Ernesto Livon-Grosman. New York: Oxford University Press, 2009. 276–79.

Pedreño, José María. "¿Qué es la memoria histórica?" *Pueblos* 12 (verano 2004): 10–12.

Ruiz Mantilla, Jesús. "Entrevista a Baltasar Garzón." *El País Semanal* 2 de febrero 2014: 28–33.

Simon, Greg and Steven F. White. "Letter *al alimón* to Rubén Darío." *Hinchas de Poesía* 10 (June 2013): n.p. http://www.hinchasdepoesia.com/wp/poesia/a-letter-al-alimon-to-ruben-dario/.

Venuti, Lawrence. "Translation, Community, Utopia." *The Translation Studies Reader*. Ed. Lawrence Venuti. London; New York: Routledge, 2000. 468–88.

White, Steven F. *Arando el aire: La ecología en la poesía y la música de Nicaragua*. Managua: 400 Elefantes, 2011.

———. *La poesía de Nicaragua y sus diálogos con Francia y los Estados Unidos*. León: Editorial UNAN, 2009.

*Chapter Six*

# Narrativa e ilusión[1]

*Argentine Historical Memory in*
Una sombra ya pronto serás *by Osvaldo Soriano*

Mallory N. Craig-Kuhn

Thirty-one years after the end of Argentina's most recent dictatorship (1976–1983), it is still a hotly debated point of contention in the country how to collectively process the violence and repression of that period, called the *Proceso de Reorganización Nacional* (National Reorganization Process).[2] After the return to democracy in 1983, the country suffered hyperinflation, and, throughout his two consecutive presidencies from 1989 to 1999, Carlos Menem implemented a sweeping policy of privatization of Argentina's economy with ripple effects that can still be detected today as we read in the news about the country's highly controversial international loan default in 2014. These recent historical events have come to form an integral part of the shared narrative that defines cultural identity in Argentina, a country at the forefront of the movement of *memoria histórica*, a collective recognition of the importance of a society's past with regard to its current sociopolitical situation.

As we will see, the trials and investigations on the crimes committed during *el Proceso* have taken place in the political, legal, and social spheres; but these are not the only realms in which the process of memory can be performed. In fact, it is in the sphere of artistic creation, which also incurs actively into the social, where much work with memory is done. Collective memory, Jeffrey Olick explains, can be understood as a shared narrative that takes into account social frameworks and contemporary circumstances, remaking the past for current circumstances (341). However, he highlights the fact that many sociologists and psychologists consider that only an individual can remember; therefore the individual mind and the act of telling are an integral part of the collected memory that comes to be shared by a certain social group. He refers to this as individualistic collective memory (338). But these memories are evoked and exchanged in social settings in the form of a dialogue which, as literary critic Mikhail Bakhtin argued, must inevitably interact with other utterances that have touched upon the same topic and become saturated with socially derived meaning (343).

This socialized evoking and exchanging is aided by the "technologies of memory" or mnemonic devices that a society uses to perpetuate the shared, identity-constructing narrative of collective memory, such as museums, archives, historiography, or the mass media; and these technologies of memory indubitably include artistic and literary production. When socialized and assimilated by the members of a society, a trauma truly comes to form part of "the legitimating narrative that we as individuals produce for us as a collectivity" (Olick 345). The literary production of Argentine writer Osvaldo Soriano (1943–1997) can certainly be seen to function in this manner. Soriano, who himself fled Argentina in 1976 to return only in 1984, after the reinstatement of democracy, narrated in his fictions the political violence that shook his country during the 1970s and 1980s. His novel *Una sombra ya pronto serás* (1990) narrates the years following the dictatorship, and its characters wander the pampas of Buenos Aires province. Largely antiheroes and marginal figures, these characters struggle to make sense of and survive in their present, the product of an incomprehensible and largely unconfronted past, and look vaguely toward an increasingly uncertain future. The allegorical nature of the novel points to the uncontrolled privatization of the national economy after its most recent dictatorship and this process's destabilizing effects on Argentine identity. In the midst of this instability, Soriano's characters are filled with *ilusiones*, hopes and dreams for the future that can also be read as pathetic illusions, the result of their unstable sense of identity.

On the stage of modern internal politics and social interaction in Argentina, the call for confronting the past holds a central role. Despite the controversial nature of historical memory work in the country for the prosecution of war criminals and the official institution of monuments and museums, there is no doubt that the most recent dictatorship is quite present in the modern shared narrative of Argentine culture. Tellingly, the death of Jorge Rafael Videla, head of the military government from 1976 to 1981, in May of 2013 was met with outright jubilance among many Argentines born during the presidencies of Raúl Alfonsín and Carlos Menem, that is, Argentines who never directly experienced the environment of fear and violence enforced by the dictatorship. This begs the question "Why the continued immediacy of the dictatorship in the collective national psyche?"

It can be explained at least in part by the official governmental support of historical memory as early as 1983, when Alfonsín's presidency created the

*Comisión Nacional sobre la Desaparición de Personas* (National Commission on The Disappearance of Persons), or CONADEP.[3] The words *Nunca más* (never again), both the axis of the investigative commission and still a unanimously socially recognized catchphrase, were born of this process begun three decades ago. This was the title given to the report published by CONADEP in 1984 reporting methods of abduction, torture, clandestine detention centers, mass executions and burials, groups targeted for disappearance, and testimonies by numerous actors involved in the dictatorship (*Nunca Más*). Despite this important first step forward in holding responsible the perpetrators of crimes against humanity during the dictatorship, the initiative suffered major setbacks. In 1986 and 1987, the Argentine Congress under Alfonsín's government passed the Full Stop Law and the Law of Due Obedience, which put time limits on trials and charges brought against members of the military and nullified culpability for soldiers following higher orders. Though both laws were repealed by the Argentine Congress in March of 1998, they obstructed the investigation of thousands of cases of forced disappearance, extrajudicial execution, and torture committed during the dictatorship. This is a source of concern for organizations such as Amnesty International (Documento—Argentina: Las Leyes de Punto Final y Obediencia Debida y el derecho internacional). These types of legal actions are the flip-side of the coin of "memory work" that aims to confront and accept trauma in order to overcome the obstacle it poses in creating a coherent shared narrative. An opposing view looks to turn the page, so to speak, and shift the focus from the past to the future, arguing that if society and the legal apparatus are occupied with processing the past, they will be unable to move forward in any meaningful way.

However, as Olick argues, trauma causes repression or a block in the mind's ability to tell a coherent narrative. Only a reconciliation with the traumatic experience, an acknowledgment of the event, can reverse this repression that hinders the construction of a coherent and constructive narrative essential, as we have seen, to the identity of an individual or a community of memory (344). The crisis of identity caused by forced disappearances, for example, is emblematic of the entire field of historical memory. In *Specters of Marx*, Jacques Derrida interrelates the concepts of inheritance, those not present, justice, and shared experience, all inextricably linked with the question of how a society can march toward the future:

> It is necessary to speak *of the* ghost, indeed *to the* ghost and *with* it, from the moment that no ethics, no politics, whether revolutionary or not, seems possible and thinkable and *just* that does not recognize in its principle the respect for those others who are no longer or for those others who are not yet *there*, presently living, whether they are already dead or not yet born. . . . Without this *non-contemporaneity with itself of the living present*, without that which

secretly unhinges it, . . . what sense would there be to ask the question
"where?" "where tomorrow?" "whither?" (Derrida xviii)

Referencing the ghostly father figure in Shakespeare's *Hamlet*, Derrida cites
the protagonist's exclamation that "the time is out of joint" (39). This disruption of a linear passing of time, the constant and unresolved incurrence of
past trauma in the present, hindering in turn the construction of the future,
will be key in our analysis of Soriano's fictions. In the case of Argentina, the
ghost can also symbolize the absent figure of the disappeared or the victim of
political violence who loses his or her life. In this sense, wresting one's
consciousness away from the lived present is fundamental both to understanding the contemporary context, inescapably linked with the "historical
entanglement" (Derrida 16) that gave rise to it, and to deciding how to
proceed toward the future. For Derrida, an inheritance, in the sense of experience, whether individual or shared, must invariably be interpreted in multiple
ways, and those doing the interpreting must come to terms with the specters
of the past. The words "ghost" and "specter," with their ominous sense of a
disembodied presence that cannot move on to a better world without securing
some kind of closure and recognition, are quite apropos in our discussion of
historical memory in Argentina.

   Soriano's novel *Una sombra ya pronto serás* presents just this: ghostly,
almost blurred characters and a lack of logical connections between different
events in the fiction. Nearly all the characters have only a first or last name,
rarely both, and the character-narrator himself is never named, but rather
confused with the former associate of another wanderer with whom he shares
the road intermittently. The characters move uncertainly through the pampas
of Buenos Aires province, circling back, getting lost, fumbling vaguely toward personal and ill-defined aspirations for the future: to make it to Brazil
or Bolivia, to Neuquén or Ohio. In this markedly allegorical novel, Soriano
approaches the problem of Argentine identity by setting his fiction in a
transitional moment after the end of the dictatorship and in the beginnings of
the widespread privatization of the Argentine economy under Menem in the
1990s. It can be noted that many Argentines now blame this process for the
current economic turmoil in the country given that the highest bidders for
Argentine enterprises during this period were often foreign, and that internal
corruption at the governmental level led to serious destabilization of the
national economy. The character-narrator's precarious economic situation
and that of the characters with whom he comes into contact play no small
role in the plot. The characters' dedication to crime, swindling, get-rich-
quick schemes, and wild pipe dreams for future business ventures all allude
to the rapid and unstable economic changes that took place in Argentina
during the late 1980s and 1990s.

In this sense, Idelber Avelar's study of postdictatorial fiction in Argentina, Chile, and Brazil is especially pertinent. For Avelar, the role of the dictatorships was to effect the "epochal transition from State to Market" (14) and, since late capitalism supposes the commodification of all aspects of life, the planned obsolescence of goods and an obsession with the latest product, this logic operates on the past, as well. In opposition to the "substitutive, metaphorical logic in which the past must be relegated to obsolescence" (2) of the capitalist market imposed in the postdictatorial societies studied, Avelar presents the allegory as "a trope that thrives on breaks and discontinuities, as opposed to the unfractured wholeness presupposed by the symbol" (11). For Avelar, the unmourned trauma lingers on as an "allegorically charged ruin" (5) represented in what he dubs postdictatorial literature. We can certainly observe the ruin or the ghost town in *Una sombra ya pronto serás*. This deeply disturbing economic shift, which, at the same time, actively seeks to bury the past in order to face a brighter future further distorts the legitimating narrative of Argentine identity on the doorstep of the 1990s.

Soriano himself wrote that deep down, his novels express the problem of identity about which, consciously or unconsciously, everyone wonders (*Soriano* 20). For literary critic Néstor Ponce, Soriano's narratives provide us with a picture of the way in which Argentines have thought and felt from the 1970s until the turn of the century (31). None of the characters in *Una sombra ya pronto serás* seem to have very precise knowledge of where they are nor how to arrive at their vague destinations. Interestingly, several of the characters' cars can't make the shift into fourth gear. They are stuck, bogged down, aimless. The character-narrator and, in fact, all of the characters in the novel can be considered representations of the collective confusion of Argentine reality and identity in the late 1980s. Several times throughout the fiction, the character-narrator is "cansado de llevarse puesto" (145), tired of running into himself, of tripping over himself, of fighting himself, among many other possible translations.

This character-narrator, an unemployed informatics engineer who has left behind a daughter in Spain (as he returns, perhaps, from exile?), meets many other dreaming wanderers in Buenos Aires province. None of the characters provide more than summary facts about their pasts or identities, focusing more on their dreams of simply getting somewhere else, always looking toward a poorly planned out future. It is telling that all of the characters travel alone and are far from their families. This isolation can well be understood to allude to those families broken by the dictatorship. Similarly, the plot is undergirded by a general ignorance (voluntary or involuntary) of the past. "The characters' incoherent destiny is completed by the memory gaps that scribble out the past, a suggestive circumstance in a country whose recent history is marked by tragedy—Lem confesses to having a ten-year gap—or by a refusal to face the present" (Ponce 33, translation is mine).[4] The unconfronted ghost of the past described by Derrida further disjoints time in the fictive world. This is evident in the narrative line that does not seem to advance, the characters' journeys lacking a clear destination or purpose, and the imprecise, blurry timeline that makes up the plot. We must also remember that Soriano wrote this fiction during the years when the Law of Due Obedience and the Full Stop Law were in effect, legally obliging society to turn a blind eye to the atrocities of the recent past, making it impossible to confront the ghost.

In fact, the protagonist and Coluccini, an obese conman, gamble both their memories and dreams, that is, their pasts and futures, playing *truco*, the most paradigmatic of Argentine card games. When asked if he has anything to bet, the character-narrator replies:

> "The trip, if you want."
> "The one from before, or tomorrow's trip?"
> "It's the same to me," I replied.
> "What did your partner bet?"
> "Hopes and dreams."
> "All right, bet yours, then."
> "I don't think I have any left." (128–29, translation is mine)[5]

It now makes no difference to the character-narrator whether he bets his memories or his hopes, because he is running short on both, and both are fading. His daughter, representative of the future, is far away in Spain, surely speaking with a Spanish accent and unaware of the feats of the Argentine forefathers. "I thought to myself that we were broken, and we would be for a long time. It made me sad to think we would walk into the abyss like blind cows, and I didn't want to be the only one to escape that destiny of ours, either" (150, translation is mine).[6] Again the sense of pity and frustration arises for the characters who, in the character-narrator's eyes, are insects caught in a spider web, just waiting for a chance to make a desperate leap. But they are bound to the destiny laid out for them by history. The character-narrator muses to himself that one day the pampas will swallow it all up, return to their calm and natural state, and show not a trace of the passing of Argentine history there.

The climax of the storyline also takes place during a *truco* game rigged by Coluccini and the protagonist in a town in the pampas in order to make a quick buck. The very nature of this card game, played by two sets of partners, is based on sending secret signals, misleading the other team, and making daring bluffs. In the context of what Avelar refers to as "Carlos Menem's neoliberal-kitsch version of Peronism" characterized by "the deregulation of the Argentine economy" (60), *truco* is highly allegorical. This rigged game meant to fleece the character-narrator's and his associate's opponents cannot help but recall to the reader's mind the going norms of behavior in Menem's questionably honest neoliberal economic reorganization. When the game turns sour and the townspeople realize they have been duped, the travelers are forced to flee. In a moment of calm during his escape, the character-narrator is overcome by a sense of returning to his childhood, as happens on various occasions in the novel: "Suddenly, I wasn't afraid anymore: I was back in my childhood and in my hometown, and everything I'd learned as a grown-up was worthless to me" (185).[7] All his experience, everything he has learned, is useless. For all the characters, their individual and collective pasts, faded and uncertain, do not provide them with tools to face the present or to understand themselves as individuals in a collective society.

In fact, this fictive world is full of figures representative of the Argentine social, political, and economic reality at the end of the 1980s. On the highway, a truck driver sits next to his broken-down rig for days, waiting in the blistering heat for someone to come to his aid while the expensive watermelons he was hauling rot away in the sun: a lack of internal infrastructure allows Argentine economic potential to be squandered. Coluccini, who claims to have owned a circus with his partner, Zárate, with whom he confuses the character-narrator, gets drunk and rides a bicycle through the sky along telephone wires only to fall pitifully and painfully to the ground because the cables have been stolen by opportunists. Watching him, the character-narrator understands the wonder and excitement Coluccini's spectators must have felt, and also why his family decided to run off with Zárate, abandoning this obese dreamer who would never achieve success. The very glory and defeat of Argentine identity, a confused product of recent history, a future stolen by shameless opportunists who themselves are responding to the chaotic present, can be read in this far-fetched but enchanting scene.

Nearing the novel's climax, the character Lem commits suicide, a poignant allegory that speaks of the hopelessness of the future and the ephemeral nature of the character's unachievable dreams of glory. After pushing Lem and his car into a riverbed by way of burial, the character-narrator stumbles across two military officers in mismatched and faded uniforms going through endless maneuvers and arbitrarily increasing their rank as they await the missing infantry. Again, we see confused, absurd, and somewhat ghostly figures quite detached from the fundamental relationships that would define their role in society. Though fuzzy on the details, the general constantly calls to mind famous defeats in Argentine military history, pathetically arguing that defeats are the most heroic, sure that one day they, too, will be remembered and celebrated. The character-narrator and the officers are forced to hide in the tent when a swarm of locusts, which have been appearing singly throughout the plot in a gradual foreshadowing of the apocalyptic closing of the narrative, now arrive in force on the pampas, devouring the Argentine flag. The allegorical power of this image is undeniable. As the plague of insects descends, Argentina's military stands disbanded and detached, almost ejected from history; the economy has been thrown into a tumultuous and unregulated free-for-all; and the citizens wander alone, disoriented, unable to distinguish a future that cannot be clearly imagined. All that is representative of Argentine political glory is faded, confused, destroyed.

When the character-narrator finds Coluccini again, they play one final game of *truco*, but now rather than memories or hopes, they bet what could better be described as surreal experiences that are likely hallucinations. Coluccini believes he has seen a crucified Christ who calls him by name, and the protagonist has been charged with finding the officers' missing infantry. Coluccini says he cannot lose because he has already reached his destination, Bolivia, and his memories are his own again. The character-narrator asks him to bet his vision of Christ, to which Coluccini agrees if the character-narrator will bet his missing infantry. Now operating on a completely muddied time-line, stuck in a hopeless present, Coluccini imagines himself fusing his lost memories, future dreams, and hallucinations in a place far from his current location. For his part, the protagonist follows the train tracks discovered by his associate all night until he finally reaches the motionless and deserted train. The schedule says it will leave at eight o'clock, but no day is listed, nor does the protagonist have any idea of the current date. Pushing his way through the weeds and noting the dead locusts and broken windows, the protagonist settles into the seat, cracks open his last warm beer, and waits for the train to depart. He again finds himself stuck in a circular journey with no destination or ultimate illumination. It is unclear whether he and the other characters are aware that their immobility stems from their inability to access or confront their elusive personal and shared pasts. The motionless locomotive is a symbol of the country at a standstill, trapped in the present. The past is a faded and incomprehensible source of pain, full of failures and losses, and the future is nothing but an uncertain *ilusión*, both "anticipation" or "hope" and "delusion" in Spanish.

Soriano's *Una sombra ya pronto serás* presents a vague and pathetic hope for a brighter future. On another occasion, the author wrote:

> All that's left is the vanity of lost courage. Nothing to evoke the passion of those founding fathers who amassed not money, but dreams (*ilusiones*). Still, ridiculous as it may seem, everything is yet to be done. In some hidden part of ourselves are the invisible threads of an unfinished dream: an equality of opportunities without misery or ignorance; an independence that does not mean isolation or hate. A utopian nation of honest men who have paid their debts to the past. (*Soriano* 26, translation is mine)[8]

For Soriano, the present is a continuation of the past, the product of the aspirations/illusions of the founding fathers and those that struggled throughout the turbulent periods about which he wrote. The future is a utopian dream, by its very definition an ideal, unreal. The confusion in *Una sombra ya pronto serás*, and the uncertainty with which his characters look toward the future, spring from the unrealized necessity of confronting the past, of speaking to the ghost, of resolving the trauma in order to seek a path forward. Even those who had first-hand experience of the turbulent years of the second half of the twentieth century in Argentina are left unsure of what has happened. Soriano once mused "Young people feel, legitimately, that we have given them a shitty country . . . We left them a ruined reality. We failed in our dreams. So we didn't even leave them our dreams as an inheritance. Our generation wanted to turn the world upside-down. It left behind great figures and great moments. Was it positive? Who am I to say" (*Soriano* 22).[9]

The writer himself feels poorly qualified to judge the value of those years. What is true, however, is that the country, the collective identity that has been handed down to younger generations, is nothing if not the product of that history forged by previous generations. Alluding to the confusion of identity discussed in his fictions, Soriano can only urge his generation to be understanding of the youth. After all, they are struggling to come to terms with the meaning of a traumatic recent national past whose repressive effects hinder their own sense of identity and clarity regarding the future.

## NOTES

1. "Narrative and illusion." The various meanings of the word *ilusión* are key to my analysis of Soriano's novel. In Spanish, this word refers not only to illusions (false in nature), but also to hopes and dreams, or aspirations for the future.

2. Though Argentina was ruled by several de facto military governments during the twentieth century, its last dictatorship, which lasted from 1976–1983, is the one most present in current memory work in the country. Jorge Rafael Videla, a senior commander of the army, was at the forefront of the military coup that overthrew the democratic government in power in March of 1976 and installed himself as the country's dictator from 1976–1981.

3. The *Nunca más* report published in 1984 by CONADEP can be accessed in its full form online in English at "Proyecto Desaparecidos" www.desaparecidos.org, which contains information on "victims of State terrorism in Latin America and the world." Finally, Argentina's *Archivo nacional de la memoria* website includes a wealth of information of interest on these topics http://anm.derhuman.jus.gov.ar/

4. The original reads, "El destino incoherente de los personajes se completa con los huecos en la memoria que borronean el pasado, circunstancia sugestiva en un país cuya historia reciente está marcada por la tragedia—Lem confiesa tener un vacío de diez años—, o con la negativa a enfrentar el presente."

5. The original reads, "—El viaje, si quiere. / —¿El de antes o el de mañana? / —Me da lo mismo —Respondí. / —¿Qué apostaba su socio? / —Ilusiones. /—Está bien, ponga la suya entonces. / —Creo que no me quedan."

6. The original reads, "Me dije que estábamos rotos y lo estaríamos por mucho tiempo. Me daba pena que camináramos al abismo como vacas ciegas y tampoco quería escapar solo a ese destino que era el nuestro."

7. The original reads, "De pronto se me había ido el miedo: estaba otra vez en la infancia y en mi pueblo y todo lo que había aprendido de grande no me servía para nada." For a more in-depth reading of childhood in the novel, see Ponce (36).

8. The original reads, "Queda, apenas, la vanidad de un coraje perdido. Nada que evoque la pasión de aquellos fundadores que no amasaban plata sino ilusiones. Sin embargo, por

ridículo que parezca, todo está por hacerse. En alguna recóndita parte de nosotros se enhebran los hilos invisibles de un sueño inconcluso: una igualdad de oportunidades en la que no haya miseria ni ignorancia; una independencia que no signifique aislamiento ni odio. Una utópica nación de hombres honestos que haya pagado sus deudas con el pasado."

9. The original reads, "Los jóvenes sienten, legítimamente, que les entregamos un país de mierda … Les dejamos una realidad hecha pelota. Fracasamos en los sueños. Y, por lo tanto, no les dejamos como herencia ni siquiera nuestros sueños. Nuestra generación quiso poner todo patas para arriba. Dejó grandes figuras y grandes momentos. ¿Fue positivo? Quién es uno para juzgarlo."

# WORKS CITED

Avelar, Idelber. *The Untimely Present: Postdictatorial Latin American Fiction and the Task of Mourning*. Durham, NC: Duke University Press, 1999.

Derrida, Jacques. *Specters of Marx: The State of the Debt, the Work of Mourning and the New International*. Trans. Peggy Kamuf. New York: Routledge, 1994.

"Documento—Argentina: Las Leyes de Punto Final y Obediencia Debida y el derecho internacional." *Amnistía Internacional*. Amnesty International, April 2013. Web. 27 Aug. 2014.

Llorente, Marina. "La *memoria histórica* en la poesía de Isabel Pérez Montalbán y David González." *Hispanic Review* 32.1 (2013): 181–200.

"Nunca Más. Report of Conadep." *Proyecto Desaparecidos*. N.p., n.d. Web. 27 Aug. 2014.

Olick, Jeffrey K. "Collective Memory: The Two Cultures." *Sociological Theory* 17.3 (1999): 333–48.

Ponce, Néstor. "Azar y derrota: El fin de las ilusiones en 'Una sombra ya pronto serás,' de Osvaldo Soriano." *Hispamérica* 30.89: 29–41.

Soriano, Osvaldo. *Soriano por Soriano*. Buenos Aires: Seix Barral, 2010.

———. *Una sombra ya pronto serás*. Buenos Aires: Seix Barral, 2010.

*IV*

# The Struggles of Memory in the
# Global Market: Venezuela and Mexico

*Chapter Seven*

# The Children of 1989

*Resurrecting the Venezuelan Dead*[1]

## George Ciccariello-Maher

The present as we receive it comes inevitably laden with residues of the past, sedimentations of the dialectical interplay between action and meaning, and contemporary Venezuela is no exception. As I write these words in 2014, Venezuela sits at the intersection of two anniversaries: twenty-five years ago marked what could be considered the violent birth of the Bolivarian revolutionary process in the riot, rebellion, and massacre known as the *Caracazo*, and we have just passed the first anniversary of the death of the single individual who has meant the most to that process, the late president Hugo Chávez Frías.

Simply observing the persistence of the past in the present, however, gives us little guidance about *what to do* with that past. Here, the Karl Marx of the *Eighteenth Brumaire* seems clear enough in his insistence that:

> Tradition from all the dead generations weighs like a nightmare on the brain of the living. And just when they appear to be revolutionizing themselves and their circumstances, in creating something unprecedented, in just such epochs of revolutionary crisis, that is when they nervously summon up the spirits of the past. (32)

It is this tendency to robe the present in the shrouds of the past—to take refuge tradition in an effort to deny or short-circuit revolutionary creativity—that leads Marx to insist that revolutionaries ought to instead, as he puts it, "let the dead bury the dead" (34). But the question for today is whether this is truly the case in contemporary Venezuela, whether the dead past indeed weighs heavily like a nightmare upon the living present, or if this history is composed of a lighter substance altogether, one capable of providing the basis for future revolutionary unfoldings. The history of Venezuela's present, I argue, liberates at least as much as it constrains, and as a result, our task is not so much to "let the dead bury the dead" as it is to reanimate those corpses, to endow them with voice and allow them to speak directly to new possible futures.[2]

What's more, as I write this, Venezuela is emerging from weeks of unrest crowning a traumatic year for *Chavismo*, with protests in the streets and sharp debates over the meaning of the moment. The loss of Chávez immediately emboldened the anti-*Chavista* opposition, which nearly defeated Nicolás Maduro in the April 2013 election, and questions of insecurity and economic scarcity—the first exaggerated, the latter at least partially manufactured—have provided fodder for the latest turn to street protests aiming at no less than that which is proclaimed in the Twitter trend "#LaSalida," Maduro's departure from power (Ciccariello-Maher, "#LaSalida?"). Proponents of the protests, many the professed enemies of the Bolivarian process, insist in not-so-subtle terms that we in fact let the dead bury the dead, urging us to forget the past so that they can seize the present. But to do so would be impossible, and this if nothing else should provide a sharp warning against any hasty forgetting.

This task of the radical resurrection of history defies many traditional methods. Properly understood, the Venezuelan present is not the product of a slow and linear progression whose truth can be gleaned from demographic data or social indicators, although the poverty rate, for example, tells us much of the motivation and later accomplishments of the process. Nor is it the heroic creation of great leaders past, to be compiled in what Foucault called "traditional history" (139–64). Instead, the Bolivarian process—as an undercurrent that preceded and provided the basis for Chávez's emergence—often emerged *despite* and even *against* such leaders. Its history is the history of small groups of guerrillas, of neighborhood assemblies, of radical women, of Afro- and indigenous Venezuelans, and of that supremely catalytic sector that is Venezuelan students. In fact, such triumphal histories played an immense role in the consolidation from the 1960s onward of a buffered, two-party political system—known as *puntofijismo*—that was impermeable to the mass dissatisfaction expressed in these movements, and that, like Sophocles's Antigone, was unable to bend and could only break.

And break it did, in spectacular fashion, twenty-five years ago, on February 27, 1989, when the political forces and popular demands that had been developing slowly, invisibly, subterraneously, exploded into a rebellion known as the *Caracazo* or *Sacudón*. After an electoral campaign critical of international lenders like the IMF and the emerging Washington Consensus, Venezuelan president Carlos Andrés Pérez had imposed his notoriously neoliberal structural adjustment program known as the *paquetazo*. Enraged by the immediate impact of the reforms—and especially the overnight doubling of transport costs due to the liberalization of domestic gas prices—as well as the "bait-and-switch" method in which this was imposed by Pérez, poor *caraqueños* and later those across Venezuela took to the streets rioting and looting for nearly a week straight. The desperately poor "swarm[ed] into the forbidden cities," in the words of Frantz Fanon, reuniting a segregated landscape if only momentarily, and in their looting of both necessities and luxuries, revealed the two-sided nature that Marx associated with the commodity, as well as their own intransigent demand that the last would soon be first (6).

The *Caracazo* was a political event of the first order, blasting a hole in what Walter Benjamin called the "continuum of history," and it was into this gaping wound in history that Chávez stepped with a failed coup in February 1992 ("Theses" 261).[3] Instead of one Venezuela, there were suddenly two, and the previously frozen dialectic of history was forced into motion in an instant, unleashing everything that has come since. There had been decades of antecedent struggles, but in 1989 the die was cast, the harmonious image of Venezuelan society irreparably smashed, and the unsustainability of both *puntofijismo* and the neoliberal reform package revealed for all to see.

Wealthy white elites were left powerfully traumatized by the temporary invasion of the poor, the dark-skinned; and responded with increasing segregation and the militarization of the urban landscape (Ciccariello-Maher, "Racial Geography"). The Caracazo simultaneously shook common understandings of who would be the historic subject of any Venezuelan revolution, as it was not the formal working class or the peasantry, but largely those informal and excluded semiperipheral urban poor so often denigrated as "lumpen" who hurled themselves decisively into the streets. Again in Fanon's words, "These vagrants, these second-class citizens, find their way back to the nation thanks to their decisive, militant action. . . . These jobless, these species of subhumans, redeem themselves in their own eyes and before history" (82).

The dead of 1989 are not mere metaphor: concretely speaking, these corpses were between 300 and 3,000, most executed at close range in their homes as the Venezuelan armed forces fired an estimated four million bullets in an attempt to do the impossible, to put the genie back in the bottle, Pandora back into her box (Grand). The dead did not, of course, bury the dead, but were instead themselves buried by the servants of a dying political order. Many, like the sixty-eight corpses later exhumed from a part of the Cemetery of the South known as *La Nueva Peste*, The New Plague, had been thrown into plastic bags and tossed into unmarked mass graves (Coronil 377).[4]

Much against the wishes of Venezuela's *ancien régime*, however, these dead would not lay quietly, would not stay silent, and nor should we wish that they inter one another in obscurity. Rather, the process of unburying those corpses, both real and metaphorical, has been a powerful catalyst for what has come since. Annual commemorations of the *Caracazo* provided the basis for a ritual repetition in which demonstrations yielded police repression—with police firing machine guns from rooftops onto the crowds gathered below—sparking increasingly militant demonstrations (Denis, *Fabricantes* 13). Alongside such moments of antagonism to the social order, popular creativity and participation also flourished and multiplied in the aftermath of the *Caracazo*, especially in the form of directly democratic *barrio* assemblies that prefigured the more recent development of communal councils (Denis, *Fabricantes* 11).

If there was such a thing as a founding moment for what has been called the Bolivarian Revolution, this was it. Nineteen eighty-nine provided a powerful example for struggle, but more concretely still, it provided the impetus for those already conspiring within the military and their civilian allies. Not only had the people in the streets acted and demanded action in turn, but it was these same troops—many poor and dark-skinned recruits—who were ordered to fire on their own in the *barrios* of Caracas and elsewhere. It was only after the *Caracazo* that, according to Chávez, "the members of the MBR 200 realized we had passed the point of no return and we had to take up arms. We could not continue to defend a murderous regime. The massacres were a catalyst" (Chávez and Harnecker 32). Chávez's failed coup attempt of February 4, 1992 was the direct *result* of 1989, and in fact had originally been scheduled to coincide with the anniversary of the massacre. As a recently spotted graffiti in Caracas by the Hip-Hop Revolución Collective puts it: "*Somos hijos del 89.* . . . [We are children of 89]."

While many accounts of foundational violence emphasize the proactive violence of establishing political community or the law at the expense of the other, the founding violence of the *Caracazo* exists between what Benjamin would call the "law-destroying" or "divine" violence of the masses and the failed "law-preserving" violence of the state that sought to restore what one government official called "normality" through massacre ("Critique of Violence" *passim*). However, the boomerang swing of this latter, "mythical" violence, fueled by the memory of the dead, would help lay the basis for new acts of lawmaking: namely the founding of a new political order with a new 1999 Bolivarian Constitution. And yet, as with all founding moments, even the most visceral memories can fade eventually if not connected and reconnected continuously with the present.

As a result, radical politics appears almost as though endowed with a half-life like Plutonium but much shorter: radical leaders come to power by the ballot or the bullet, and move—gradually or swiftly—from left to center, from challenging the status quo to faithfully upholding it. Venezuela, by contrast, has seen the opposite trajectory: elected as a moderate in 1998, Chávez was powerfully radicalized through a combination of pressure from below and antagonism from the right. Here too, the question of the political event as a moment of rupture is central: rather than rely on a single, founding moment, which then fades in the popular memory as it is gradually betrayed by governing practice, the Bolivarian Revolution has instead, as longtime militant Roland Denis explained to me, "moved from event to event" (Denis, Personal Interview).

From 1989 came 1992, which laid the groundwork for Chávez's 1998 election. But crucially the progression did not stop there: almost immediately following the approval of the new Constitution, the Bolivarian process confronted an increasingly combative opposition, culminating in the short-lived opposition coup that unseated Chávez for forty-eight hours in April of 2002. Hundreds of thousands mobilized in the streets on April 12th and 13th, defying a press blackout to insist that not only their president, but also the constitution they had participated in drafting, be reinstated. The successful reversal of the coup that resulted largely from such mobilizations was a powerful reminder not only of the dangers faced by the Bolivarian process, but also the ability of popular movements to intervene decisively. Through this chain of events—1989, 1992, and 2002—the memory of struggle has been periodically reinvigorated in a way that condenses within itself not only the continuity of the Chávez government but also its process of radicalization.

The unavoidable resonances of 2002 today are yet another reminder that our task is not to liberate present from past à la Marx, but to instead deepen continuities and make such bonds not only perpetual but also palpable. The history of the Venezuelan present has thus been a history of momentary and decisive rupture, of 1989 but also of many moments before and since. It moves forward as with the momentum of a catapult, of previously unforeseen and unforeseeable qualitative leaps that suddenly become historically possible. But rather than cede to this unforeseeability and neglect historical tasks, and rather than dissolve this history into a multiplicity of micropolitical moments without any overarching meaning, our task is instead to grasp, in reverse, the dialectic which draws them together and around which they coalesce gradually, with the barely visible becoming undeniable in an instant.

All of this is not to say that Marx is fundamentally wrong, or that we should never "let the dead bury the dead" (after all, it was Marx himself who criticized others for treating the always relevant Hegel like a "dead dog") (*Capital* 102). In fact, Marx himself drew attention to historical moments and contexts in which memory served quite the opposite function, in which "the resurrection of the dead . . . served to glorify new struggles, not parody the old; to magnify fantastically the given task, not to evade real resolution; to recover the spirit of revolution, not to relaunch its spectre" ("Eighteenth Brumaire" 33). There is much in Venezuela's recent past that "weighs like a nightmare" on the present: the bureaucracy and corruption, the petro-state centralism, the ingrained tendency to see solutions only from the top-down, and the resurrection of some dead at the expense of others. Our question instead begs a response like Lenin's famous "Who? Whom?": *who* is being resurrected and *for what purpose?*

Even Simón Bolívar, for whom the revolution draws its contested name, has been resuscitated for both radical and conservative purposes in the past and the present. Chávez himself drew attention to the ways in which "traditional elites 'sanctified Bolívar' in an effort to 'depoliticize him.'" But according to the contemporary writer Íñigo Errejón, the legacy of the late Chávez runs precisely the same risk today: "In a remarkable historical paradox, the 'Chávez myth/faces a similar situation today . . . transforming Chávez into a beautiful historic memento and Chavismo into the non-political act of missing an individual, with no implication for current political loyalties" (Errejón). Hugo Chávez was above all a figure of combat, but in his death his opponents are attempting to rob him of this elemental content, doing so ironically through a feigned affection: today the Venezuelan opposition that demonized Chávez in live celebrates him in death, all in an attempt to hide him away in the national pantheon as a figure of unity rather than rupture, class reconciliation rather than class combat.

This question throws the protests that today dwindle in Venezuela into sharp relief: the rancid leadership of the Venezuelan opposition—heirs of the *ancien régime*—would like nothing more than to let the half-buried corpses of the *Caracazo* lie, and thus their own attempts to compare the current protests to events of twenty-five years ago are halfhearted at best. This is, firstly, because they need to privilege the exaggerated violence of the present—to which they contribute decisively, and most of which has fallen on bystanders—at the expense of the undeniable violence of the past. For the thousands of Venezuelan revolutionaries who lived through the *Caracazo*, present comparisons with that moment predictably ring hollow. Secondly, moreover, it is because some of these opposition leaders—notably, Antonio Ledezma, mayor of metropolitan Caracas—participated directly in past repression that far exceeded even the most exaggerated claims of the present.[5] This is simply one of the many details that those in the streets today would ask us to forget.

As the revolutionary Venezuelan folk singer Alí Primera put it, "Those who die for life cannot be called dead, and from this moment forth, mourning them is prohibited." Our task is instead to distinguish between the corpses, to bury some and unearth those that resonate with the demands of contemporary struggles in a manner that far distinct from mourning. Whether it be the late President and Comandante Hugo Chávez, gone nearly a year, or the thousands massacred twenty-five years ago in the *Caracazo*, some of our dead simply cannot be left buried.

# NOTES

1. An earlier version of this chapter appeared in *History Workshop Online* (November 5th 2012). More recently, it was presented on the twenty-fifth anniversary of the Caracazo at the Embassy of the Bolivarian Republic of Venezuela in Cairo, Egypt (February 27, 2014) and at the University of Jordan in Amman (March 2, 2014).

2. This task informs much of my work in Ciccariello-Maher (2013).

3. As though answering Marx in a Marxist way, Benjamin further notes the task of revolutionary resurrection in the way that Robespierre "blasted" the example of ancient Rome "out of the continuum of history" as a motivation for the present: "This same leap in the open air of history is the dialectical one, which is how Marx understood the revolution" ("Theses" 261).

4. The name of the area derives from its previous role as burial site for the victims of an epidemic (Coronil 377).

5. As mayor, Ledezma oversaw part of the repression during the Caracazo. While he has denied this recently, a video surfaced of his public press statements prior to the massacre, in which he explained the deployment of security forces and promised to restore order—see http://www.youtube.com/watch?v=8DWKaURpmqI. Ledezma also restored order through the massacre of dozens of prisoners at the notorious Retén de Catia on November 27, 1992, coinciding with a second coup attempt against the Pérez government.

# WORKS CITED

Benjamin, Walter. "Critique of Violence." *Reflections: Essays, Aphorisms, Autobiographical Writings*. Ed. Peter Demetz. New York: Schocken, 1978: 277–300.

———. "Theses on the Philosophy of History." *Illuminations: Essays and Reflections*. Ed. Hannah Arendt. New York: Schocken, 1968: 253–64.

Chávez, Hugo, and Marta Harnecker. *Understanding the Bolivarian Revolution*. Trans. C. Boudin. New York: Monthly Review Press, 2005.

Ciccariello-Maher, George. "#LaSalida for Venezuela?," *The Nation*, 24 March 2014: 4–5.

———. *We Created Chávez: A People's History of the Venezuelan Revolution*. Durham, NC: Duke University Press, 2013.

———. "Toward a Racial Geography of Caracas: Neoliberal Urbanism and the Fear of Penetration." *Qui Parle* 16.2 (2007): 39–71.

Coronil, Fernando. *The Magical State: Nature, Money, and Modernity in Venezuela*. Chicago: University of Chicago Press, 1997.

Denis, Roland. Personal interview. 14 Oct. 2012.

———. *Los fabricantes de la rebelión: Movimiento popular, chavismo y sociedad en los años noventa*. Caracas: Editorial Primera Linea, 2001.

Errejón, Íñigo. "We Are (Almost) All Chávez: Challenges in the Deployment of Chavista Political Identity." Trans. George Ciccariello-Maher. *Venezuela Analysis* 15 Sept. 2013. Web. http://venezuelanalysis.com/analysis/10024.

Fanon, Frantz. *The Wretched of the Earth*. Trans. Richard Philcox. New York: Grove Press, 2004.

Foucault, Michel. "Nietzsche, Genealogy, History." *Language, Counter-Memory, Practice: Selected Essays and Interviews*. Ed. Donald F. Bouchard. Ithaca, NY: Cornell University Press, 1977: 139–64.

Grand, Emma. "El Caracazo: Cuatro millones de balas se dispararon contra un pueblo desarmado." *YVKE Mundial*. 26 Feb. 2010. Web. http://www.radiomundial.com.ve/yvke/noticia.php?43605.

Marx, Karl. "The Eighteenth Brumaire of Louis Bonaparte." *Later Political Writings*. Ed. Terrell Carver. Cambridge: Cambridge University Press, 1996: 31–127.

Marx, Karl. *Capital, Volume I* (Postface to the Second Edition). Trans. Ben Fowkes. London: Penguin, 1976.

Primera, Alí. "Los que mueren por la vida." *Canción mansa para un pueblo bravo*. Venezuela: Cigarrón-Promus, 1976.

*Chapter Eight*

# Depoliticization, Historical Memory, and Resistance to Obliviousness

*The Case of Feminicide and the Cotton Field Memorial in Ciudad Juárez, Mexico*

Martha I. Chew Sánchez and
Alfredo Limas Hernández

This chapter explores the context of feminicide in Ciudad Juárez and the importance of the decision by the Inter-American Court of Human Rights (IACHR) against the Mexican State in the *Case of González et al. ("Cotton Field") vs. Mexico*, widely known as the El Campo Algodonero case. In an effort to move away from the binaries of memory and countermemory[1] as two opposing sites of contention and representation, this work tries to present some of the contradictory frames of historical memory that are actively produced in relation to the Cotton Field memorial among the various actors: the regional and global oligarchy as well as the parents and relatives of victims of feminicide.

## CONTEXT OF FEMINICIDE IN MEXICO

Most feminicide victims are students or workers. These women have been kidnapped, held for days, tortured, raped, mutilated, and strangled. The victims tend to have a well-defined physical profile: between 14 and 25 years of age, brown, long-haired, and good-looking. Violence against women in Ciudad Juárez has increased as the types of victimization have multiplied.[2] Feminicide near the border is especially controversial because nearly all the cases are still unresolved.[3]

The pattern of violence has deeper roots, however. According to Fregoso and Bejarano, "feminicide is systemic violence rooted in social, political, economic, and cultural inequalities" (5). Feminicide cannot be explained simply as a series of individual attacks; it requires an understanding of the systemic and structural forces that are in place. Feminicides in Ciudad Juárez can be considered state crimes because the state has acted with negligence or collusion, blocking access to justice in many cases. In many cases, the evidence of the crimes has been deliberately lost by the police or government agents. Relatives, lawyers, journalists and scapegoats of the crimes have been harassed, tortured, and killed.[4] Feminicide and abduction of girls and young women in Ciudad Juárez is central to a trajectory of hate crimes not only against these young women, but also against their relatives, who have been impoverished and continuously revictimized over a period of at least twenty years.[5] Such practices have forced some relatives of victims of feminicide to seek political asylum, a status that has been granted by the United States of America (IAHCR 107).[6]

The phenomenon of feminicide in Ciudad Juárez can be divided into three main periods: mergence phase, 1995–2003; the period of "contention," 2004–2008; and the period of consolidation and upturn, 2008–2012.[7] Feminist analysis offers solid arguments showing the relationship between neoliberal capitalism and the rise of feminicidal violence.[8] Since the end of the occupation of northern Mexico (what is now known as the Southwest of the United States), the border between Mexico and the United States has been a site of global projects of capitalism predicated on a number of factors: the denial of citizenship, the exercise of terrorism against racialized and sexualized subjects, the impunity enjoyed by the aggressors, and the official insistence on the erasure of such cruelties from the border consciousness (Guidotti-Hernández 5). There has been a long history of systematic destruction of brown bodies, which has taken the form of lynching, public punishment, genocide, and other extreme forms of violence.[9] According to Guidotti-Hernández, exclusionary practices of membership, made manifest in policing racialized, gendered, and sexualized subjects, have obscured the physical and psychological pain and trauma inflicted on borderland communities (6). The moments and markers of differentiations in citizenship are inscribed through violence and the obstruction of access to justice, land, resources, and control of the body, and through vigorous policing. The exhibition of ritualized sexual violence and pain inflicted upon mainly brown (and female) bodies— Apache, Pima, Yaqui, and Mexican women in the newly conquered territory of the Southwest, Chicanas, undocumented women and children, migrant women, maquiladora[10] workers, and others—has served as a disciplining tool of racialized and gendered subjects in particular moments of economic change in the borderlands.

In the case of Mexico, neoliberal policies have been applied dogmatically, in favor of national and global financial institutions at the expense of social, economic, and political marginalization in both rural and urban areas, with an increasing severity of human rights violations.[11] Mexico is Latin America's second largest economy after Brazil. Since the end of the U.S. military takeover of what was northern Mexico during the Mexican-American War, Ciudad Juárez has been strategically situated for business, both legal and illegal, for both countries.[12] In Ciudad Juárez, the process of industrialization was carried out through the maquiladora industry in the late 1960s.[13]

Ciudad Juárez has become an emblematic city of an apparent paradox in which the major manufacturing operations of Fortune 500 firms coexist with a vast organized crime economy based on drug smuggling and sexual violence against women.[14] From 2008 to 2010, while Ciudad Juárez´s murder rate was the highest in the world, this urban center was also one of the most promising places for foreign investment (Washington Valdez, "Juárez Valle in Ruins" 1).[15] In its publication *The Foreign Direct Investment Magazine*, the Financial Times Group ranked Ciudad Juárez as the "City of the future" and the "Winner of the overall and most cost effective" rankings.[16]

As the city's main economic activity, the maquiladora industry influences the everyday lives of residents in both tangible and symbolic ways. It provides a strategic site for the local elite to gain local and regional political and economic power by helping the industry operate in the city with minimal problems and advantageous economic conditions.[17] The city has about 350 maquiladoras and employs over 300,000 direct workers who are experiencing the effects of increasing social, economic, and urban marginalization.[18] How can we explain that Ciudad Juárez—which was the most dangerous city in the world for three consecutive years (2008–2010)—was also ranked during those very same years, and thereafter, as the best city in the American continent for foreign investment? The war on drugs has been intrinsically linked to the expansion of foreign investment, that is, to transnational corporate control over labor, minerals, and land.[19]

## DRUG ECONOMY IN CIUDAD JUÁREZ

Part of the socioeconomic and political context of sexual crimes in the region involves the drug economy. The emergence and sustained drug economy in Mexico is directly linked to the United States' drug prohibition laws.[20] According to Bunker, Mexican cartels employ about 450,000 people, and the livelihood of about 3.2 million people in Mexico depends on the drug trade (41). In Ciudad Juárez, from 30 percent to 60 percent of the economy depends on laundered money (Bowden 45). Most of the drug cartels in the region have operations throughout the United States and in some parts of Central America, South America, and Europe; and most of the cartels dispute Ciudad Juárez as one of the most strategic areas for their smuggling operations.[21] The fact that Ciudad Juárez is a hotbed for drug trafficking contributes to the escalation of homicides, sex traffic, prostitution, and other crimes. It is important to point out that during the "war on drugs"—which was waged for six years under Mexico's last president, Felipe Calderón—160,000 people were killed and over 50,000 people, men and women, "disappeared," that is, were abducted, tortured, killed, and dumped into clandestine cemeteries or burnt.[22] The Mexican State, which is becoming more militarized, promoted the discourse of a necessary war against the drug cartels to justify the human rights violations suffered by civilians.[23] In 2006, the Mexican State deployed 10,000 soldiers in Ciudad Juárez for the war against drugs. This militarization caused an increase in violence and public insecurity, stimulated the flow of drugs, and led to a massive exodus. In fact, abductions and feminicide have become part of the everyday life of the city since the early 1990s, with a sharp increase during President Calderón's war on drugs and the tenure of the current president, Enrique Peña Nieto.[24]

## NATIONAL MEMBERSHIP, HUMAN RIGHTS, AND THE EXPANSION OF CAPITALISM

Citizenship is an essential locator and marker of national subjects and legal processes that emerge in the ongoing construction of a nation, which in turn produces hierarchies. Nation-states create and monitor changing boundaries of difference between those who enjoy full citizenship and those who do not. Such boundaries become visible, in part, through the failures of a justice system that does not deliver. In the case of feminicides in Ciudad Juárez, working-class brown women are not considered full citizens. In many cases, the state has acted with negligence by colluding with the perpetrators or blocking access to justice, as the verdict of the IACHR in the El Campo Algodonero case has proven.

Mexicans have paid a high social price for sustaining structural inequality through terror, war, and apartheid. Most neoliberal structural projects require processes of exclusions. One of the most pivotal exclusions in periods of political and economic change, such as the one Mexico has experienced since the signing of NAFTA, involves the construction of the citizen-subject. Ironically, Ciudad Juárez has been presented to the world as the best city in Latin America for investment. The Mexican State, in alliance with global capital, has made incredible efforts to rebrand the nation as well as the city as a global capitalist "player."

In a way, Ciudad Juárez is emblematic of the new world order, where organized crime displays a modus operandi so close to the global corporations that the oligarchies are often the same. Both the state and organized crime take advantage of the geopolitical location of the Mexico-U.S. border to profit from labor exploitation and human rights violations in order to supply not only the drug demand but also the cheap goods guaranteeing the affordable high standard of living associated with the United States. The Mexican State and organized crime use terrorism against the Mexican population, and even more against the dissident population, in order to maintain a labor force and a population in constant fear, and therefore, docile.

## EL CAMPO ALGODONERO (THE COTTON FIELD) CASE

On November 16, 2009, at the conclusion of the *Case of González et al. ("Cotton Field") vs. Mexico*—widely known as El Campo Algodonero case—the Inter-American Court of Human Rights declared a landmark verdict, holding the Mexican government accountable for the murders of Esmeralda Herrera Monreal, 15; Laura Berenice Ramos Monárrez, 17; and Claudia Ivette González, 19. Although eight corpses were found in the clandestine cemetery of El Campo Algodonero, the case names only three women because only three of the bodies could be properly identified. El Campo Algodonero case has implications for other kinds of social and political reform projects regarding women's citizenship. In the operative paragraphs of the verdict, the court declared that the Mexican State "violated the rights to life, personal integrity and personal liberty . . . [and] failed to comply with its obligation to investigate—and thereby guarantee—the right to life, personal integrity and personal liberty. . . . The State violated the obligation not to discriminate" (IACHR 146–47). Accordingly, the Mexican State was given twenty-six directives that constituted "per se a form of reparation" (IACHR 147).[25] However, according to the families of the victims, only one—the financial compensation to the families of feminicide—of the thirteen IACHR resolutions has been entirely fulfilled by the Mexican State. The verdict includes a statement regarding a memorial to the victims of gender-based murders:

> The Tribunal considers that, in the instant case, it is pertinent for the State to erect a monument to commemorate the women victims of gender-based murder in Ciudad Juárez, who include the victims in this case, as a way of dignifying them and as a reminder of the context of violence they experienced, which the State undertakes to prevent in the future. The monument shall be unveiled at the ceremony during which the State publicly acknowledges its international responsibility (*supra para*) and shall be built in the cotton field in which the victims of this case were found. 2. Since the monument relates to more indi-

viduals than those considered victims in this case, the decision on the type of monument shall correspond to the public authorities, who must consult the opinion of civil society organizations by means of an open, public procedure in which the organizations that represented the victims in this case shall be included. (IACHR 114)

Although sexual violence and feminicide in Ciudad Juárez have attracted worldwide attention over the past two decades, all feminicide cases are still unresolved and without delivery of justice.[26] The Mexican State has displayed a lack of political will to eradicate sexual violence and feminicide through judicial and criminal investigation. Mainly, no legislation has been enacted to prevent and punish sexual and gender violence and to monitor procedures that would ensure the implementation of new protocols. Evidence of these failures can be seen in the fact that reports of feminicide and abductions have increased year to year.

## EL CAMPO ALGODONERO MEMORIAL

On November 8, 2011, a memorial to the eight victims of feminicide was built in El Campo Algodonero, in the same place where their bodies were found ten years earlier.[27] The memorial, which cost 16 million pesos (about $1.19 million dollars), features the eight pink crosses that were planted in the cotton field a few weeks after the young women's bodies were found. Rosa-Linda Fregoso provides a useful description of the memorial:

To the right of the entrance, a plaque dedicates the memorial 'To the memory of the women and girl victims of gender violence in Ciudad Juárez.'[28] . . . [T]he names of the women found at El Campo Algodonero (Claudia Yvette González, Laura Berenice Ramos Monárrez, Esmeralda Herrera Monreal, María de los Angeles Acosta Ramírez, Mayra Juliana Reyes Solís, Verónica Martínez Hernández, Merlín Elizabeth Rodríguez Sáenz, María Rocina Galicia) are engraved on a wall, in a marble-encased panel. An adjacent memory wall is partially filled with the names of additional women who were murdered in the city. . . [There is a] shrine bearing a large cross, painted in the iconic pink, a tribute to and recognition of the mothers' cross campaign for justice. ("For the Women of Ciudad Juárez")

On the far side, there stands a large bronze sculpture, *Flor de Arena* (*Sand Flower*), which was designed by Verónica Leiton, a Chilean artist who has lived in Ciudad Juárez for the past twenty years.[29] *Flor de Arena* was inspired, as the artist explained to Fregoso, in the rose-shaped fossils that are formed by layers of salts, water, and sand in the desert area of Ciudad Juárez ("For the Women of Juárez"). At the center of the sculpture, a young woman reaches out looking up to the sky.

The legal team representing the victims of feminicide proposed the memorial at the beginning of the legal process in the IACHR. The Mexican State repudiated many of the IACHR's recommendations without any formal follow-up; in particular, the recommendation regarding the development of educational initiatives that would help generate cultural and historical memory. Quite the opposite happened: threats and attacks intensified against human rights leaders, researchers, and civil organizations. In theory, of all the remedial measures stipulated by the IACHR, the El Campo Algodonero memorial may have been one of the simplest and least taxing for the Mexican State. However, it was one of the most draining for the individuals concerned with justice for the victims of feminicide. Making sure that the state complied with this resolution meant a lengthy confrontation with the authorities.[30] The memorial has been a major embarrassment to the local and national oligarchy because it represents a public acknowledgment of the state's failure to protect women and to carry out the proper investigation necessary to follow international protocols and carry out justice. But the site is even more significant with regards to its denunciatory message because it is located in one of the expensive business areas of the city, just one block from the United States Consulate and directly in front of the headquarters of the Association of Maquiladoras.[31] Despite the fact that the memorial does not fully comply with the stipulations of the IACHR, it has nonetheless vindicated the struggle of those who fought for it.[32]

The memorial has become a site of protest, information, and mourning. Many family members go to the memorial and place a pink cross when they learn that their daughter is missing or has been killed or abducted. Since the beginning of the phenomenon of feminicide in Ciudad Juárez, the families have placed pink crosses with the names of the victims and the dates their bodies were found or when they disappeared. This kind of painful collective action calls for justice and condemns state terrorism. At the same time, it mobilizes and triggers human rights movements and gives testimony to human rights violations. The pink crosses, the photographs, and at times the memorial serve to destabilize the state's contrived consensus of peace. Despite the violence under which they live, family members have persisted in recounting the effects of living with their losses and injustices. The relatives of the young women buried at El Campo Algodonero, however, did not attend the inauguration of the memorial.[33]

The families of victims of feminicide and abduction have faced enormous pain, yet they are the ones who have insisted on the creation of democratic and just models of prevention of violence and alternative approaches to human security. Despite the fact that they face indignities in their claims for justice, they have persevered in demanding the delivery of justice and an end to the practices of denying and erasing these crimes in the national consciousness. Many families were present in the opening ceremony to protest, yet again, the injustices and the constant threats they faced. They carried candles, banners, and photographs of their children. They continually expressed one of the main maxims of feminicide protests in Mexico: "They were abducted alive, we want them alive!"[34] Some of the protesters expressed, "We are forced to do this in public, so that we get your attention. Why are you not doing anything about the crimes? Why are you not willing to solve the crimes? We do not want memorials." Still, others interrupted the representatives of the State with the chant, "No more killing!"[35]

Families have expressed their refusal to accept the way the Mexican State and the mainstream media around the world have constructed the Cotton Field memorial and the phenomenon of feminicide as "neutral" and non-political, or merely as a result of delinquency. By rejecting the social costs of authoritarianism, the families have exposed the fact that the bodies of women have paid for Mexico's entrance into the realm of market-driven globalization, a global economic model that is based on gross inequalities and the dismantling of social safety nets of entire communities. These families have revealed the impossibility of reintegrating such communities to national hegemonic projects. They have recounted how the tortured bodies of the population of the "best city for investment in Latin America" cannot be separated from the neoliberal turn in the nation, from the moment the military state imposed its multifold project of adjustment plans, free trade, and a narcotics-centered economy through extreme violence.

The failures by part of the Mexican State have opened more wounds and further disempowered families by its attempt to dehistoricize the killing and abduction of young women. The official narrative representing the victims of feminicide does not incorporate the memory of women with identities as social actors invested in a variety of personal, family, and community ties. Such narrow framing actively pursued by the Mexican State—which never accounts for the broader life story that could bestow a more complex identity to the victims—has been challenged by the historical memory constructed by the families of the victims with every commemorative act, protest, and denunciation. Instead, the state and mainstream media present a ritualized repetition of traumatic and dark stories. The families of the victims, however, refuse the tautological interpretation of feminicide as a consequence of a culture of violence, a reductive version that relocates responsibility in the victims themselves and their families. Instead, they denounce the government's failure to implement socially responsible policies. The parents, extended family, and communities of the victims of feminicide have refused to participate in the concealment brought about as a consequence of unresolved justice, of a forced closure. Nevertheless, the state's superficial approach to reconciliation has not contained historical memory, particularly with such levels of violence and neglect. While the Cotton Field memorial has not brought closure, it has played an important role in the process of healing; it has paved the way for the demands for human rights and the dignified treatment of the families of the victims and the community in general. Violence against activists and sympathizers has been used repeatedly as a means to disarticulate mass social mobilizations. As Guidotti-Hernández states, the racialized exercise of power requires the constant threat of terror tactics in order to maintain its grip (8).[36]

The Cotton Field memorial has become a critical arena of struggle, engagement, and identification, where the families directly affected by paramilitary violence have represented symbolically their experiences and their demands. The opening ceremony of the memorial was marked by a sense of emotional incompleteness and the unwillingness of the state to work within the law to uphold the political democracy that is supposed to be the basis of the current democratic transition.

## CONCLUSIONS

Ciudad Juárez has experienced over twenty years of terrorism by the state, transnational factories, military and paramilitary forces, and organized crime. These actors have not been antagonistic with each other altogether. Often times, they have indeed benefitted from each other's activities and thrived in the context of deregulated national industries, dismantled national and social safety networks and programs, a corrupt judiciary, state-inflicted violence, and a general disregard for human rights. Feminicide in Ciudad Juárez marks one of the most violent episodes in the history of the Mexico-U.S. border, where women are stripped of their citizenship and historical identities. The state policy of *desmemoria* of feminicide—this manufactured oblivion in the national consciousness—is achieved in various ways: by obliterating the humanity of its citizens and treating them as labor force without public safety mechanisms and safeguards; by disrupting the social fabric while stigmatizing the families of the victims and movements struggling for justice; by enforcing and naturalizing a policy of terror to discipline its population; and lastly, by creating and promoting official symbols—such as *La Monumental "X"*—to overshadow El Campo Algodonero Memorial.

## NOTES

1. Countermemory is understood as a manifestation of resistance to hegemonic and official versions of historical continuity. Countermemory questions the context of official memory; represents the voices that remember but are suppressed; and at the same time examines the political, social and economic reasons that lead to changes in the perception of memory and its reproduction.

2. These cemeteries are emblematic given the sexual nature of the crimes and the randomness of the discovery of the clandestine cemeteries. In fact, for the past twenty years, these makeshift graves have been detected only because passersby have reported them to the police.

The following list, which indicates the year that the sites were reported to the police, includes some of the most important clandestine cemeteries located in Ciudad Juárez: Lote Bravo, 1995; Lomas de Poleo, 1996; El Campo Algodonero (Cotton Field), 2001; La Zona Dorada de Juárez, 2001; El Cristo Negro, 2003; and El Arroyo del Navajo/Valle de Juárez, 2011–2013. This last one contains the bodies of women who were found from 2011 to 2013.

3.  Fregoso and Bejarano problematize the term *femicide*, which conceptualizes the murder of women on the basis of their gender (5). Fregoso and Bejarano state that *feminicide* is a more comprehensive approach to gender violence; it is the murder of women involving a crime "that is both public and private" and implicates "both the state (directly or indirectly) and individual perpetrators (private or state actors)" (5). Therefore, this type of crime "encompasses systematic, widespread, and everyday interpersonal violence" (5).

4.  During the trial of the *Case of González et al. ("Cotton Field") vs. Mexico* in the IACHR, evidence emerged showing that the Chihuahua state police had randomly planted evidence against working-class men, most of them bus drivers, and tortured them. In fact, one of them died while in custody at the state prison. Their lawyers were also murdered.

5.  Since 1993, hundreds of women and girls have been violently murdered in Ciudad Juárez, Chihuahua, Mexico. In light of the government's inaction in preventing further cases, as well as the lack of investigation and mishandling of evidence, these murders have received international attention.

6.  For more information on this case, see *Case of González et al. ("Cotton Field") vs. Mexico* Judgment of November 16, 2009, by the Inter-American Court of Human Rights; and the article "Forced North by Drugs, but United in Exile," by Julián Aguilar.

7.  From 1995 to 2007, there were no more than five victims of feminicide in Ciudad Juárez, whereas in 2008 there was a substantial increase to sixteen cases that year. Then, in 2009, there were twenty feminicide cases and twenty-seven reports of disappeared women. In 2011, fifty-seven reports of disappeared women were filed. Now, in 2014, there are already over one hundred reports of disappeared women, of which thirty-six are under eighteen years of age.

8.  For more information see the following studies: *Terrorizing Women: Feminicide in the Americas*, edited by Rosa-Linda Fregoso and Cynthia Bejarano; *Seguridad y equidad social y de género*, by Alfredo Limas Hernández and Myrna Limas Hernández; and *Geografía de la pobreza en Ciudad Juárez* and *Desarrollo y pobreza en México*, both by Myrna Limas Hernández.

9.  This has been the case for indigenous people and Mexicans of non-European descent on both sides of the border, as seen particularly during the Spanish conquest, the Mexican-American War, the Indian Wars, and the last two decades of feminicide.

10.  A maquiladora is an assembly factory where all the material that is assembled is exempted from import and export, as well as national and local taxes. There are over 3,000 maquiladoras in Mexico that employ over a million workers. Most of the maquiladoras are located in the Mexico-U.S. border.

11.  The signing of NAFTA was a turning point in Mexico's economic, social, and political history. Prior to the 1980s, the Mexican government had accepted the Import Substitution Industrialization (ISI) economic model, where Mexico enjoyed food sovereignty and there was a protection of domestic industries and a captive national market. In the so-called "lost decade" that lasted from 1980 to 1991, Mexico experienced (a world record) thirteen structural adjustment plans with the World Bank alone, due to its national debt. In 1994, NAFTA locked Mexico into a series of reforms that resulted in greater control of private foreign investment, the widespread sale of government industries, and the termination of state programs that had provided a health and social safety net for millions of Mexicans. NAFTA displaced millions of people from rural areas when the agricultural sector was left without any protection from the government, and brought levels of inequality similar to those before the Mexican Revolution at the turn of the twentieth century. NAFTA was part of an increasingly unequal global project with one unaccountable power and many unaccountable regional and local forces that have left the nation-states without much power in the world of economics and politics.

12.  The Paso del Norte area—consisting of the hub cities El Paso (Texas, USA), Ciudad Juárez (Chihuahua, Mexico), and Las Cruces (New Mexico, USA)—is especially important

because it is the midway point on the Mexico-U.S. border, 814 miles from the Port of Long Beach and 739 miles from the Port of Houston. The region's geographic position is supported by a strong infrastructure where three major highways, U.S. Interstates 10 and 25 and the Pan-American Highway in Mexico, connect the region to major hubs in both countries. The rail service to the region is provided by three major rail lines: Union-Pacific and Burlington Northern-Santa Fe (U.S.) and Ferromex (Mexico). There are three commercial ports of entry—two in El Paso and one in New Mexico—featuring the dedicated truck lane known as FAST (free and secure trade) Lane and two dedicated commuter lanes (DCL). Maquiladoras are twenty minutes away from El Paso; more than 3,000 US maquiladora managers work in Ciudad Juárez but live in El Paso.

13.   At the end of the bracero program in 1964, Ciudad Juárez became even more attractive for global capital to set up multinational assembly factories (maquiladoras) focused mainly on automotive and electrical products, which are Mexico's manufacturing industries served by the near-shore production plants in Ciudad Juárez. However, there is a significant presence of companies involved in the production of appliances, industrial machinery, transportation equipment, aerospace and plastic parts, as well as communications, electronic, and computer equipment. ADC Telecommunications, Electrolux, Bosch, Foxconn, Flextronics, Lexmark, Delphi, Visteon, Johnson Controls, Lear, Boeing, Cardinal Health, Yazaki, Sumitomo, and Siemens are some of the foreign companies that have chosen Ciudad Juárez as the site of their near-shore manufacturing facilities. These companies are quite important for the production of goods used in hospitals, the automotive industry, and telecommunications.

14.   "The cartel leaders 'don't want to interrupt the legal trade,'" says Manuel Ochoa, vice president of bi-national development at the El Paso Regional Economic Development Corporation, a nonprofit organization that advises companies on doing business in El Paso" (Parish Flannery 1).

15.   From 2007 to 2009, Ciudad Juárez's murder rate was the highest reported in the world, exceeding the holders of the second and third highest rates by more than 25 percent. The war on drugs that President Calderón waged from 2006 to 2012 increased Mexico's national homicide rate from 8.1 homicides per 100,000 in 2007 to 23.7 homicides per 100,000 in 2011 (Washington Valdez, "Juárez Valle in Ruins" 1).

16.   The city also received a top five ranking for best infrastructure among 2007/2008 North American cities. Multinational capital has shaped the local social, political, and economic spaces of the city to satisfy the needs of the maquiladora industry.

17.   The city's economic and political elite, in close partnership with the maquiladora industry, has actively participated in city planning. This planning has benefited the development of the urban infrastructure almost exclusively within the areas in which the maquiladoras are located. This partnership greatly explains the city's extreme and growing urban marginality.

18.   The urban infrastructure is new and visibly developed on the east side, the area where the maquiladoras are situated. However, it is the west side, at the foot of the mountains, where the oldest settlements can be found and where about 48 percent of the population lives. The western part of the city lacks a basic social infrastructure. There are no hospitals and no emergency services, there are no police, very few streets are paved, plumbing is rare, and water is scarce. There are no daycare centers, and there are only two high schools for a population of about 500,000 (Limas Hernández and Limas Hernández 1). These social and economic hardships have accelerated due to internal migration.

19.   From this perspective, the Plan Mérida works in favor of those who are sponsoring and financing a war that is increasingly against Mexico's civil population. The war on drugs in Latin America has meant U. S. military, economic and political intervention and social control (Hernández 5). Paramilitary groups have been the most effective in creating displacement, controlling labor, dissuading labor organizing, and terrorizing union organizations for capital expansion. All these crimes require considerable levels of organizational sophistication and resources.

20.   The emergence of the drug economy in Mexico is directly linked to the United States' drug prohibition laws. Since the 1860s, the U.S. government had passed laws in an attempt to control alcohol, cocaine, heroin, morphine, and cannabis production, distribution, and consumption. In 1814, the Harrison Narcotics Act created a drug economy, mainly along the

Mexico-U.S. border, based on smuggling drugs to reach the consumer market in the United States.

21. A turning point was seen in the early 1990s, when the Colombia-Miami drug route was blocked by the United States. This change in routes meant that almost all drug smugglers had to negotiate with Mexican cartels to go through Mexico. Since 95 percent of the cocaine trade now goes through Mexico, the redirection of vast amounts of money and power caused by the disruption of the Colombia-Miami drug route has resulted in the weakening of the Mexican State (Bowden 3–4).

22. This war on drugs was partly financed by the United States with the Plan Mérida.

23. The number of abductions and victims of political repression from the state has increased well after the end of Felipe Calderón's presidency.

24. Paramilitaries have been able to impose "political" demands on governments at the city, county, state, and federal levels. Paramilitarism in Mexico is continuously fed by mass defection. For instance, since 2005 there has been a mass defection of members of the army's airmobile elite division (GAFES, Grupo Aeromóvil de Fuerzas Especiales), an elite group who left to be part of the Zetas, "one of the most powerful drug cartels in Mexico" (Aranda 1).

25. Sonia Torres was the common intervener in the case (IACHR 2). Some of the most important directives are the following:

> "The State shall . . . conduct the criminal proceeding that is underway effectively and, if applicable, any that are opened in the future to identify, prosecute and, if appropriate, punish the perpetrators and masterminds of the disappearances, ill-treatments and deprivations of life of Ms. González, Herrera and Ramos, in accordance with the following directives . . . provide the victims' next of kin with information on progress in the investigation regularly and give them full access to the case files, and be conducted by officials who are highly trained in similar cases and in dealing with victims of discrimination and gender-based violence;. . . . The State shall, within a reasonable time, investigate, through the competent public institutions, the officials accused of irregularities and, after an appropriate proceeding, apply the corresponding administrative, disciplinary or criminal sanctions to those found responsible. . . . The State shall, within six months of notification of this Judgment, publish once in the Official Gazette of the Federation, in a daily newspaper with widespread national circulation and in a daily newspaper with widespread circulation in the state of Chihuahua. . . . The State shall, within one year of notification of this Judgment, organize a public act to acknowledge its international responsibility in relation to the facts of this case so as to honor the memory of Laura Berenice Ramos Monárrez, Esmeralda Herrera Monreal and Claudia Ivette González . . . continue standardizing all its protocols, manuals, prosecutorial investigation criteria, expert services, and services to provide justice that are used to investigate all the crimes relating to the disappearance, sexual abuse and murders of women. . . . The State shall, within one year of notification of this Judgment, erect a monument in memory of the women victims of gender-based murders in Ciudad Juárez. . . . The monument shall be unveiled at the ceremony during which the State publicly acknowledges its international responsibility, in compliance with the decision of the Court specified in the preceding operative paragraph." (IACHR 145)

26. According to Amnesty International, there are inadequate official data on the crimes committed in the state of Chihuahua, Mexico, particularly those related to feminicide and abduction of young women (1). Some researchers make a distinction between those that bear the evidence of serial killing and those that do not. However, according to Amnesty International, as of February 2005, more than 370 young women and girls have been murdered in the cities of Ciudad Juárez and Chihuahua (1). More recently, prosecutors from the state of Chihuahua reported that in 2010, of the 270 women who were killed in the state, 247 of them died in Ciudad Juárez (Ortega Lozano 1).

27.  Ironically, the bodies were found in a vacant lot in one of the most expensive areas of Ciudad Juárez, in front of the Association of the Maquiladora Industry headquarters, a couple of blocks away from where the new United States Consulate stands today.

28.  "A la memoria de las mujeres y niñas víctimas de la violencia de género en Ciudad Juárez."

29.  There was a national call and the mothers and the legal committee read the proposals and voted for Leiton's.

30.  In one meeting in Mexico City between the mothers of the four identified victims of El Campo Algodonero, their legal representatives and Felipe de Jesús Zamora Castro, vice-secretary of judicial matters of the Ministry of the Interior under President Felipe Calderón, Zamora Castro threatened the legal representatives and the families and persisted in pointing his finger at them. At one point the vice-secretary even pounded the table. The Mexican oligarchy clearly expressed its unwillingness to ask for the forgiveness of these poor women.

31.  In place of a memorial in the Cotton Field, where the young women were found, the government proposed a flower arrangement in a large pot in another part of the city.

32.  The verdict of the IACHR stated that the Mexican State should invite these mothers of victims of feminicide to recognize that the memorial was built for them and to accept that their children were still missing. At the same time, the memorial did not meet the deadline. The inauguration ceremony was cancelled twice because it was far from ready. To this day, there is no water in the statue, no gardens, no parking space, and the memorial is missing many other details that were stipulated in the sentence.

33.  The absence of the families was meant to show their disappointment and frustration with the Mexican State's blatant disregard for the standards set by the court for El Campo Algodonero memorial and the failure of high-level Mexican officials to extend their apologies.

34.  *¡ Vivas se las llevaron, vivas las queremos!*

35.  *¡Ni una más!*

36.  There is little to no legal or formal recourse in the face of state-sponsored terror. The deficiencies of the legal system are exemplified by the fraught and stacked court system that dramatically limits any possibility for citizenship participation in a traditional sense.

## WORKS CITED

Aguilar, Julián. "Forced North by Drug Wars, but United in Exile." *The New York Times*. 12 April 2012. Web. http://www.nytimes.com/2012/04/13/us/forced-north-by-mexican-drug-wars-but-united-in-exile.html?pagewanted=all.

Amnesty International. "Mexico: Justice Fails in Ciudad Juárez and the City of Chihuahua." *Amnesty International*. 27 Feb. 2005. Web. http://www.amnestyusa.org/node/55339.

Aranda, Jesús. "Alarmante deserción en el ejército; casi 100 mil durante este sexenio." *La Jornada*. 7 Aug. 2005. Web. http://www.jornada.unam.mx/2005/08/07/index.php?section=politica&article=003n1pol.

Bowden, Charles. *Murder City: Ciudad Juarez and the Global Economy's New Killing Fields*. New York: First Nation Books, 2010.

Bunker, Robert. *Narcos over the Border: Gangs, Cartels, and Mercenaries*. New York: Routledge, 2010.

Cárdenas, Lourdes. "Exodus from Juárez Will Continue, Researchers Warn." *El Paso Times*. 21 Jan. 2011. Web. http://elpasotimes.typepad.com/mexico/2011/01/exodus-from-ju%C3%A1rez-will-continue-researchers-warn.html.

Fregoso, Rosa-Linda. "For the Women of Ciudad Juárez." *The Feminist Wire*. 12 Dec. 2012. Web. http://thefeministwire.com/2012/12/for-the-women-of-ciudad-juarez/.

Fregoso, Rosa-Linda, and Cynthia Bejarano. "Introduction." *Terrorizing Women: Feminicide in the Americas*. Ed. Rosa-Linda Fregoso and Cynthia Bejarano. Durham, NC: Duke University Press, 2010. 1–42.

Gavin Marshall, Andrew. "Security and Prosperity Partnership of North America (SPP): Security and Prosperity for Whom?" *Global Research*. 17 March 2008. Web. http://www.

globalresearch.ca/security-and-prosperity-partnership-of-north-america-spp-security-and-prosperity-for-whom/8375.

Guidotti-Hernández, Nicole. *Unspeakable Violence: Remapping U.S. and Mexican National Imaginaries*. Durham, NC: Duke University Press, 2011.

Hernández, Anabel. *México en llamas: El legado de Calderón*. México, D.F.: Editorial Grijalbo, 2013.

IAHCR (Inter-American Court of Human Rights) *Case of González et al. ("Cotton Field") vs. Mexico* Judgment of November 16, 2009 (Preliminary Objection, Merits Reparations, and Costs). Washington, D.C. November 16, 2009. Web. http://www.rtdh.eu/pdf/seriec_205_ing.pdf.

Limas Hernández, Alfredo, and Myrna Limas Hernández. *Seguridad y equidad social y de género. Consideraciones sobre un índice y estudios de caso en Ciudad Juárez*. Ciudad Juárez: Editorial Universidad Autónoma de Ciudad Juárez, 2010.

Limas Hernández, Myrna. *Desarrollo y pobreza en México. Los índices IDH y FGT en la primera década del Siglo XXI. Estudios regionales en economía, población y desarrollo. Cuadernos de trabajo de la Universidad Autónoma de Ciudad Juárez. No. 4*. Ciudad Juárez: Editorial Universidad Autónoma de Ciudad Juárez, 2010.

———. *Geografía de la pobreza en Ciudad Juárez. Una perspectiva de género*. Ciudad Juárez: Editorial Universidad Autónoma de Ciudad Juárez, 2011.

Ortega Lozano, Marisela. "130 Women Killed in Juárez this Year; Chihuahua AG Says Fight for Women's Rights Painful and Slow." *El Paso Times*. 24 Aug. 2011. Web. http://www.elpasotimes.com/ci_18747536?IADID=Search-www.elpasotimes.com-www.elpasotimes.com.

Parish Flannery, Nathaniel. "Big Business Boom in an Unlikely Mexican City." *Global Post*. 22 Aug. 2012. Web. http://www.globalpost.com/dispatch/news/regions/americas/mexico/120822/mexican-economy-juarez-exports-outsourcing-multinationals-business.

Scherer García, Julio. "Calderón, tal cual es . . . Reporte Especial." *Revista Proceso*. 11 Feb. 2012. Web. http://www.proceso.com.mx/?p=298097.

Vergara, Rosalía. "Elección comprada: El escándalo Peña Nieto-Soriana." *Revista Proceso*. 7 July 2012. Web. http://www.proceso.com.mx/?p=313518.

Washington Valdez, Diana. "Juárez Falls to No. 37 on World's Most Violent Cities List." *El Paso Times*. 16 Jan. 2014. Web. http://www.elpasotimes.com/latestnews/ci_24926073.

———. "Juárez Valle in Ruins: Drug Violence Economically, Socially Devastating." *El Paso Times*. 25 Feb. 2011. Web. http://www.elpasotimes.com/business/ci_17475882.

———. *The Killing Fields: Harvest of Women*. Burbank: Peace at the Border Film Productions, 2006.

Washington Valdez, Diana, and Aileen B. Flores. "Court Blasts Mexico for Juárez Women's Murders." *El Paso Times*. 12 Dec. 2009. Web. http://www.elpasotimes.com/news/ci_13981319.

*V*

# The Palimpsest of Memory: Reconstructing Race, Culture, and Religion from Colonial Times to the Present in Peru, Mexico, and the Dominican Republic

*Chapter Nine*

# Mystic Ringing of Stone Bells[1]

*A Case of Annihilation of Cultural Memory in Peru*

Beatriz Carolina Peña

Most of the international community was horrified to learn that the former Taliban government had destroyed the two standing stone Buddhas of Bamiyan in March 2001 in order to "purify" Afghanistan of its past non-Islamic religions. A similar horror might overcome us to learn how, at Morro de Eten[2] (Mount Eten), in Lambayeque, coastal Northern Peru, there used to be two large phonolites (alkaline igneous rocks that produce a ringing sound when struck by other stones or metallic objects)[3] that, like the monumental statues of the Buddhas, were also destroyed by explosives. The stupendous stone Buddhist statues were carved into the cliffs of the Bamiyan valley while the phonolites were wonders of the natural world, unique ancient rocks that took millions of years to be formed.[4] Yet, despite their distinct origins, those awe-inspiring monuments were linked at some point in history to vibrant religious rituals, and they also constituted the property and cultural symbols of the local peoples they moved.

The gigantic empty niches of the Buddhas stand today in the Bamiyan valley, "as a monument to the crime of their destruction" and "a defeat for those who tried to obliterate its memory with dynamite" (Hegarty). In contrast, there are no material remnants of the Peruvian phonolites—called *piedras campanas*: literally "bell stones"—tragically reduced to dust at the beginning of the twentieth century. Not even the textual evidence about *piedras campanas* constitutes a solid memory of them. The written legacy is limited to mainly passing mentions in some colonial texts[5] and other Peruvian sources of the late nineteen and early twentieth centuries.[6]

Despite the radical decision of the Spanish to destroy any images, festivals, and monuments of precolonial religious practices, the large phonolites

127

of Morro de Eten survived colonial times, perhaps thanks to the reverence these natural phenomena inspired in the Europeans who stroked them and heard their melodious tones. As an alternative to such violent destructive actions, a deliberate act of erasure of the cultic preconquest significance of those rocks started after the mid-seventeenth century. This article argues that the *piedras campanas* were invested with new meanings so that their identity as relics of indigenous religious practices would cease to exist; instead of anchoring them to pre-Hispanic ritual ceremonies interpreted as devil-worship, they would serve the new Christian identity that the Spanish were trying to impose on the Viceroyalty of Peru. This annihilation of cultural collective memory was accomplished by constructing new Catholic memories linked to the rocks in order to purge them of their ancient sacred meaning.

## FORGETTING: WHY DOES IT MATTER?

As Greg Woolf has pointed out, "anthropological and historical studies of tradition have focused on memory" (367); but some have occasionally addressed forgetfulness as well. Simon Price argues that "the process of constructing memories needs to be accompanied by analysis of its counterpart, forgetting" (27), and that historians tend to be so interested in memory that they put forgetting aside. Forgetting is germane to the study of historical memory because "societies shape stories about their histories through selectivity, a process of forgetting as well as remembering." Equally important, memory erasure is "usually inadvertent rather than self-conscious" (Levene 217). However, when memory erasure is the result of a process brought about by colonial policy, the phenomenon might be unforeseeable for the colonial subjects, but it is generally intentional for those with the power to exercise it. Thus, if oblivion constitutes a form of "memory sanction," as termed by Harriet Flower (xix), and can be carried out through stealth methods by groups interested in transforming collective memory, it should be the historian's responsibility to track those forms of suppression that have impoverished cultural memory.

Images, objects, or sounds, as in the case analyzed here, of a community's past represent their identity. When negotiations of that past are necessary to propel a new religious practice, instead of destroying the ancient elements of ritual significance, the strategy of forging fresh ties between ancient and encroaching beliefs might be put to advantageous use. One of the tactics in accomplishing this is what Mary Carruthers calls "crowding" or "overlay," a mnemotechnical resource "mastered by the Christians" since the Middle Ages, which consists of carefully "blocking one pattern of memories by another" (54).

The phonolites of Eten aroused admiration in the Spaniards, as it is evi-dent in the travel account by the Castilian Hieronymite friar Diego de Ocaña (c. 1570–1608). The monk suggested that, because of the majesty of the rocks, the king should order them to be taken to Spain. For their unique-ness—"more of such kind of stones surely do not exist in the world" (242),[7] he affirms—Ocaña considered them a creation worthy of royal attention and enjoyment. The same appreciation was most likely common among the Fran-ciscan missionaries who were evangelizing in the area. Therefore, rather than opting for physical obliteration of the stones, the sounds of the phonolites were reinterpreted to connect them to Catholic rituals and beliefs. A network of associations, triggered by miraculous events at the local church in Puerto Eten, was the platform for a mnemonic replacement. The study of these associations could offer understanding into the ways collective cultural mem-ory operates.

## MORRO DE ETEN: A CUPINISQUE ARCHAEOLOGICAL SITE

In 1978, Carlos G. Elera detected and excavated an archeological site at Morro de Eten. There he discovered the undisturbed tomb of an elderly man, whom the archeologist identified as a shaman. Elera was able to recognize the occupation of the man whose skeleton he unearthed through the tools placed next to the body, particularly those laid above his head. He deter-mined that these instruments were the objects still used in shamanic practices in the Peruvian north coast today. Also, the osteological evidence showed that the individual in the burial had carried throughout his life a rattle in-serted in his right thigh. The archeologist located the instrument, carved from deer bones, underneath his right femur (Elera, "El shaman" 22–42; Cardoza 46–47). The painful effects of carrying that foreign object implanted in the body were apparent in the signs of arthrosis. Both the slow piercing process and the rattle's weight created deep scarring of the bone and muscle tissue (G. Elera 48–50). The burial paraphernalia located in the interment proved not only the sacred role the deceased shaman had performed in life but also the relevance of Morro de Eten as a site of ancient religious significance.

The archaeological site at Morro de Eten is from the Middle Formative Period (500–200 B. C.) of the Cupisnique culture (Elera, "El shaman" 41), which dominated in the area from 1500 to 1 B.C. "Cupisnique society is seen as one strongly rooted and absorbed by religion . . . it seems fair to refer to the Cupisnique people as a 'cult,' probably a shamanistic one" (Cordy-Col-lins 22). The Cupisnique influenced other north-coast cultures that rose later: Moche, Salinar, Vicús, and Virú. "Of these, by far the most vigorous and enduring was the Moche, spanning almost six centuries (ca. 300–800 A.D.)" (Cordy-Collins 22). Similarities between the Cupisnique and Moche religious art support "a continuing tradition of belief" (Cordy-Collins 22; Larco Hoyle 8–9, 150–51). Thus, the basic cosmological system of the Cupisnique and the basic cosmological system of the Moche are closely related, for the latter derived from the former.

It is difficult to know exactly how the two successive north-coast cultures, Lambayeque (800–1350 A.D.) and Chimú (1100–1550 A.D.), incorporated Morro de Eten into their religious practices. Yet various elements make the site blatantly obvious as an ideally situated temple-mountain: its location is right by the sea; its elevation, according to Italian naturalist Antonio Raimondi, allowed the travelers to see it from far away, and would guide them, like a lighthouse, to not stray from the right path (328); its ancient ceremonial architecture, formed by "a temple, an overlook, a ritual path, and the cemeteries," was erected by the sea (Alva Alva, "Tempranas manifestaciones" 71–72; Elera, "El Complejo Cultural" 252). The two large phonolites completed the maritime ceremonial center. The rocks, positioned on top of another rock serving as a pedestal (see figure 9.1), could have being used as signal gongs, while ascending the mount, or as divine musical instruments.[8] For their uniqueness, the *piedras campanas* were most likely considered manifestations of the sacred or, as termed by Mircea Eliade, "hierophanies" (11); and as such they must have been perceived as very powerful magnets for supernatural power.

Figure 9.1.   *The "piedras campanas" of Eten* (1904). The picture by Hans Heinrich Brüning (1848–1928) belongs to the collection of the Museum für Völkerkunde Hamburg: Inv. Nr. 17.140, Brüning, Eten/Peru, 1904, "Piedra de campana." A copy was kindly provided by the archeologist Carlos Wester La Torre, director of the Museo Arqueológico Nacional Brüning, Lambayeque, Peru. Copyright: Museum für Völkerkunde Hamburg.

## THE MOCHE AT PUERTO DE ETEN

Even without elucidating the symbolism of the Cupisnique ceremonial center of Morro de Eten at the time of the Spanish conquest, the pristine preservation of the space shows that, for the local Moche or Yungas, as the Spanish called them, the place represented not only the home of the venerated long-deceased lineage founders, but also the point at the edge of the sea where the local gods would replenish the community with divine grace.[9] That the Moche of Eten were able to hold on to their language up until the beginning of the twentieth century proves that conservation of their traditions and customs was a strong characteristic of these people. When Antonio Raimondi traveled to Eten in 1868, he commented that the indigenous people there spoke a language different from the one the natives used in the rest of Peru (328). Ricardo Palma emphasizes how, despite the Inca and Spanish efforts to impose Quechua and Spanish respectively, the locals remained attached to their ancestor's tongue:

> The truth is that today people from Eten are custodians of the language and traditions of the old Yungas, and that they sum up their pride in staying true to their origin. Although many people spoke the Yunga language at one time, Cuzcan as well as Spanish conquerors were determined to make it disappear. (390)

In 1930, Kroeber records that Eten is "the one pueblo in which the native Mochica or Yunca language is still to some degree remembered, though no longer a living speech" (92).

The same resolution the Moche demonstrated in keeping their language was most likely shown in the persistence of their religious practices. Pablo José de Arriaga points out how in his visits to many Andean localities between 1617–1618 and also in places inspected by other *visitadores* (inspectors and judges with a mission of annihilating native religious practices) who went over the Peruvian coast, like Alonso Osorio, they discovered that the indigenous peoples continued to honor and care for their gods and ancestors (198–201).[10] Despite the severe repression, persecution, and punishments the visitors and missionaries inflicted on those found guilty of the offense of idol worship, the religious leaders and many in their communities steadfastly continued to hold celebrations and offerings to those divinities. The sanctions—public lashes, scalping or shaving off of hair, humiliating donkey rides, isolation, jail, confiscation of properties, and so forth—were consequences of the *Extirpation of Idolatry*, an intense campaign to eradicate native religions. This treatment of regional, local, and individual religious practices began in 1610 (Duviols xxvii), after the colonial authorities faced the futility of previous efforts to convert the indigenous population to Christianity.

## FROM CHILD SACRIFICES TO CHILD CHRIST SACRIFICED

It is in a climate of re-indoctrination and ardent, anti-idolatry campaign, retaken with renewed vigor during the archbishopric of Pedro de Villagómez, between 1641–1671 (Duviols xxxiii), that those present at church in the town of Eten on Wednesday, June 2, 1649, the day before the feast of Corpus Christi, witnessed the apparition in the blessed sacrament of the half-body image of a blond child dressed in purple. Spontaneously, filled with joy and wonder, some of the participants began to play instruments and to ring the bells of the church. The supernatural phenomenon, considered a miracle, happened a second time, on July 22, 1649, before the four Franciscan friars Marcos López, Jerónimo de Silva Manrique, Tomás de Reluz, and Antonio Crespo. This time the priests saw the half-body image of a child in the sacred host and, minutes later, three gleaming white hearts (Pini Rodolfi 33–74).

The documents that record the eyewitness testimonies of the miracles of 1649 are housed at the historical archive of the Convent of San Francisco of Lima. Neither Pini Rodolfi, who in his 1999 book shows a thorough review of those documents, nor Diego de Córdova Salinas, who as a Franciscan friar had unlimited access to the same archives in 1650, when he composed his *Crónica Franciscana de las Provincias del Perú*, linked in any way the apparitions of Jesus as a child in Eten to the Morro's phonolites. However, while the missionaries employed the narrative of the miracle as a medium for evangelization and indoctrination, the ringing of the church bells at the moment of the first apparition started to being connected, imperceptibly and gradually, to the sounding rocks. By the late nineteenth century, when Ricardo Palma (Lima, 1833–1919) collected the oral materials to write his *tradition* entitled "The Bells of Eten," erasure of the ageless function of the phonolites in the local native rituals of the ancestors had been achieved. [11]

In "The Bells of Eten," published in the eighth part (1891) of his *Peruvian Traditions* (1859–1910), Ricardo Palma relates that on the eve of the feast of Corpus Christi in 1649, "the priest Fray Jerónimo de Silva Manrique and the five hundred souls who were part of the local community of Eten saw in the Divine Host the image of a very blond boy with a purple little tunic" (390). Later, "to honor even more the miracle of the apparition of the Child, the people of Eten say that, when it happened, the angels, chiming in the said stones, bestowed upon them the metallic sound they have today" (390). Yet in a much earlier account, the travel narrative of the Hieronymite Diego de Ocaña—who passed through Eten in 1599 and records this experience in a chapter titled "How I went from Chiclayo to Puerto de Eten, where there are two stones worthy of memory" (239)—the friar writes that the rocks were used in pre-Hispanic times to summon people to ancient sacrificial rituals. His passage is the most complete reference to the phonolites of Eten:

> Here, then, in this town, half a mile away, close to the sea, there is a small elevation where the sea batters on one side and on which there are two stones . . . so remarkable and exquisite that I understand is one of the worthiest things to store in the memory . . . because of the attribute they have, which is to sound like a large sonorous bell when struck with other stones. On this hill, according to the tradition of the old Indians, it is said that the Inca worshiped the sun and sacrificed many children whom he decapitated there at the top . . . And to summon people to the sacrifice . . . he placed close to the center of the hill two identical long stones, which must be three yards long by a little over one and one-quarter yard wide and thick . . . the thickness must be a one-fourth larger than the width. They are on top of another stone, not lying flat, but rather with their ends in the air and set in the middle, because the bottoms are carved like a crescent. When the ends are struck with other stones, they make a sound so loud that they are heard from half a league away and . . . they seem like enormous bells. (240)

This passage of Ocaña's experience in 1599 belies the origin that Palma's account attributed to the stones' ringing. The oral narrative of the supernatural phenomenon of the image of the Child Jesus in the consecrated host in 1649 generated new meanings for the natural prodigy of the phonolites. First, it transformed the rocks from immemorial manifestations of the sacred in the world, as they may have been perceived by the indigenous collective cultural memory, to inanimate ordinary natural objects, originally lacking any special property. Second, it was only when touched by angels, who God sent to proclaim the miracle of the appearance of the Child Jesus in the consecrated host during mass in 1649, that those stones acquired their extraordinary sounding quality. Therefore, heavenly angels instituted the igneous rocks as divine Christian instruments. Thus, the story propels a new explanation for the origin of the chiming sound of the phonolites. Another key aspect is that, according to Ocaña, who cites old natives as sources,[12] in the Inca tradition—which in his account could be interpreted as pre-Columbian local cults rather than official Inca religion—the sound of the stones at Morro de Eten were used in pre-Hispanic times to announce child sacrifices. In the reinvented colonial tradition, the ringing sounds of the phonolites are established as the synchronized background or "soundtrack" to the miracle in 1649 of the apparition of Child Jesus.

In the Catholic liturgy, the color purple symbolizes the passion of Christ (Oesterreicher-Mollwo 227). The image of the divine child in the Eucharist wearing a purple tunic, after the celebration of Jesus Christ's sacrifice, is meant to evoke the Nazarene's death. Consequently, the blond child's visible impression in the sacred host, after Mass—the liturgy of the transubstantiation—substitutes that of the adult Jesus who dies on the cross. Once the image of the child as Lamb of God is instituted, the transposition of this new religious notion over the former one of a child's life offered to the native gods is in motion. That is, the potential connection with the sacrifice rituals at Morro de Eten is fortified by the parallelism of children as ceremonial offers. Incorporating in the narrative the element of the musical stones, located at the hill, further strengthened that relationship.

At Morro the Eten, the excavation of a shaman's tomb facing the sea, the existence of other internments known to be previously looted in the hill (Elera, "El shaman" 27) and the ancient marine ceremonial architecture suggest that the site was of religious importance for the native inhabitants of Puerto Eten and the region. The two phonolites that used to be part of the complex were of religious significance for those peoples as well. The connection between the seventeenth century Eucharistic miracles at the town's church and the former sacrificial rituals at the elevation was cleverly established and conveyed through the superposition of the image of the Child Jesus sacrificed on the cross and the native child sacrifice at the mount. What further and mainly secured that link was the incorporation of the phonolites as the instrument delivering the ringing sound produced by angels during the first Eucharistic miracle; thus, purging the rocks of their traditional role in the chastised evil pagan past.

The Christian divinization of the origin of the rocks' sound avoided the less sophisticated and more generally used colonial recourse of renaming indigenous worshipped natural marvels with a form of Spanish damnation, which would have caused initial resentment and repudiation in the native population. The clever strategy indeed must have prevented the alienation of the people from the local church. The contrast between the opposite tactics is shown in Raimondi's allusion to the name of the phonolites at the Morro of Eten and that of others located elsewhere: "Half a league from Eten in the slopes of the hill are some very sonorous dioritic rocks that the inhabitants know as Miracle Bells, as opposed to the name of other rocks of the same kind located in the Caldera' highlands, on the road from Arequipa to Vitor, known by the name of Devil's Bells" (1:329).

Jan Assmann observes that the "past has always to be reconstructed and tradition has always to be (re-)invented." He asserts that while "every collective memory is, in a way, 'distorted memory,' there are, however, degrees of distortion. The most extreme case of distortion is the eradication of memory" (366). The case of *piedras campanas* is indeed one of cultural amnesia that resulted from an act of erasure. The emergence of new oral traditions obliterated the connection of the rocks to the native religious practices. The community of Eten thus lost the information pertinent to the use of the rocks in the preconquest past.[13] Moreover, the Christians adopted the phonolites after creating a more acceptable origin for them. By instituting the rocks as the device the angels chose to create a sound effect for the Eucharistic miracle at Eten, a new tradition is superimposed upon the previous collective memory associated with the phonolites. The Child's sacrifice on the cross is the intentional mnemonic replacement of the child sacrifices at Morro de Eten. Eventually, as Palma's narrative shows, the old instrument formerly called *alecpong* or "Indian chief's stones" (Middendorf 2:295–96) is renamed *piedras campanas*, and the elevation where they were situated became *Cerro de las campanas*. Sadly, the stone monuments of Morro de Eten cannot be a sight for sore eyes. Let us recapture their memory for sore minds.

## NOTES

1. My thanks to Stella Boghosian, Barbara Simerka, and Gerald McElroy for their suggestions and corrections. Any errors remain my own. I am grateful to Glyphos Publications for their permission to publish in English a section of my book *Fonolitos. Las piedras campanas de Eten: Rituales, milagros y codicia* (Valladolid, 2014).

2. The Morro de Eten is an elevation "of igneous origin along the Pacific Ocean" (Elera, "El Complejo" 252; "El shaman" 23). It is formed by three hills: 1) Cerro de Eten, located at 9'232, 576.81N, 626, 444,68E, elevation 103,46 meters above sea level; 2) at the north of Cerro de Eten, a second hill with no name at 9'233,389N, 625,880.39E, elevation 128.06 meters above sea level; and 3) at the southeast of Cerro de Eten, Punta Farola, located at 9'232.220.00N, 625,60.00E, elevation of 62.50 meters above sea level (Puican Carreño).

3. A phonolite is a fine-grained alkaline igneous rock consisting of essentially alkali feldspar, nepheline, and possibly other feldspathoids (Gill 296).

4. Most phonolites are of Cenozoic age and therefore formed within the last 65.5 million years (Lleras Codazzi 45).

5. Besides a reference to the *piedras campanas* by friar Diego de Ocaña—whose account is the most substantial of the ones I know and which will be analyzed later in this chapter—other authors offer brief allusions to the phonolites located near the town of Eten: Antonio de Alcedo (1735–1812) in his *Diccionario geográfico-histórico de las Indias Occidentales ó América: es á saber: de los Reynos del Perú, Nueva España, Tierra-Firme, Chile, y Nuevo Reyno de Granada (1786–1789)*; Joseph Ignacio Lequanda (1748–1800) in an article published in the *Mercurio Peruano* in 1793; and Ernst W. Middendorf y Fröbel (1830–1908) in his *Perú: Observaciones y estudios del país y sus habitantes durante una permanencia de 25 años*, published after his travels in the area in 1885. In 1862, Mateo Paz Soldán, in his posthumous *Geografía del Perú*, refers succinctly to the phonolites as a noteworthy element of Eten: "That of the utmost importance are two big stones at the sea shore, which hit with another stone, sound like bells" (224).

6. Two publications, one from 1921 by Carlos J. Bachmann and another from 1927 by Ricardo A. Miranda, make references to the *piedras campanas* of Morro de Eten offering the impression that the rocks still existed at those times.

7. All translations from Spanish to English in this chapter are mine.

8. The Uruguayan oboist and musicologist Mariana Berta published a brief study of two phonolites located in Arroyo de la Virgen in Uruguay. Called "piedras campana" by the locals, they are placed about ten feet one from the other. The bigger of the two phonolites weighs between five and six tons, while the other weighs close to two tons. Both are positioned on top of other minor rocks. Berta argues that they were native musical instruments. She recorded the sounds of the rocks having three players hitting the biggest phonolite with stones and two performers playing the smaller one. She proposes the need for an interdisciplinary approach to the study of the *piedras campanas* as indigenous musical instruments.

9. The sea is also of utmost importance to the ancient cultures of the area as a food source (Alva Alva, "Historia" 52).

10. The effects of the Extirpation of Idolatry in the Andes are better known than the results of the same process in the Peruvian north-coast. Historians have concentrated their efforts on studying the documents housed at the Archivo Arzobispal de Lima and much less on transcribing and analyzing those kept at Archivo Arzobispal de Trujillo (Larco 16).

11. The *tradición*, literally "tradition," is a genre created by Ricardo Palma. It is a short story characterized by the mixture of history and fiction, a good dose of humor, an unexpected ending, and use of colloquialisms. The topic of each *tradición* could be generated by a popular saying, joke, custom, or legend, a curious historical fact, among other themes.

12. These testimonies were probably collected through a third party. Likely, the informant was the Franciscan priest who Ocaña visited in Eten. Despite being a town inhabited mainly by natives, the place was part of Ocaña's itinerary since one of the priests who taught the Christian doctrine there had been raised at the Royal Monastery of Saint Mary of Guadalupe, in Cáceres, Extremadura. The institution was also Ocaña's home in Spain, from where his superiors sent him in 1599 to collect alms in the Indies for the Spanish convent.

13. This is proven when Doctor Carvallo, as cited in Bachmann, advanced his idea that the stones were used as grinders. The theory is not dispensable, however, since Carlos G. Elera ties up the ceremonial center at Morro de Eten with the existence of a gold mine ("El Complejo" 252). However, from my point of view, if the grinding of metal was performed with the phonolites, the process must have been related to rites and cults.

# WORKS CITED

Alcedo, Antonio de. *Diccionario geográfico de las Indias Occidentales o América*. 4 vols. Ed. Ciriaco Pérez-Bustamante. Madrid: Atlas, 1967.

Alva Alva, Walter. "Historia general de Lambayeque. Pampa de Eten." Ed. Eric Mendoza Samillán. *Presencia histórica de Lambayeque*. N.p.: Ediciones y Representaciones H. Falconí, 1985. 52.

———. "Tempranas manifestaciones culturales en la región de Lambayeque." Ed. Eric Mendoza Samillán. *Presencia histórica de Lambayeque*. N.p.: Ediciones y Representaciones H. Falconí, 1985. 53–75.

Arriaga, Pablo José de. *Extirpación de la idolatría del Perú*. Ed. Francisco Esteve Barba. Biblioteca de Autores Españoles. Vol. 209. Madrid: Atlas, 1968. 191–277.

Assmann, Jan. "Ancient Egyptian Antijudaism: A Case of Distorted Memory." Ed. Daniel L. Schacter. *Memory Distortion: How Minds, Brains, and Societies Reconstruct the Past*. Cambridge, MA: Harvard University Press, 1980. 365–76.

Bachmann, Carlos J. *Departamento de Lambayeque: Monografía histórico-geográfica*. Lima: Imp. Torres Aguirre, 1921.

Berta, Mariana. "Informe sobre las 'piedras campana' del Arroyo de la Virgen en Uruguay." *Revista Musical Chilena*, 210 (2008): 39–45.

Brüning, Hans Heinrich (1848–1928). *H. E. Brüning*. Lima: Goethe-Institut Lima y Embajada de la República Federal de Alemania, 2006.

Cardoza, Carmen Rosa. "Estudio de los artefactos de hueso que formaban parte del ajuar funerario del entierro 4 de la unidad 14-D del Morro de Eten." Ed. Luis Millones y Moisés Lemlij, con la asistencia de Dana Cáceres. *En el nombre del Señor: Shamanes, demonios y curanderos del norte del Perú*. Lima: Biblioteca Peruana de Psicoanálisis, 1994. 46–47.

Carruthers, Mary. *The Craft of Thought: Meditation, Rhetoric, and the Making of Images, 400–200*. Cambridge, MA: Cambridge University Press, 1998.

Córdova Salinas, Diego de. *Crónica franciscana de las Provincias del Perú*. Ed. Lino G. Canedo. Washington, D.C.: Academy of American Franciscan History, 1957.

Cordy-Collins, Alana. "Decapitation in Cupisnique and Early Moche Societies." Ed. Elizabeth Benson and Anita G. Cook. *Ritual Sacrifice in Ancient Peru*. Austin, TX: University of Texas Press, 2001. 21–33.

Duviols, Pierre. *Cultura andina y represión: Procesos y visitas de idolatrías y hechicerías, Cajatambo, siglo XVII*. Cusco: Centro de Estudios Rurales Andinos "Bartolomé de las Casas," 1986.

Elera, Carlos G. "El shamán del Morro de Eten: antecedentes arqueológicos del shamanismo en la costa y sierra norte del Perú." Ed. Luis Millones y Moisés Lemlij, con la asistencia de Dana Cáceres. *En el nombre del Señor: Shamanes, demonios y curanderos del norte del Perú.* Lima: Biblioteca Peruana de Psicoanálisis, 1994. 22–51.

———. "El Complejo Cultural Cupisnique: Antecedentes y desarrollo de su ideología religiosa." *Senri Ethnological Studies* 37 (1993): 229–57.

Elera, Gustavo. "Análisis radiográfico, comentarios y resultados de los fémures derecho e izquierdo del individuo correspondiente al entierro 4 de la unidad 14-D del Morro de Eten." Ed. Luis Millones y Moisés Lemlij, con la asistencia de Dana Cáceres. *En el nombre del Señor: Shamanes, demonios y curanderos del norte del Perú.* Lima: Biblioteca Peruana de Psicoanálisis, 1994. 48–51.

Eliade, Mircea. *The Sacred and the Profane: The Nature of Religion.* Trans. Willard R. Trask. Orlando, FL: Harcourt, 1987.

Flower, Harriet I. *The Art of Forgetting: Disgrace & Oblivion in Roman Political Culture.* Chapel Hill, NC: University of North Carolina Press, 2006.

García y Merino, Manuel. "Cerros sonoros." *Boletín de la Sociedad Geográfica de Lima.* 4:7–9 (1894): 359–62.

Gill, Robin. *Igneous Rocks and Processes. A Practical Guide.* Oxford: Wiley-Blackwell, 2010.

Hegarty, Stephanie. "Bamiyan Buddas: Should they be rebuilt?" *BBC News Magazine* 13 Aug. 2012. Web. 28 Jan. 2014.

Kroeber, A. L. *Archaeological Explorations in Peru. Part II: The Northern Coast.* Chicago: Field Museum of Natural History, 1930.

Larco, Laura. *Más allá de los encantos: Documentos históricos y etnografía contemporánea sobre extirpación de idolatrías en Trujillo siglos XVIII–XX.* Pról. Luis Millones. Lima: Instituto Francés de Estudios Andinos, 2008.

Larco Hoyle, Rafael. *Los Cupisniques. Trabajo presentado al Congreso Internacional de Americanistas de Lima, XXVII sesión.* Lima: Casa Editora "La crónica" y "Variedades," 1941.

León Barandiarán, Augusto D. *Mitos, leyendas y tradiciones lambayecanas.* N.p.: n.p., 1938.

Lequanda, Joseph Ignacio. "Descripción del partido de Saña ó Lambayeque." *Mercurio peruano de historia, literatura y noticias públicas que da a luz la Sociedad Académica de Amantes de Lima. Tomo IX que comprende los meses de septiembre, octubre, noviembre y diciembre de 1793. Edición Facsimilar.* Lima: Biblioteca Nacional del Perú, 1966. Fol. 54–61.

Levene, D. S. "'You shall blot out the memory of Amalek': Roman Historians on Remembering to Forget." Ed. Beate Dignas and R. R. R. Smith. *Historical and Religious Memory in the Ancient World.* Oxford: Oxford University Press, 2012. 217–37.

Lleras Codazzi, Ricardo. *Notas geográficas y geológicas.* Bogotá: Imprenta Nacional, 1926.

Middendorf, Ernst W. *Perú: Observaciones y estudios del país y sus habitantes durante una permanencia de 25 años.* Trad. Ernesto More. Lima: Universidad Nacional Mayor de San Marcos, 1973. 2 vols.

Miranda, Ricardo A. *La monografía del departamento de Lambayeque.* Chiclayo: Talleres Tipográficos "El tiempo," 1927.

Moisés Lemlij, ed., con la asistencia de Dana Cáceres. *En el nombre del Señor: Shamanes, demonios y curanderos del norte del Perú.* Lima: Biblioteca Peruana de Psicoanálisis, 1994. 48–49.

Ocaña, fray Diego de. *'Memoria viva' de una 'tierra de olvido': Relación del viaje al Nuevo Mundo de 1599 a 1607.* Ed. Beatriz Carolina Peña. Barcelona: CECAL / Paso de Barca, 2013.

Oesterreicher-Mollwo, Marianne. *Diccionarios Rioduero: Símbolos.* Versión y adaptación de Purificación Murga. Madrid: Ediciones Rioduero, 1983.

Palma, Ricardo. "Las campanas de Eten (1649)." *Tradiciones peruanas completas.* Ed. Edith Palma. Madrid: Aguilar, 1964. 390.

Paz Soldán, Mariano Felipe. *Diccionario geográfico estadístico del Perú, contiene además la etimología aymara y quechua de las principales poblaciones, lagos, cerros, etc., etc.* Lima: Imprenta del Estado, 1877.

Paz Soldán, Mateo. *Geografía del Perú, obra póstuma*. Corregida y aumentada por Mariano Felipe Paz Soldán. Vol. 1. París: Librería de Fermín Didot Hermanos, 1862. 2 vols.

Pini Rodolfi, Francesco. *El milagro eucarístico de Eten (1649)*. Lima: Colibrí, 1999.

Price, Simon. "Memory and Ancient Greece." Ed. Beate Dignas and R. R. R. Smith. *Historical and Religious Memory in the Ancient World*. Oxford: Oxford University Press, 2012. 15–36.

Puican Carreño, Godofredo. "Las piedras de las campanas de Puerto Eten, fueron destruidas por un cónsul chileno." Web. 14 Dec. 2013.

Raimondi, Antonio. *El Perú*. Vol. 1. Lima: Imprenta del Estado, 1874.

Woolf, Greg. "The Uses of Forgetfulness in Roman Gaul." Ed. Hans-Joachim Gehrke and Astrid Möller. *Vergangenheit und Lebenswelt: soziale Kommunikation, Traditionsbildung und historisches Bewußtsein*. Tübingen: Gunter Narr Verlag, 1996.

*Chapter Ten*

# The Memory of Black Womanhood in Mexico

## *La Mulata de Córdoba*

## Selfa A. Chew

In 1997, Mexican archeologists unearthed the remains of a woman of African descent along with those of four white women, several Spanish conquista-dores, and hundreds of indigenous men killed in Tlaxcala in 1520, thus providing unequivocal proof of the female African presence in Mexico since the first years of the conquest. While it is not known if the woman was born in the Caribbean or in Europe, or whether she was originally from Africa, Mexican archeologists have classified her as a *mulata*, or a woman of mixed, black and white ancestry (Martínez Vargas and Jarquín Pacheco 3; Ortiz Pedraza 9).[1] They determined that she arrived in Mexico with other Spanish women participating in Hernán Cortés's invasion. Her presence signals the importance of women of African descent in the crux of the Spanish conquest and the development of the Mexican nation's African roots.

As Spanish colonization displaced African women from their homeland and forced them to remain in New Spain during the colonial period, the contributions of black women to the history and culture of Mexico became significant in the formation of a Mexican identity. Currently, Afro-mestizas form part of the most vulnerable populations of Mexico and have joined the Mexican immigrant communities in the United States as a result of their economic disfranchisement (Lewis 190–95). In spite of their historical role and survival as a distinct ethnic group in Mexico, their presence has been ignored or distorted in the national memory (Vinson and Restall 1–3; Cuevas 31–49).

This chapter analyzes the legend of *La Mulata de Córdoba* and its insertion in the historical memory and counter-memory of Mexicans. A brief study of black womanhood and its representations throughout history and in current popular culture may assist our understanding of social processes that simultaneously negate and affirm the contributions of African women to the economy and culture of Mexico. Although the persistence of the story of *La Mulata de Córdoba* in popular culture provides evidence of the strong presence of African women in Mexico, the appropriation of the narrative by intellectual elites reflects distinctive political objectives in the creation of a collective identity.

In addition to anthropological discoveries, evidence of the indigenous encounter with Africans around 1519 can be found in the Nahuatl term "soiled gods," which the Mexicans used to describe black persons travelling with Cortés (Bennett, *Africans* 14). The language defining black men and women conveyed admiration, but that first impression would change once the conquerors imposed a racial hierarchy that established a slave society in New Spain in which African men and women occupied the lowest ranks and shared with indigenous peoples the burden of sustaining the most arduous economic activities of the colonial domain (Ortiz Pedraza and Weckmann 336, 65, 95; Bennett, *Africans* 14–16; Simms 229–30). Notwithstanding the agency, freedom, and social mobility that some African men and women and their descendants enjoyed, the presence of slaves defined the legal, religious, moral, and sexual lives of Spaniards. The existence of oppressed black men and women was continuously acknowledged and enunciated to signify the sumptuous lifestyle and superiority of those who could claim *pureza de sangre*, meaning a "pure" white ancestry (Bennett, *Africans* 31; Bennett, *Colonial Blackness* 50).

The idea that colonial Mexico was inhabited by highly mixed, yet racially classifiable human beings, was vividly reflected in a series of paintings that attempted to illustrate multiple racial combinations and their results. *Casta* paintings indeed depicted multiracial families, thus conveying the impression that women could easily achieve economic mobility through their marriage with men holding a superior social position. Historian Susan Kellogg argues, however, that *casta* paintings do not reflect the actual and high frequency with which women married men in inferior social ranks. The laws that maintained the privileges of "pure" Spanish men and women—such as the right to acquire certain land, pensions, or official positions—discouraged the marriage of Spaniards with non-Spaniards. Social mobility was not, therefore, universally accessible to women of color. Imagining a colonial racial fluidity was necessary, nonetheless, to set apart the American territory from the restraints of colonial power (Kellogg 70; Bennett, *Africans* 31).

Racialized women were rather limited in their election of sexual partners and spouses; yet, the colonial social dynamics allowed for the procreation of persons of mixed descent whose freedom depended on the status of their mother. Slaves, consequently, were particularly motivated to form families with indigenous women since their children would be born free under the Spanish slave laws. *Mulatos*, originally thought of as the children of Spanish fathers and black mothers, were, thus, also the children of Spanish and indigenous persons. They held an ambiguous social standing in the new colonial society, often occupying a higher racial stratum than African-born men and women (von Germeten 137–38; Kellogg 81).

The images of black women with different skin tones that recurrently appear in *criollo* paintings confirm the African character of the Mexican identity. The depiction of their alleged reckless behaviors, nevertheless, tended to emphasize the Spaniards' determination to control the assumed proclivity of blacks to reject the principles of the Spanish culture (Kellogg 76; Vinson 3; Bristol 32). *Mulatas*, in the world the *criollos* imagined, were evidence of a new social reality that the Iberian monarchy could not totally regulate from a distance. The origin of the term *mulato,* meaning "mule," reflects the contempt with which the dominant Spanish society, in both Europe and America, regarded interracial children (Nutini and Isaac 46–47; von Germeten 137). While a patriarchal society muted white women's sexual desire for black men, Spanish men allowed themselves, however, to engage in out-of-wedlock sexual relations with racialized women of inferior economic status. Because their white lineage was inscribed in their phenotype, *mulatas* became the evidence of socially objectionable sexual relations, embodying sexual power and desire that crossed social conventions and norms. Their ambiguous role in the formation of a New World character—one distinct from Spanish identity—made women of partial African descent appear, on the one hand, as a sign of the fluidity of racial identities, and on the other, as the incarnation of concubinage, racial impurity, and the indignity of slavery (Lovell Banks 205, 207; Carrera 13).

The recognition of Afro-mestizas as integral to New Spain's society continued through the Mexican War of Independence of 1810, when Afro-descendants actively fought against Spain in all ranks of the insurgent army, thus promoting the abolition of slavery in Mexico (T. Vincent 257–58; T. G. Vincent 148–49). The persistence of white supremacy in Mexico and the erasure of official racial categories under a new political system were, nonetheless, factors promoting social discrimination based on skin tones (*colorismo*). The disappearance of Africans and their descendants from the national historical narrative was accelerated by the racialization of Mexicans in the United States. At the conclusion of the war against Mexico in 1848, the new colonial subjects of the United States, if classified as whites, would be entitled to certain civil rights denied to black persons. By distancing themselves from any trace of African blood, Mexicans thought they would achieve a higher status not only in the United States, but also in the international racial hierarchy (Lovell Banks 215–18).

In spite of the prevalence of racism, the new ruling class in independent Mexico saw itself as a progressive force in charge of forming a democratic society. Mexican rulers decided to build a clear separation between their previous colonial administrators representing monarchy and a Mexican state free of absolutism. Mexican politicians—particularly after the inauguration of the Mexican Republic in 1867—established "reason" as the main social force and valued the liberal aspirations that would, in their view, lead the way towards an equalizing political existence. Racial divisions ceased to exist officially, but they actually kept in place social hierarchies that had a meaning in the context of a Eurocentric world order enforced by the United States (Lovell Banks 218). The *criollos'* thought adapted to internal and external racism anticipating the problematic Vasconcelian theory of the *Raza Cósmica*: they too conceived the Latin American region as the place where whitening would result in the improvement of the human species (Medina 103; Kellogg 70).

## *LA MULATA DE CÓRDOBA*

At the conclusion of the independence war, the search for a Mexican identity occupied artists and scholars. By collecting and distributing stories or legends from the "dark ages" of monarchic rule, Mexican writers in the newly created nation offered their readers the opportunity (a) to assert themselves in a better social place than that occupied by colonial subjects, (b) to emphasize their distance from periods of uncertainty and superstition under monarchic rule, and (c) to believe that their history had a distinctive national character (Medina 104; Corral Rodríguez 91–92). Variations on the narrative of *La Mulata de Córdoba* reveal the new place women of African descent occupied, or ceased to occupy, in the formation of a national, independent identity after 1821.

The first published narrative of *La Mulata de Córdoba* was authored in 1837 by José Bernardo Couto, a prominent moderate liberal politician who became minister of justice in 1845. Couto participated directly in the historically traumatic signing of the Treaty of Guadalupe, which stipulated the conditions under which his country would surrender Mexican territory to the United States in 1845. As a *criollo* seeking to reaffirm the Mexican character, Couto thought important to document folklore to assert his nationalist stance; consequently, he wrote, among other Mexican legends, *La Mulata de Córdoba* for *Mosaico Mexicano* (Corral Rodríguez 99).

Couto had originally composed *La Mulata de Córdoba* as the introduction to *Historia de un peso falso* (*Story of a Counterfeit Coin*). The humor with which Couto presents La Mulata is enhanced with his use of an allegorical Medea to describe the woman in his short story. A princess in the Greek mythos, Medea is a malignant sorcerer whose desire for Jason drives her to murder her own children, carrying out other vindictive acts that build her destructive image. Equally revealing symbolic representations of La Mulata as a negative or ambiguous character were built into other literary, performative, and musical genres in subsequent generations (Cuoto, *Obras* 373–74).

La Mulata appears in all versions as a famous sorceress in Córdoba, Veracruz, imprisoned by Inquisition officers expecting to prove that she is a witch. The woman remains calm as she spends days in a sordid cell. But on one particular day she draws a ship on a wall and asks her jailer what improvements the vessel needs. Her keeper responds disapprovingly that it is La Mulata who needs to cleanse herself of her sins. Marveled by her art, however, he adds that it needs only to sail to be perfect (Cuoto, *Obras*; Janvier). Leaping onto the deck of the ship to sail away, La Mulata replies, "If you desire it, it will sail!" (Janvier 19).[2]

*La Mulata de Córdoba* continued her travels through the pens of other artists. In February 1869, Aurelio Luis Gallardo, a writer living in exile in San Francisco, wrote the drama *La Hechicera de Córdoba*, which was translated to English and staged in San Francisco. *La Mulata* reappeared as a short story in *Calendario Antiguo* (1882) and was included again in the *Obras del doctor D. José Bernardo Couto* (1891) (Wilson and Fisk; Cuoto, *Obras*). Other artists, all of them male, who appropriated the story were Manuel Ramírez Aparicio (1861); Vicente Riva Palacio and Juan de Dios Peza (1922); Luis González Obregón (1923); Xavier Villaurrutia and Agustín Lazo in their opera musicalized by José Pablo Moncayo (1848); Heriberto Frías (1899); and José Emilio Pacheco (1990) (Ramírez Aparicio; Mejía Núñez; Algaba; Corral Rodríguez; Obregón; Pacheco).

In spite of the nationalist drive in the use of *La Mulata de Córdoba,* its plot is not exclusively Mexican. Riva Palacio and Peza's publication of an anthology of colonial legends was echoed by Ricardo Palma in Peru, who enthusiastically addressed obvious similitudes between *La Mulata* and *La Voladora,* a Peruvian woman's story: "*La Mulata de Córdova's* (sic) ship is the same on which our Inés, the Flying Woman, sailed away to escape from an official of the Inquisition" (Palma 129; Algaba 188).[3] A nationalist pride has continued to inspire Mexican artists who insist in providing the same colonial historical context in their different versions of *La Mulata de Córdoba.* Furthermore, currently, the Mexican government, through the administration of the National Archives of Mexico, verifies the story by featuring the legend on its website. Its readers are assured that the archives hold the Inquisition files documenting the existence of La Mulata although the precise location of the files has never been released (AGN).

As the relationship between collective memory and collective identity has been established, the analysis of certain cultural productions that are assumed to be the creation of marginalized social groups may reveal whether they support hegemonic ideas of memory and identity or are counternarratives (Confino 149). Recent attention to the role of oral history in the construction of memories that challenge dominant narratives has revitalized the art of storytelling, a practice previously undervalued by elitist cultural gatekeepers. Radio and television shows, street and school performances, as well as other forms of popular culture, such as puppet theater, currently attempt to address issues of marginalization by validating stories allegedly created from the bottom up. In Mexico, however, storytelling that attempts to critique social inequalities may, inadvertently, endorse racism or *colorismo*.

A performance that can assist our understanding of Mexican racism is presented by Martha Escudero, a contemporary actress and storyteller born in Mexico City. Escudero resides now in Barcelona, where she is an accomplished cultural activist with a presence in international storytelling circuits (Escudero "Narradora Oral"). I use the video recording of her performance in the 2011 edition of the International Meeting of Oral Narrators in the Pyrenees to analyze contemporary representations of black womanhood in colonial Mexico (Escudero "La Mulata").

To preface the story of *La Mulata de Córdoba* in her performance, Escudero starts by mentioning the exploitative nature of Spanish imperialism resulting in the distortion of history (0:05). She lists several racial classifications in New Spain, changing her tone of voice to accentuate the ridiculous nature of such discriminatory categories, eliciting laughter from her audience. After signaling their agreement with Escudero's explicitly anti-racist description of how colonial stratifications worked, the viewers learn her interpretation of Vasconcelos's theory of the *raza cósmica*: she explains that the *Raza Mestiza* is made up of five races (Vasconcelos 39). Like other Mexican artists, Escudero applies the term "race" as a biological reality and not as a social construction (Escudero "La Mulata" 2:40).[4]

Escudero's performance does not differ a great deal from other versions of La Mulata (DIF; RRRU; COVAEB). She attributes a fantastic wealth to the nameless woman, "a very strange thing because she was a woman of mixed-descent, a pariah!" (5:10)[5] La Mulata, states Escudero, was a "mysterious," extremely beautiful woman who did not age. It was "very strange" to see her living by herself, attended by her servants, and she would only leave her magnificent house to attend mass (5:27). She could grant the wishes of anyone who made a request to her as she exited the church; she was considered "the patron saint of impossible things" (7:25).[6]

In Escudero's view, La Mulata's beauty was such a spectacle that men would attend mass only to see her. The fragile relationship between the extraordinary woman and the rest of the community is altered when a young *hidalgo*, a noble Spanish man, attempted to marry La Mulata to improve his economic situation. Escudero marks the racial distance between them by affirming that "even though she was *mulata*, it didn't matter (to him), that's right, because she was very wealthy" (8:31).[7] Rejected, the aristocratic Spanish man took his revenge by accusing La Mulata of witchcraft. "That was a period in which rumors for that kind of suspicion could grow," explains the story teller (9:54).[8] Escudero's remark supports the idea that the colonial world ruled by the Spanish monarchy was populated by superstition, in contrast to reason and the scientific principles that eventually would build, according to the *criollos*, an independent republic (Medina 103; Kellogg 70).

Oblivious to the ecclesiastic powers of New Spain, La Mulata embodies an alternative power that overrules the unjust colonial system and ambiguously attracts the sympathy of Escudero's listeners. Imprisoned in a cage, "as a beast" the woman without a name looked comfortable on her way to the Inquisition (10:15).[9] A multitude of people stood along the road only to admire La Mulata's exotic beauty while in transit to Mexico City to receive her punishment for sorcery. Once in the Inquisition's dungeons, La Mulata is said to have adorned herself with diamonds, brocade, and gold, only to sail away after drawing a ship, as in every other retelling of her exploits. Joining previous and contemporary attempts to underscore the vernacular African Spanish of the region called *jarocho*,[10] Escudero impregnates with that particular accent her explanation for the idiomatic expression found in Veracruz, "Do you think I am the mulata, boy?"—the traditional response to an impossible request (13:25).[11]

Escudero's use of the *jarocho* accent and traditions attracts a public willing to consume some aspects of the Mexican popular culture, those that have been tempered through a liberal view of the conquest of Mexico. Escudero expresses her admiration for Mexico during her presentation of *La Mulata de Córdoba* by mentioning the wealth that the conquerors were able to extract from New Spain. In addition, the performer educates her international audience in the culture of indigenous peoples, the mixing of peoples, and even the genocide inscribed in the Spanish conquest. She critiques the imposition of the Spanish empire on the indigenous communities of Mexico (Escudero "La Mulata" 13:00).

In spite of her empathy for the conquered peoples of Mexico, Escudero's attempt to revise the dominant narrative falls short of highlighting the importance of the population of African descent in Mexico noted by Bennett and other historians of the African Diaspora. Escudero places the Inquisition arrest of La Mulata around 1650 (2:16). While describing a *variopinta* ("multicolored") population, the storyteller mentions that Mexicans are the product of the mixing between Spanish conquerors and indigenous individuals, plus "some black men who had been taken to America to work" (2:20).[12] She uses two different terms, *mestizo* and *mulato*, to emphasize different racial classifications for persons of African descent, excluding the African element as an important contributor to the mestizo population. Escudero not only ignores the violence of the racial mixing that took place in New Spain, but she also negates the high proportion of African men and women and their descendants in relation to the Spanish population of the colony during the seventeenth century. Her oversight alters significantly the historical narrative: in this period, the African population was particularly high in Veracruz, a port receiving migrants across the Atlantic, and it is currently a state referred to as *negro* due to the strong presence of Afro-mestizos (Aguirre Beltrán; Bennett *Africans* 22, 26; Carroll 76).

The demographic component represented by persons of dark skin in the Córdoba of the seventeenth century is not only omitted in most narratives of *La Mulata de Córdoba* but is linguistically accentuated in Escudero's narrative. She repeats the adjectives *sola* ("lonely"), *misteriosa* ("mysterious"), and *rara* ("rare") to describe, incorrectly, the presence of La Mulata as an isolated event. The image of numerous Mexicans lining up along the road between Córdoba and Mexico City to admire her tells us that La Mulata was a spectacle not only for her supposed supernatural powers but because of the rarity of her looks and calm poise (9:24–10:50). In other narratives in which women of African descent appear, *mulatas* seem to have a large amount of control over their own lives and those of the men in their proximity thanks to their physical charm. [13]

In sharp contrast with Escudero's view, historian Cameron Bristol reports the presence of Afro-mestizas and the processes through which the Inquisition frequently targeted them in the seventeenth century. During this period, *mulatas* were often denounced and subjected to public punishment for their healing knowledge and alleged practices of witchcraft. As other women in the colonial world, some Afro-mestizas used the power Spaniards, and others, believed black women held. As healers or witches, they received payment for their services and gained temporary control over their oppressors. La Mulata's legendary arrest by the Inquisition would not be, therefore, a rare occurrence, but an event that, when placed within its historical context, reflects how fragile was the status of *mulatas* within a colonial structure that may have granted agency and certain privileges for women of mixed descent (Bristol 165).

Martha Escudero's oral history, similar to previous and posterior versions of *La Mulata de Córdoba*, assists us to note the discrepancy between the imagined historical context of the story and actual racial relations in the seventeenth century. In 1640, New Spain had the second largest enslaved population in the American continent, after Brazil (Bennett, *Africans* 14). By 1650, the African-descended population in Mexico City was estimated at 50,000; the indigenous at 80,000; and Spaniards numbered approximately 15,000 (Proctor 30). By 1793, half of the residents of the haciendas in the area of Córdoba were classified as *pardos* or *mulatos* (Carroll 61–78). Escudero's narrative, thus, fits into a pattern that negates the significance of the presence of African women in the racial formation of Mexico. It embodies the refusal to acknowledge an Afro-mestizo collective identity emerging out of the womb of a black woman.

In all literary versions, including the contemporary narrative of Escudero, La Mulata decides not to have descendants, much less with the devil, with whom most writers suggest she has sexual intercourse. La Mulata complies with Vasconcelos's prescription for the improvement of the human race, "The inferior races, when educating themselves, will become less prolific, and the best specimens will ascend in a scale of ethnic improvement" (32).[14] According to this logic, then, the best human being possesses the characteristics of whites and does not manifest an African ancestry. La Mulata does not attempt to reproduce herself, but her existence represents an instant in the mythological creation of *la raza cósmica*, previous to the creation of the "perfect" human being (Vasconcelos 40). Those Mexicans who reject the African component of their culture and DNA pool can rest assured: the ideal Spanish/Indigenous *mestizaje* has been saved through the telling and retelling of *La Mulata de Córdoba*. Having no progeny and disappearing into the ocean on her own will, La Mulata is indeed a convenient icon, one with no traces of a history of sexual violence, labor, or *mulataje*. Inhabiting the collective memory of Mexicans, black womanhood may be beautiful and even powerful; yet, it is misrepresented and excluded from the Mexican collective identity.

## NOTES

1. *Casta* paintings explained that the product of the union of a "Spanish man and a black woman" was "mulato" (Carrera viii). However, the term was popularly used also for any person of mixed descent who showed in his or her phenotype an African ancestor (Schwaller 889–90).
2. "–Pues si usted quiere –dijo la encantadora–, él andará." Unless otherwise noted, all translations are mine.
3. "El barquichuelo de *La Mulata de Córdova* (sic) es el mismo en que se embarcó nuestra Inés La Voladora para burlarse de un Inquisidor."
4. The location in the video recording is noted in minutes and seconds.
5. "Cosa muy rara porque ella era una mezclada . . . ¡una paria!"
6. "La patrona de los imposibles"
7. "Era mulata, sí, pero no importaba porque era muy rica."
8. "Eran tiempos en que el terreno estaba abonado para ese tipo de rumores."
9. "Como una bestia"
10. Jarocho is the term applied to Afro-mestizos in Veracruz. It comes from the Spanish term *jaro*, or wild pig (Aguirre Beltrán 179; González 56).
11. "¿Qué acaso soy la mulata, chico?"
12. "*Algunos* negros que habían llevado a América para trabajar" (Emphasis added).
13. Example of this type of representation is the main female character of the Mexican comic titled *Rarotonga*.

14. "Las razas inferiores, al educarse, se harían menos prolíficas, y los mejores especímenes irán ascendiendo en una escala de mejoramiento étnico."

# WORKS CITED

AGN. "La Mulata de Córdoba." *Leyendas*. Archivo General de la Nación 2013. Web. 5 May 2013.

Aguirre Beltrán, Gonzalo. *La población negra de México*. México: Fondo de Cultura Económica, 1972.

Algaba, Leticia. "Una amistad epistolar: Ricardo Palma y Vicente Riva Palacio." *Secuencia* Septiembre–Diciembre 30 (1994): 179–206.

Bennett, Herman. *Africans in Colonial Mexico: Absolutism, Christianity, and Afro-Creole Consciousness, 1570–1640*. Bloomington, IN: Indiana University Press, 2003.

———. *Colonial Blackness: A History of Afro-Mexico*. Bloomington, IN: Indiana University Press, 2010.

Bristol, Joan Cameron. *Christians, Blasphemers, and Witches: Afro-Mexican Ritual Practice in the Seventeenth Century*. Albuquerque, NM: University of New Mexico Press, 2007.

Carrera, Magali Marie. *Imagining Identity in New Spain: Race, Lineage, and the Colonial Body in Portraiture and Casta Paintings*. Austin, TX: University of Texas Press, 2003.

Carroll, Patrick J. *Blacks in Colonial Veracruz: Race, Ethnicity, and Regional Development*. Austin: University of Texas Press, 2001.

Confino, Alon. "Collective Memory." *Encyclopedia of Social History*. Ed. Peter N. Stearns. New York: Garland Publishing Inc, 1994. 194-96.

Corral Rodríguez, Fortino. "Génesis del relato fantástico en México." *Ruta crítica. Estudios sobre literatura hispanoamericana*. Ed. Fortino Corral Rodríguez. Hermosillo: Universidad de Sonora, 2007. 97–116.

Couto, José Bernardo. "La Mulata de Córdoba y La historia de un peso." *Obras del Doctor D. José Bernardo Couto*. Ed. Victoriano Agüeros. Vol. I. México: Imprenta de Victoriano Agüeros, 1898. 371–87.

———. *Calendario Antiguo*. Mexico: Casa de Munguía, 1882.

COVAEB. "Obra de teatro *La Mulata De Córdoba*." *113 B Bachillerato en Artes del COBAEV 35*. 2011. Web. 12 Feb. 2014.

DIF. "Cuento La Mulata de Córdoba." *Viva la pelota*. Undated. Web. 23 July 2013.

Escudero, Martha. "La Mulata de Córdoba." *V Encuentro Internacional de Narradores Orales en el Pirineo* 2011. Web. 20 Jan. 2013.

———. "Martha Escudero: Narradora Oral." Web. 5 Feb. 2013.

González, Anita. *Jarocho's Soul: Cultural Identity and Afro-Mexican Dance*. Lanham, MD: University Press of America, 2014.

González Obregón, Luis. *Las calles de México*. México, D. F.: Ediciones Botas, 1947.

Hernández Cuevas, Marco Polo. *African Mexicans and the Discourse on Modern Nation*. Lanham, MD: University Press of America, 2004.

Janvier, Thomas A., ed. *Legends of the City of Mexico*. New York: Harper & Brothers, 1910.

Kellogg, Susan. "Depicting Mestizaje: Gendered Images of Ethnorace in Colonial Mexican Texts." *Journal of Women's History* 12.3 (2000): 69–92.

Lewis, Laura A. "'Afro' Mexico in Black, White and Indian." *Black Mexico. Race and Society from Colonial to Modern Times*. Ed. Ben Vinson III and Matthew Restall. Albuquerque, NM: University of New Mexico Press, 2009. 183–208.

Lovell Banks, Taunya. "Mestizaje and the Mexican Mestizo Self: *No Hay Sangre Negra*, So There Is No Blackness." *Southern California Interdisciplinary Law Journal* 15 (2006): 199–234.

Martínez Vargas, Enrique and Ana María Jarquín Pacheco. "El Tzompantli de Zultépec-Tecoaque." *Letras Libres*. 2010. Web. 17 Feb. 2012.

Medina, Rubén. "El mestizaje a través de la frontera: Vasconcelos y Anzaldúa." *Mexican Studies/Estudios Mexicanos* 25.1 (2009): 101–23.

Mejía Núñez, Guadalupe. "La Mulata en la expresión artística." *Sincronía* (Fall 2002). Web. 8 Jan. 2013.

Nutini, Hugo G. and Barry L. Isaac. *Social Stratification in Central Mexico, 1500–2000.* Austin, TX: University of Texas Press, 2009.

Ortiz Pedraza, Francisco. "El Caribe en la Conquista de México." *Cuicuilco* Nueva Epoca 10.29 (2003).

Ortiz Pedraza, Francisco, and Luis Weckmann. *The Medieval Heritage of Mexico.* Trans. Frances M. López-Morillas. New York: Fordham UP, 1992.

Pacheco, José Emilio. *La sangre de Medusa y otros cuentos marginales.* México: Era, 1990.

Palma, Ricardo. "Letter." Ed. Riva Palacio, Gral. Don Vicente, 1885. "Una amistad epistolar: Ricardo Palma y Vicente Riva Palacio": Algaba, Leticia. *Secuencias* 30 (1994) 179–208.

Proctor, Frank "Trey" III. "Slave Rebellion and Liberty in Colonial Mexico." *Black Mexico. Race and Society from Colonial to Modern Times.* Ed. Ben Vinson III and Matthew Restall. Albuquerque, NM: University of New Mexico Press, 2009. 21–50.

Ramírez Aparicio, Manuel. "La Mulata de Córdoba." *Obras de Don Manuel Ramírez Aparicio.* Ed. V. Agueros. Vol. 59: Imprenta de V. Agueros, 1908. 169–77.

RRRU. "La Mulata de Córdoba." *Leyendas Mexicanas.* RRRU. Web. 15 Jan. 2013.

Schwaller, Robert C. "'Mulata hija de negro y india': Afro-Indigenous Mulatos in Early Colonial Mexico." *Journal of Social History* 44.3 (2011): 889–914.

Simms, Ellen Yvonne. "Miscegenation and Racism: Afro-Mexicans in Colonial New Spain." *The Journal of Pan African Studies* 2.3 (2008): 228–254.

Vasconcelos, José. *The Cosmic Race: La raza cósmica.* Trans. Didier T. Jaén. Baltimore: Johns Hopkins University Press, 1997.

Vincent, Ted. "The Blacks Who Freed Mexico." *The Journal of Negro History* 3.79 (1994): 257–76.

Vincent, Theodore G. "The Contributions of Mexico's First Black Indian President, Vicente Guerrero." *The Journal of Negro History* 86.2 (2001): 148–59.

Vinson, Ben III. *Bearing Arms for His Majesty: The Free-Colored Militia in Colonial Mexico.* Stanford, CA: Stanford University Press, 2003.

Vinson, Ben, and Matthew Restall, eds. *Black Mexico: Race and Society from Colonial to Modern Times.* Albuquerque: University of New Mexico Press, 2009.

von Germeten, Nicole. "Colonial Middle Men? Mulatto Identity in New Spain's Cofraternities." *Black Mexico: Race and Society from Colonial to Modern Times.* Ed. Ben Vinson and Matthew Restall. Albuquerque: University of New Mexico Press, 2009. 136–54.

Wilson, James Grant, and John Fisk. *Appleton's Cyclopædia of American Biography.* Vol. 2. New York: D. Appleton, 1889.

*Chapter Eleven*

# Casting Traitors and Villains

*The Historiographical Memory of the 1605 Depopulations of Hispaniola*[1]

## Juan José Ponce-Vázquez

Thinking about the colonial past is still today a painful and contradictory subject in the Dominican Republic. Spanish colonialism is interpreted as a time of violence, death, and exploitation of Native American and African peoples. At the same time, however, according to the island's history, different sectors of the population have claimed and even defended their Spanish heritage as an important marker of Dominican national identity.

Of all the events that make up the colonial history of Hispaniola, the 1605 depopulations arguably still loom largest in the Dominican imagination. Any teenager or adult who went to school on the island can tell the story of *las devastaciones* (the devastations), or even *las devastaciones de Osorio* (Osorio's devastations), as it is popularly known, indicating the name of the governor who carried out the orders of the Spanish crown to destroy a number of towns on the island.

In 1605, the destruction of villages in the north and west of the island, as well as the forced relocation of the then homeless villagers to an area closer to the capital Santo Domingo stirred an open rebellion among some of the villagers, and agitated locals across the island. There were many reasons for the relocation of these frontier villages, the most important being the desire on the part of the Spanish authorities to curtail the increasing participation of local peoples in Atlantic contraband networks that connected these small Caribbean villages with merchants from England, France, and the Netherlands. These commercial contacts challenged the trade monopoly that Spanish merchants and the crown had established in the American colonies in the last decades of the sixteenth century. Letters and memorials sent back to Spain from Hispaniola also indicate a growing anxiety concerning the influence that these northern European merchants had acquired on the island and the possible sway of Protestantism among the local population. Previous attempts to curb the contraband trade by means of judges, ships patrolling the island's shores, or inspections of ships had proven ineffective. In the minds of the royal officials in Spain and some on the island, the relocation of the population to the area around Santo Domingo became the only means by which contraband and contact with northern European traders could be stopped. Despite ample local opposition, the relocation plan was carried out by governor Osorio with the help of troops sent from Puerto Rico.[2]

An informal survey of Dominicans about the topic would likely yield an opinion much like this: *las devastaciones* were an example of Spanish imperialism on the island and its people, as well as a brute imposition that deprived locals of their livelihood and forced them to a life of poverty near the capital. The depopulations are still commonly perceived to be the moment in which the island fractured into two polities: the Spanish colony of Santo Domingo and the French colony of Saint Domingue; the *devastaciones* removed all the Spanish settlers from the western lands, thus allowing the first European foreigners to settle there and fracture the unity of the island into two polities represented today by Haiti and Dominican Republic.

This national memory of the depopulations was not born in a vacuum: it is the result of a Dominican historiography, which has struggled to find the essence and origin of Dominican nationhood in the island's turbulent past while denying a common past with its island neighbor. Dominican nationhood has been constructed and is recreated everyday in opposition to Haiti. Still today, Haiti and Haitians are perceived by certain sector of Dominican population and political class as the most important threat to the Dominican nation. A recent 2013 judgment of the Constitutional Court of the country suspended the Dominican nationality of four generations of Dominicans whose Haitian parents had an "in transit" status. According to a Dominican member of Parliament, he was very satisfied with people's "growing awareness of the real dangers of Haiti's silent invasion towards the Dominican Republic" (qtd. in Pérez 246).[3] Anti-Haitian sentiment in Dominican Republic has a well-established scholarship (Matibag and Sagás). The bases of anti-Haitian rhetoric, however, rest on a particular narrative of the island's past that sees the depopulations as the event that made possible the split of the island into two polities and thus the rise of Haiti in the early nineteenth century. The historical memory of these events serves as an ideological justification of the political climate that the Dominican Republic is experiencing today.

This chapter will analyze the place that the narratives of the depopulations occupy in the Dominican national imagination. I will argue that in the

process of creating a national discourse, twentieth-century Dominican intellectuals of diverse ideological leanings agreed that the depopulations constituted the crossroads in the history of the nation. When looking at the depopulations through the eyes of Dominican scholars, the key protagonists of this
historical event seem typecast into unchangeable roles that define them more
than their actions. Out of that germinating moment, they created a pessimistic narrative of a poor and fractured nation. In its ultimate consequences,
these narratives sustain an anti-Haitian rhetoric and became a justification for
acts of violence and exclusion against Haitians and Dominicans of Haitian
descent.

   In this chapter I will talk about Baltasar López de Castro and Antonio
Osorio, two protagonists of the depopulations turned by Dominican
historiography into what I have called the traitor and the villain, thus becoming the foundation on which the rest of this national narrative was sustained. I
will briefly look into Dominican pessimism as a historiographical narrative
with solid roots among historians and thinkers of the Dominican Republic,
going as far back as the colonial period. I will then provide examples of how
Dominican historiography has understood two historical figures active in the
depopulations in light of this pessimistic current in historical studies.

## DOMINICAN PESSIMISM

Pedro L. San Miguel has argued that Dominican scholars across time and
ideological stances have used certain literary archetypes borrowed from clas-
sical tragedy to create a pessimistic narrative of the Dominican past. "Dominican pessimism" is in fact a well-known intellectual trend in the Dominican social sciences and humanities (Tejada *n.pag.*). Danilo de los Santos has
argued that it originated with the late-nineteenth-century and early-twentieth-
century intellectual elites of the island, whose views were rooted in the
perception of the Dominican masses as indolent, ignorant, and mixed-raced,
and therefore responsible of the country's backwardness (San Miguel 9).

   San Miguel has traced the roots of that characterization of the history of
the island further back into the late colonial period and the writings of early
local writers such as Antonio Sánchez Valverde (1734–1790), who penned
the first historical narrative of the island written by someone born in Hispaniola (San Miguel 9). Sánchez Valverde viewed the sixteenth century as the
golden age in the history of the island. In his telling, *las devastaciones*
represented the beginning of what he viewed as a long period of Spanish
neglect of its oldest American colony (San Miguel 11).

   Luis José Peguero, a contemporary of Valverde's, also presented Spanish
neglect as the defining historical marker in the island's past. Using earlier

works as reference, Peguero compiled a local history of the island[4] (Enríquez Ureña 56–57). Referring to the early colonial period, Peguero stated:

> During the sixteenth and seventeenth centuries, our island Hispaniola was forgotten by our Catholic kings when sending their provisions, for neither the three Philips nor the second Charles appreciated it. Until the year 1701, when the king our lord Philip the Fifth entered to govern the Spains [sic], the French of his nation reminded him of the continued losses since they were already in control of a third of the island. But in his great prudence, he saw it as a jewel of the Royal Patrimony of his Crown and denied it to them [the French]. (Peguero 12)[5]

Peguero thus denounced what he viewed as a history of metropolitan neglect that extended from the early years of the colony until the early eighteenth century.

The constant lamentation over the island's past and the role that the depopulations had on its decline continued well through the nineteenth and twentieth century. Using the legacy of nineteenth-century liberal historians such as José Gabriel García, scholars under the auspices of Rafael Trujillo's dictatorship (1930–1961) collaborated with the dictator in the reshaping of the island's past to match Trujillo's record of accomplishments on the island. These scholars built a self-serving version of the past that placed the Trujillo dictatorship at the cusp of the island's meteoric rise towards modernity. The history of the Dominican Republic had thus risen from the ashes of its forgotten colonial past thanks to the efforts of the "Benefactor of the Nation."

Of all the intellectuals working for Trujillo, Manuel Arturo Peña Batlle (1902–1954) was arguably the regime's most important ideologue. Conservative thinkers in the Dominican Republic still look to him as their intellectual forerunner. Peña Batlle's long essay, *"Las devastaciones de 1605 y 1606"* (*"The Devastations of 1605 and 1606"*), which he later included in his book *La cuestión fronteriza dominico-haitiana, (The Dominican-Haitian Frontier Question)* has long been one of the canonical works about the depopulations, and despite having been published over seventy-five years ago, still carries a lot of weight on Dominican scholars of the colonial period. The fact that he published his essay about the depopulations in a volume dedicated to an analysis of the border conflict between the Dominican Republic and Haiti reveals the ideological space that the depopulations occupy in the island's history. For Peña Batlle, the depopulations opened the doors to the enemies of the Spanish crown to settle the western part of the island and allowed the rise of Saint-Domingue, which in turn led to the foundation of the Haitian nation. For Peña Batlle, Haiti represents the threat of the black uncivilized savage, as opposed to the Spanish Catholic tradition that Dominican Republic theoretically embodies. Therefore, in the mind of Peña Batlle, and many of the intellectuals who followed him, the depopulations in 1605 constitute the beginning of all Dominican national woes. José Gabriel Garcia had already made this claim in the nineteenth century, but Peña Batlle's influential work crystalized it in the Dominican national myth. In his view, Dominicans are the victims of a defeated history that started in 1606.[6]

Peña Batlle's success in raising the depopulation to the level of national lore is rooted in his ability to dramatize the events in 1605–1606. Many scholars during and after Peña Batlle have recognized the narrative power of the depopulations. Dominican intellectual Emilio Rodríguez Demorizi (1904–1986) believed that the depopulations were "fascinating . . . of bigger dramatic intensity and with more elements for literary creation than the Enriquillo revolt" (Rodríguez Demorizi 108).[7] Historian Carlos Esteban Deive, possibly acknowledging Rodríguez Demorizi's suggestion, wrote an award-winning novel in 1979 titled, of course, *Las devastaciones*. The writings of Dominican historians and intellectuals also show an inclination to portray historical figures in dramatic roles that support their construction of a pessimistic narrative about the nation's past. I will focus on two protagonists of the depopulations, Baltasar López de Castro and Antonio Osorio, and the way they have been depicted by Dominican historiography. In this historical episode, they respectively embody the dramatic roles of the traitor and the villain.

## THE TRAITOR

Baltasar López de Castro was born in Santo Domingo to a prominent local family, probably sometime in the 1550s. He inherited the post of *escribano de cámara* (scribe of the court) of the *Audiencia* of Santo Domingo after his father, Nicolás López, died in 1569. The office of scribe of the *Audiencia* was one of the most influential posts in the colonial administration of the island, since it was charged with crafting the paperwork for all cases that passed through the court.[8] Baltasar was still a child when his father died, and therefore unable to occupy the post personally. Other members of the city's elite held the office in his stead, and it seems that some of them might have grown attached to the post, because Baltasar was unable to serve until 1580, when he was finally sworn in (Rodríguez Demorizi 161–63).

During Francis Drake's attack on Santo Domingo in 1586, López de Castro was one of the sixteen men who rode to oppose the English forces attacking the city. Even though their efforts were not sufficient to stop Drake's forces, such an act of courage might have earned him a certain social and political capital among his peers. Maybe because of that newly acquired capital, in 1592, he was also sworn in as *alférez real* (standard bearer) of the *Cabildo* (city council) of Santo Domingo, thus crowning him as a member of the city's elite, and giving him the opportunity to serve as a powerful local connection between the affairs of the *Audiencia*, the royal court on the island, and the city's most powerful men (Rodríguez Demorizi 161–63).

The work of *escribano de cámara* of the Audiencia was not free of tensions. Sometime before 1597, López de Castro directed some unrestrained words to one of his superiors, and as a result was held in contempt. At trial, he was sentenced to banishment from his office, fined 500 ducats, and exile from Santo Domingo for four years. Forced to leave his household and city, López de Castro appealed his case to the Council of the Indies in Madrid and marched to the Spanish capital to plead his case in person.[9]

López de Castro's fall from grace motivated him to write several memorials to the Council of the Indies, in the hopes that they would grant him the political favor he so desperately needed in order to have his sentence revoked. Thanks to his post of *secretario de cámara* of the Audiencia, he was well aware of the crown's concern with contraband and foreign influence on the island and probably thought that his direct knowledge on the issue might become his most valuable asset. On November 20, 1598, he wrote two memorials describing the natural wealth of Hispaniola and its current poverty, which he attributed to the inhabitants' practice of trading with foreigners. Following common economic assumptions of his time, he believed that this unlawful trade was siphoning away the island's riches for the benefit of the enemies of the Spanish crown (primarily England and France) and that such contact also posed serious risk of religious contamination to the Catholic residents of the island.

His first memorial provided a list of the unsuccessful measures that the authorities on the island had attempted in hopes of curbing the contraband trade, such as the use of galleys to patrol the waters off Hispaniola, or the commission of judges to apprehend the smugglers (Ponce-Vázquez 64–68). López de Castro suggested some possible measures to supervise cattle owners who were selling hides in exchange of foreign merchandise, such as counting and regulating the herds, or insuring that the herds were brought back to Santo Domingo (where many ranchers kept them previously before moving them to the north for sale). In his second memorial, López de Castro proposed a much more vigorous approach. Since the villages in the north were small and sparsely populated, he believed that a definitive solution would be to relocate the inhabitants of those villages to the region around Santo Domingo. This measure would provide the capital with abundant meat, which had become scarce due to the relocation of the cattle to the north. It would also provide the needed manpower to defend the city in case of attack. Most important, smugglers would be under the close supervision of the authorities in Santo Domingo.[10]

Initially, the Council of the Indies ignored López de Castro's ideas and petitions. The arrival of Philip III to the throne in 1598 precipitated changes within the Council, and the new councilors might have been more open to

López de Castro's ideas. At the same time, letters from Santo Domingo detailing how entrenched contraband was within the culture of Hispaniola continued to be sent to the Council of the Indies. The *oidor* (judge) of the Audiencia Pedro Saenz de Morquecho wrote one of such letters in 1599. The *oidor* had been conducting an investigation of the contraband trade on the north side of the island when he was attacked by a group of villagers who were angered by the meddling of the judge in their affairs. Once back in Santo Domingo, he wrote, "As I have already informed Your Majesty, the only remedy I can find for this land is doing with these peoples of the northern coast what was done with the *moriscos* of the kingdom of Granada: take their farms and move them to other parts."[11] Morquecho's suggestion to treat the northern resident of Hispaniola like the morisco rebels in the mountains of Granada (Spain) seems to indicate that López de Castro was not alone in envisioning the depopulation of the north as the only possible solution to the contraband culture of the island.

It is impossible to know from whom the Council of the Indies originally received the idea, but the chronology and chain of events indicates that López de Castro's memorial played an important part in the decision. In February 1602, the Council of the Indies moved ahead with the plan and approved the depopulation of the northwest of the island and the relocation of the villagers to the area surrounding Santo Domingo. López de Castro himself had his banishment lifted and was allowed to return to his post after paying the 500 ducats penalty he owed. He was also entrusted to carry the depopulation orders to Hispaniola. Once in Santo Domingo, he applied himself to the execution of the royal orders, becoming one of the governor's closest allies on the island.

While Lopez de Castro's fortunes rose again, many of his neighbors resented what they perceived as the Crown's intrusion in their lives and the role that López de Castro had in the loss of their lands and houses, to the point that López de Castro often feared for his life and that of his family. As soon as the depopulations were completed, he went back to Spain to claim a reward for his efforts and died sometime before 1608. For his services, the king granted his son the title of *alguacil mayor* (high constable) of the *Audiencia* of Santo Domingo in perpetuity to him and his descendants.

Dominican historical memory has been unkind to López de Castro. In 1945, the words of Emilio Rodríguez Demorizi aptly summarized the collective historiographical assessment of López de Castro's legacy in the eyes of the contemporaries of this Dominican scholar. López de Castro was to be blamed, he stated, for "the greatest misadventure suffered by the Dominican peoples; the loss of the political unity of the island in the benefit of former servants of Spain and France, transported to the lands that had been the cradle of the American civilization!" (Rodríguez Demorizi 113).[12] In other words, López de Castro became Rodríguez Demorizi's scapegoat for every single event considered detrimental to the Dominican nation, namely, the French settlement in the western coasts of the island, the Haitian revolution, and the rise of Haiti as an independent nation, and possibly even the Haitian annexation of Santo Domingo (1822–1844).

The intellectual Américo Lugo, still a revered pioneer in Dominican historical studies, penned one of the few articles dealing exclusively with López de Castro and his role in the depopulation. Even though Lugo and Rodríguez Demorizi were on the opposite sides of the Dominican political spectrum (Rodríguez Demorizi was one of the intellectuals who served and collaborated with the Trujillo regime, while Lugo opposed the dictator), they both coincided in their opinion about López de Castro. Lugo had few kind words to spare about him. Talking about López de Castro's origins, Lugo wrote:

> He was a native of that land [Hispaniola]. . . . And what if he was not? He would be in line with other precursors of the national character like bishop Bastidas, Miguel de Pasamonte, the bigamist Luis Colón, or the magnate Rodrigo Pimentel, residents in the land in whom the custom of bastardizing or purifying themselves can be observed as a territorial footprint; and without mentioning others like Cristopher Columbus, philanthropist Las Casas, or the benefactor Gorjón, whose profound love for the land, clear and indelible, can be seen in their hearts. (68)[13]

Although Lugo is unable to dispute the claim that López de Castro was a *criollo* (born on the island), he places him in the company of other historical figures, most of them Spaniards (but adopted by the Dominican national rhetoric) to whom he attributed the worst traits of the Dominican national character. He then juxtaposes those unwanted "sons" of the nation (Bastidas, Pasamonte, Luis Colón, and Pimentel) with those he deemed worthy of praise (the "discoverer" Christopher Columbus, the friar Bartolomé de Las Casas, and the sugar planter turned philanthropist Hernando Gorjón). *Criollo* or not, López de Castro represents for Lugo the worst possible kind of Dominican man: a traitor to his own people, someone willing to do anything to advance his own career and ambitions, even to the detriment of his countrymen.

Lawyer and intellectual Socrates Barinas Coiscou shared this negative view, except that he went so far as to add a number of false claims about López de Castro's life to make his case. Barinas Coiscou wrote that

> circumstances aligned so "López de Castro's sick and coward mind could come up with the idea that culminated in the division of the island. He was a resentful officer who, since the moment he ran away in cowardice from the city of Santo Domingo when Drake attacked, swore to win the trust of the king of Spain and obtain the orders to move the towns in the north of the island with the intention of stopping their inhabitants from trading with corsairs and pirates."[14]

As mentioned earlier, López de Castro was actually one of the few who rose to the challenge and actually faced Drake. Furthermore, he did not run away, but was exiled and went to Spain to appeal his sentence. By the 1980s, when Barinas Coisou was writing, the myth of López de Castro as the ultimate traitor had long since taken hold of the Dominican intellectual imagination.

Professional historians have tried to explain the reasons that animated López de Castro's proposal to destroy and depopulate the northern villages. Even though their arguments are more nuanced and sophisticated than Lugo's, they continue to depict López de Castro as an outsider, someone whose interests were not aligned with his origin. Frank Moya Pons believes that Lopez de Castro, "like the other bureaucrats in Santo Domingo identified with Sevillian and royal interests, outlined the situation in terms of the officialist needs of the capital" (119).[15] In other words, López de Castro's post as *secretario de cámara* of the *Audiencia* of Santo Domingo conditioned him to perceive the topic of local smuggling in the same light as that of his peninsular colleagues. At the same time, his inability to see his world just like his *criollo* neighbors made him something less than a real *criollo,* an outsider.

Historian Genaro Rodríguez Morel chooses a different path to condemn López de Castro's ideas while depicting him as a different type of outsider. He believes that the *secretario* was the only royal official on the island who believed in the depopulations. "The Crown," writes Rodríguez Morel, "opted to give credit to the memorials written by a *criollo* of dubious reputation called Baltasar López de Castro" (26).[16] Rodríguez Morel does not explain what makes López de Castro's reputation dubious, but we can assume he refers to the fact that López de Castro had been found guilty of a crime and was in Madrid seeking the commutation of his sentence. Questioning his standing as a member of Santo Domingo's society allows Rodríguez Morel to delegitimize López de Castro and his ideas, while at the same time raising suspicions about the sincerity of his intent. Like Moya Pons, Rodríguez Morel does not accept the possibility that individuals, regardless of their birthplace, might have held diverse opinions about the depopulations, and therefore needs to find fault in López de Castro's ideas.

In fact, many other members of the local elite got into trouble with the colonial administration throughout their lives without a loss in their social standing. Although the elites of Santo Domingo were inevitably linked to the contraband trade taking place in the north of the island, their attitudes towards smuggling was diverse and at times conflicted. They purchased smuggled goods and simultaneously disapproved of smugglers. López de Castro's ideas about the depopulations did not make him a less-than-perfect *criollo.* The fact that someone like López de Castro articulated his ideas about the depopulation is actually an eloquent proof of the very contradictory relationship that residents of Hispaniola had with the contraband trade, their most profitable source of wealth and well being, and at the same time, a serious risk to the colony.

It is impossible to know to what degree López de Castro believed in the benefits of the implementation of the depopulations in Hispaniola. The zeal that he demonstrated in the application of the royal orders against the wishes of many of his neighbors and friends, and despite threats against himself and his family, seems to indicate that his actions were driven by more than mere opportunism, but it is impossible to make that claim definitively. Being born in Hispaniola did not presuppose opposition to the depopulations, just as being born in the Iberian Peninsula did not guarantee that one would favor the plan either.

Turning Baltasar López de Castro into a traitor to his neighbors, and by extension, to the Dominican nation as a whole, has become a common and powerful trope in Dominican historiography. López de Castro might have been the person who best articulated the reasons why the depopulation would have been advantageous for both the Crown and the island population, but he was certainly not the first—nor the only one—to do so, as we saw with the example of *oidor* Pedro Saenz de Morchecho. López de Castro's persuasiveness may have played as large a role in the authorities decision to move forward with the plan as the sense of urgency distilled from the letters arriving in Santo Domingo describing the relationships of local inhabitants with foreign smugglers, or the political changes in Spain after the rise of Philip III to the throne. Yet, instead of grappling with these complicated motivations and political realities, Dominican intellectuals latched onto López de Castro as an accessible and convenient scapegoat to explain an important yet extremely complex event in the island's colonial past.

## THE VILLAIN

Although López de Castro has received a good share of the blame for the depopulations, Governor Antonio Osorio is the most vilified individual in contemporary narratives of the depopulations, and arguably, the most maligned historical figure in Dominican history. His last name, connected to the plan that he executed (las devastaciones de *Osorio*), is inexorably linked in the minds of contemporary Dominicans with images of authoritarianism, cruelty, and injustice, all accusations that convey the extent to which Osorio was not just the executor of the depopulations, but the mastermind behind it. Some Dominican intellectuals have gone so far as to wrongly attribute to him the initial idea of the depopulations. Scholar Joaquín Balaguer, who would become president of Dominican Republic numerous times, accused Osorio of suggesting the idea of the depopulations to the king himself (Balaguer 67). Likewise, after proposing that Osorio's "ill-fated name should be execrated by future generations," Rodríguez Demorizi said that the north of the island was "devastated by Osorio without consultation" (vol. I 73–74).[17]

Rodríguez Demorizi's prediction regarding the way future generations would think of Osorio did come to pass. Historians have almost unanimously condemned Osorio's character and participation in the depopulations. He has been described as a "sinister actor," "perverse," "dissolute," "one of the bloodiest and the most ill-fated governors that the island ever had," "the prototype of a despot," "unbalanced," and more (Peña Pérez 11). Dominican scholars have often referred to the *juicio de residencia*, an investigation conducted at the end of the term of a government official by his successor to determine the rectitude of his actions during his term.[18] The *residencia* was conducted in the aftermath of the depopulations, and the local residents tried to mobilize in order to extract some revenge against their governor. Scholars have uncritically repeated the accusations that the island residents made against Osorio, and by doing so, they have contributed to the construction of the figure of a perfect villain, a character risen from historical sources that fits perfectly within these scholars' narratives of the depopulations and over-all decline of the island, as well as the future of the nation, during and beyond the seventeenth century.

Antonio Osorio was a knight of the order of Santiago, which he was awarded for his military service to the Crown. He spent most of his military career serving in the Mediterranean and Northern Europe. He fought in the battle of Lepanto in 1571, and while stationed in Italy, fought aboard the royal galleys until 1579. He also fought in Flanders for fifteen years, was promoted to the rank of captain, and might have been part of the troops that the Duke of Parma assembled in Dunkirk for the failed invasion of England. Osorio also led 1,000 men in the defensive rebuilding efforts in Cádiz (Spain) after the English sack of the city in 1596. He was serving near Cádiz when he was named to succeed his brother Diego Osorio as the new governor of Santo Domingo.[19]

Osorio arrived in Santo Domingo in 1602, before the depopulation plans had been approved. Even though he was not specifically appointed for the depopulations, his relentless military discipline moved him forward despite the aggressive opposition he encountered. Even before the arrival the depopulation orders, Osorio petitioned the king to let him retire back to Spain. He did it again in numerous occasions without avail. His requests were ignored, and he continued in his post until his replacement arrived after he had completed the depopulations in 1608. Without any further evidence, it is impossible to know whether he completed such arduous task out of his sense of duty or in order to be granted a pension to retire. Except for the documents of his *residencia*, which the crown dismissed knowing that they were part of a local plan seeking revenge from Osorio, all the sources we have paint a very different portrait from that of the villain that the Dominican historiography has created.

Dominican scholars tended to mistake Osorio's military approach with obstinacy or even fanaticism. Peña Batlle is once again at the center of this trend. He attributed the depopulations to the "obsessions of a mad man," thus linking the evils of the depopulations to Antonio Osorio's character and blaming Osorio for all the ills that Dominicans have faced as a nation since the early colonial days. "Don Antonio Osorio," he claims, "is the father of the social and ethnic duality in which [the island] has grown to be, and the cause of the listlessness and the dejection with which the Dominican nation has developed. We Dominicans owe much of our vices and all of our deficiencies to Osorio's disastrous and tyrannical administration" (Peña Batlle, *Historia* 22).[20] In Peña Batlle's narrative, the Spanish crown disappears from sight and it is Osorio, the inflexible villain, the only person responsible for the depopulations and everything that followed. That social and ethnic duality that he refers to is the division of the island into the Dominican Republic and Haiti. He sees the African influence of the latter as a corrupting influence on the Dominican nation, which he envisions as white and European. For Peña Batlle, the entire history of the island after 1605 unravels around the depopulations, and, as the enforcer of the plan, Osorio himself bears the full responsibility for the fate of the nation.

More recent scholars have moved away from such interpretations, and have instead focused on explaining the negative economic consequences that the depopulations had on the island. For these historians, the depopulations were motivated exclusively by economic forces, which they have explained as the desire of the crown and Spanish merchants to preserve their commercial monopoly. Any other ideological factors (such as religion) are merely considered to be excuses for the execution of the plan. In these narratives, Osorio's participation in the depopulations has deserved passing though often unflattering remarks. Frank Moya Pons, for instance, believes he was merely a "victim in the hands of an ignorant king" or an "instrument of the world forces in conflict" (*Dominican Republic* 49). For Genaro Rodríguez Morel, Osorio was an outsider and so also ignorant of the colony's affairs, voiding any rationale for his involvement in the population, while Roberto Cassá sanctions the view of the residents of Hispaniola in 1605, and believes that due to a technicality, Osorio did not have the authority to carry out the plan. In these economic explanations of the depopulations, Osorio becomes a pawn in the hands of others (35). This transition in the historiography, from viewing Osorio as evil mastermind to ignored and ignorant puppet, has done little to change the memory of Osorio as a tyrant. In the mind of ordinary Dominicans, Osorio's name has become inextricably intertwined with that of the plan that he was ordered to execute.

Baltasar López de Castro and Antonio Osorio are only two examples of historical figures who have been transformed into stock characters of a dramatized version of the history of Hispaniola. Dominican historians have placed the depopulations at the center of the unraveling of a Dominican national history constructed on a foundation of pessimism. Even today, Dominican historians and scholars have been unable to completely dispose of the pessimism that has engulfed historical narratives of the island since the colonial period, and particularly, under the dictatorship of Trujillo. In the early twentieth century, such narratives were used to explain the backwardness of the Dominican nation by the liberal elites. In the years of the Trujillo dictatorship, this pessimistic narrative placed Trujillo at the center of a national discourse of redemption and progress that the dictator's rule represented. Today, these narratives are still alive in part due to the compelling nature of these representations. I suspect that they are also alive because they serve as the foundation of anti-Haitian sentiments that run deep in the country's collective identity. Once used to elevate Trujillo's achievements, today they serve to denounce past injustices of the colonial state and create a compelling yet deeply anachronistic and nationalistic view of the island's past. In this view, true Dominicans, like those who suffered the depopulations, are portrayed as victims while the blame is squarely placed on particular individuals, "traitors" like López de Castro and "villains" like Osorio.

The 1605 depopulations sit at the crossroad of the collective memory of the tragic past in Hispaniola because scholars have privileged anachronistic analyses that try to explain the centuries after the depopulations, instead of focusing on the depopulations themselves and its immediate context. Any future reconceptualization of the depopulations must be anchored in rigorous historical analysis instead of teleological national narratives.

## NOTES

1. All quotes in this chapter were translated from their original Spanish by the author.
2. For a more detailed look at the depopulations, see Concepción Hernández Tapia 286, and Ponce-Vázquez, chapters 2 and 3.
3. "La toma de conciencia de los peligros reales de la invasión silente de Haiti hacia República Dominicana."
4. Max Enríquez Ureña 56–57; Mercedes Román Fernández 499.
5. "Corrieron los siglos seiscientos, y setecientos dada la nuestra isla Española al total olvido de nuestros Catholicos Reyes, en mandar sus provisiones, pues ni los tres Filipos, ni el Carlos segundo le hicieron aprecio; hasta el año 1701 que entró en la gobernación de las Españas el Sr. Rey nuestro Don Felipe quinto, que los franceses de su nación se la acordaron con sus continuas pérdidas, como ya señoreados de un tercio de la isla, pero esta la miró su gran Prudencia como Joya del Patrimonio Real de su Corona y se la negó."
6. Tejada, "Apuntes. . ."; Henríquez Gratereaux, chapters 23 and 24; González de la Peña 159–92; Medar Cruz Serrata, chapters 1 and 2.
7. "Apasionante . . . de mayor intensidad dramática y de mayores elementos para una obra literaria que el alzamiento de Enriquillo." Enriquillo was a Taino leader who led a revolt

against the Spanish colonists in Hispaniola between 1519 and 1533. Already in the sixteenth century, Bartolomé de las Casas chronicled his struggle against the Spanish colonists. Enriquillo's story has been amply romanticized in historical narratives and novels, and other forms of popular culture. The first of these representations was the 1879 novel *Enriquillo*, written by Manuel Jesús Galván.

8. For a study on the importance of scribes and clerks in Spanish colonial courts, see Herzog.

9. Utrera 122; Memorial from Baltasar López de Castro to the Council of the Indies, May 20, 1596. Archivo General de Indias, Santo Domingo 70, Ramo 1, Number 40 (henceforth AGI, SD 70, R. 1, N. 40).

10. Both memorials can be found in Rodríguez Demorizi (161–87).

11. "No hallo remedio por tierra como tengo avisado a Vuestra Majestad si no es hacienda a esta gente de la banda del norte lo que se hizo con los moriscos del reino de Granada, quitándoles las haciendas y pasándolos a otra parte." Dr. Pedro Saenz de Morquecho to the Council of the Indies. January 5, 1599. AGI, SD. 81, R. 5, N. 124.

12. "La más grande desventura del pueblo dominicano: la pérdida de la unidad política de la isla en beneficio de antiguos siervos de España y de Francia, transportados del Africa a las tierras que habían sido cuna de la civilización americana!"

13. "Era natural de aquella tierra, según Osorio. ¿Qué mucho, si no lo fuera? Estaría en la línea, precursora del carácter nacional, como el obispo Bastidas, Miguel de Pasamonte, el bígamo don Luis Colón o el magnate don Rodrigo Pimentel, moradores de la isla en los cuales se observa la huella territorial, hábito o costumbre, bastardeando unos o bien purificándose; sin mencionar a otros, como Cristóbal Colón, al filántropo Las Casas o el benefactor Hernán Gorjón, a quienes se les ve la huella en el corazón, clara e indeleble, cautivados de particular y profundo amor por ella."

14. "Todo parece que se conjuró para que la mente enfermiza y cobarde de Baltasar López de Castro concibiera la idea que culminó con la división de la isla. Funcionario resentido, desde que huyó cobardemente de la ciudad de Santo Domingo cuando la invasión de Drake, juró ganar la confianza del Rey de España y obtener la orden del traslado de las ciudades del norte de la isla e impedir así que sus habitantes pudieran comerciar con los corsarios y piratas" (Barinas Coiscou 179–80).

15. "López de Castro, lo mismo que los demás burócratas de Santo Domingo identificados con los intereses reales y sevillanos, planteó la situación en términos de las necesidades oficiales y capitaleñas" (Moya Pons, *Historia colonial de Santo Domingo* 119). He also made a similar point in one of his most recent books on Caribbean history, where he once again identifies López de Castro as "a colonial official associated with Sevillian commercial interests" (Moya Pons, *History of the Caribbean* 42).

16. "La Corona optó por darles crédito a los memoriales redactados y llevados personalmente por un criollo de dudosa reputación llamado Baltasar López de Castro" (Rodríguez Morel 26).

17. "Osorio, cuyo fatídico nombre debería encomendarse a la excecración de las generaciones"; "inconsúltamente devastada por Osorio."

18. A good result in the *residencia* ensured the officer in question a new appointment and a promotion within the royal bureaucracy, while a negative result could end up in pecuniary fines, prison, confiscation of property, or even a death penalty for the most exceptionally egregious charges.

19. Antonio Osorio to the Council of the Indies, October 1, 1603. AGI, SD. 1, N. 56. Also in Inchaustegui Cabral 797.

20. "Don Antonio Osorio es el padre de la dualidad social y étnica de que aquella se ha repartido y el causante de la languidez y el abatimiento con que se ha desarrollado la nacionalidad dominicana. A la desastrosa y tiránica administración de Osorio debemos nosotros, los dominicanos, muchos de nuestros vicios y casi todas nuestras deficiencias de conjunto."

# WORKS CITED

Balaguer, Joaquín. *Historia de la literatura dominicana.* Ciudad Trujillo: Editorial Librería Dominicana, 1956.

Barinas Coiscou, Sócrates. *Las rebeliones negras de la Española; La isla dividida.* Santo Domingo, 1988.

Cruz Serrata, Medar. "Epic and Dictatorship in the Dominican Republic: The Struggles of Trujillo's Intellectuals." Diss. University of Texas at Austin, 2009.

Deive, Carlos Esteban. *Las devastaciones.* Santo Domingo: Alfa y Omega, 1978.

Enríquez Ureña, Max. *Panorama histórico de la literatura dominicana.* Santo Domingo, 1965.

González de la Peña, Raymundo Manuel. "Peña Batlle, historiador nacional." *Clio* 174 (2007):159–92.

Henríquez Gratereaux, Federico. *Un ciclón en una botella. Notas para una teoría de la sociedad dominicana.* Santo Domingo: Alfa y Omega, 1996.

Hernández Tapia, Concepción. "Despoblaciones de la isla de Santo Domingo en el siglo XVII." *Anuario de Estudios Americanos* 27 (1970): 281–320.

Herzog, Tamar. *Upholding Justice: Society, State, and the Penal System in Quito, 1650–1750.* Ann Arbor, MI: University of Michigan Press, 2004.

Inchaustegui Cabral, Joaquín Marino. *Cédulas y Correspondencia de Gobernadores de Santo Domingo de la Regencia del Cardenal Cisneros en Adelante.* Madrid, 1958.

Lugo, Américo. "Baltasar López de Castro y la despoblación del norte de la Española." *Revista de Historia de América* 23 (1947): 281–301. Rpt. in *Colección pensamiento dominicano.* Vol. V. Santo Domingo: Sociedad Domincana de Bibliófilos, 2009. 67–77.

Matibag, Eugenio. *Haitian-Dominican Counterpoint: Nation, State, and Race on Hispaniola.* New York: Palgrave Macmillan, 2003.

Moya Pons, Frank. *The Dominican Republic, a National History.* New Rochelle, NY: Hispaniola Books, 1995.

———. *Historia colonial de Santo Domingo.* Santiago, República Dominicana: Universidad Católica Madre y Maestra, 1977.

———. *History of the Caribbean: Plantations, Trade, and War in the Atlantic World.* Princeton, NJ: Markus Wiener Publishers, 2007.

Peguero, Luis José. *Historia de la Conquista, de la isla Española de Santo Domingo trasmutada el año de 1762: traducida de la Historia general de las Indias escrita por Antonio de Herrera coronista mayor de Su Magestad de las Indias, y de Castilla, y de otros autores que han escrito sobre el particular.* Vol. 2. Santo Domingo: Museo de las Casas Reales, 1975.

Peña Batlle, Manuel Arturo. *Las devastaciones de 1605 y 1606. Contribución al estudio de la realidad dominicana.* Ciudad Trujillo, 1938.

———. *Historia de la cuestión fronteriza dominico-haitiana.* Ciudad Trujillo, 1946.

Peña Pérez, Frank. *Antonio Osorio. Monopolio, contrabando y despoblación.* Santiago, República Dominicana: Universidad Católica Madre y Maestra, 1980.

Pérez, Amín. "'Yo no soy racista, yo defiendo mi patria:' Síntomas y efectos nacionalistas en República Dominicana." *Caribbean Studies* 41.2 (July–December 2013): 245–55.

Ponce-Vázquez, Juan José. "Social and Political Survival at the Edge of Empire: Spanish Local Elites in Hispaniola, 1580–1697." Diss. University of Pennsylvania, 2011.

Rodríguez Demorizi, Emilio. *Relaciones históricas de Santo Domingo.* Vol I. Ciudad Trujillo: Montalvo, 1942.

———. *Relaciones históricas de Santo Domingo.* Vol II. Ciudad Trujillo: Montalvo, 1945.

Rodríguez Morel, Genaro. *Cartas del cabildo de la ciudad de Santo Domingo en el siglo XVI.* Santo Domingo: Patronato de la Ciudad Colonial de Santo Domingo/Universidad Católica Santo Domingo: Centro de Altos Estudios Humanísticos y del Idioma Español, 1999.

Román Fernández, Mercedes. "Estudios de los clíticos en un texto dominicano del siglo XVIII." *Actas del II Congreso Internacional de Historia de la Lengua Española.* Tomo II. Madrid: Pabellón de España, 1992. 499–507.

Sagás, Ernesto. *Race and Politics in the Dominican Republic.* Gainesville, FL: University of Florida Press, 2000.

San Miguel, Pedro L. *The Imagined Island. History, Identity, and Utopia in Hispaniola*. Chapel Hill, NC: University of North Carolina Press, 2005.

Tejada, Rita María. "Apuntes para una bibliografía del pesimismo dominicano." Web. http://cielonaranja.com/ritatejada1.htm.

Utrera, Cipriano de "Sor Leonor de Ovando." *Boletín del Archivo General de la Nación* 68 (1951): 120–50.

# Index

# About the Contributors

**Selfa A. Chew** is a poet, novelist, playwright and scriptwriter. She holds a bachelor's degree in communication science from Universidad Nacional Autónoma de México. She received a MFA in creative writing and her PhD in borderlands history from The University of Texas at El Paso. Dr. Chew is an editor for *Border Senses Literary Review* and translator for *Memorias del Silencio*, a migrant workers' publication. She coordinated the *Mexican Contemporary Literature Journal* and Conference from 1999 to 2012. Her work (poetic, graphic, narrative, and editorial) has been published in Peru, Spain, Argentina, Mexico, the Netherlands, and the United States. Dr. Chew's research focuses on racial relations, the Asian and African diasporas, and World War II. Her dissertation title is *Race, Gender and Modernity: The Removal of Japanese and Japanese Mexicans from the Mexican Borderlands during World War II*. She currently teaches United States History, Afro-Mexican History, Contemporary Latin America, and African American History at the University of Texas at El Paso and New Mexico State University.

**Martha I. Chew Sánchez** is an associate professor in the Department of Global Studies and Caribbean and Latin American Studies Program at St. Lawrence University. Her lines of research are related to cultural identities in the U.S.-Mexico border, and the effects of globalization on human rights. Chew Sánchez is the author of the book *Corridos in Migrant Memory* (University of New Mexico Press, 2006), and has written articles on militarization and paramilitarization in Mexico. Chew teaches courses on Critical Race Theory, Border Theory, Qualitative Methods, Migration and Cultural Studies.

**George Ciccariello-Maher** teaches political theory from below at Drexel University in Philadelphia, after having previously taught at the University of California, Berkeley, San Quentin State Prison, and the Venezuelan School of Planning in Caracas. He is the author of *We Created Chávez: A People's History of the Venezuelan Revolution* (Duke, 2013), as well as numerous articles and book chapters. He is currently completing two books, one on revolutionary identity entitled *Decolonizing Dialectics* and an analysis of Venezuela's communes entitled *Building the Commune*.

**Mallory Craig-Kuhn** is a literary critic and translator. She earned her B.A. magna cum laude at St. Lawrence University with a double major in political science and multi-languages. She then studied a master's program at the Universidad de Buenos Aires in Argentina in Spanish and Latin American literature with a thesis analyzing the urban novels of Colombian author Rafael Chaparro Madiedo. She is currently continuing her graduate studies at the Universidad de Antioquia in Colombia. Her literary studies focus on urban and crime novels in Latin America and comparative literary studies (crime novels in Latin America and the western genre in the United States).

**Aída Díaz de León**, visiting assistant professor of Spanish in the Department of Modern Languages and Literatures at St. Lawrence University, earned her PhD at the University of Kansas, at Lawrence. She has presented a number of papers on film and testimony in Latin America. Her research focuses on the development of individual, communal, and historical memory in Latin America as represented in film, autobiography, *testimonio*, and confession. She has also taught at Bowdoin College, Grinnell College, and Colgate University.

**Alfredo Limas Hernández** is professor at the Universidad Autónoma de Ciudad Juárez, Chihuahua, México. His lines of research and teaching are: human rights education, citizenship, gender equality and sociocultural intervention, clinical and social pedagogy, and international advocacy. He is one of the three legal representatives of the families of the victims of *El Campo Algodonero vs. Mexico* case in the Inter-American Court of Human Rights. Limas Hernández actively participates in the defense of human rights in cases of feminicide and trafficking and disappearance of women. He does pro bono legal representation for many abduction cases. Limas Hernández is a founder member of the Red Ciudadana de No Violencia y Dignidad Humana and Observatory of social and gender violence of the Universidad Autónoma de Ciudad Juárez. He is the author of several chapters and co-author of six books with his sister Myrna Limas Hernández on gender violence, gender citizenship and women's human rights.

**Marina Llorente**, professor of Spanish in the Department of Modern Languages and Literatures at St. Lawrence University, has published *Palabra y deseo: Espacios transgresores en la poesía española, 1975–1990*, and coedited the anthology *Abuelas hispanas: Desde la memoria y el recuerdo*. Her latest monograph, *Poesía en acción: Poemas críticos en la España contemporánea*, was launched by Baile del Sol in Spain in June of 2014. She has written articles on the intersections between Hispanic literatures, gender and social justice with a focus on contemporary Hispanic poetry analyzed within the theoretical framework of cultural studies. Her current research addresses ethics, the politics of memory and contemporary literature and film in Spain and Latin America. Llorente is presently coediting the anthology *Activism through Poetry: Critical Poems in Translation from Latin America and Spain*, which will be published in 2016.

**Beatriz Carolina Peña** is an assistant professor at Queens College (CUNY). Her areas of interest are colonial Latin American literature, culture, history, and iconography. Peña is the author of *Fonolitos. Las piedras campanas de Eten: Rituales, milagros y codicia* (Valladolid: Glyphos Publicaciones, 2014), winner of the IV Edition of the "Juan Antonio Cebrián" Award of Historical Dissemination (Madrid and Crevillente, Spain, 2014). She is also the editor of *"Memoria viva" de una "tierra de olvido": Relación del viaje al Nuevo Mundo de 1599 a 1607* (Barcelona: CECAL/Paso de Barca, 2013), a critical annotated edition of friar Diego de Ocaña's travel narrative. Her *Imágenes contra el olvido: El Perú colonial en las ilustraciones de fray Diego de Ocaña* (Lima: Fondo Editorial Pontificia Universidad Católica del Perú, 2011) was awarded the *Premio de Historia Colonial de América "Silvio Zavala,"* 2013 Edition and the *2012 Premio Alfredo A. Roggiano de Crítica Literaria y Cultural Latinoamericana*. Before publication, this work also received an Honorable Mention in the forty-ninth edition of the *Premio Literario Casa de las Américas* 2008, in the category of *Ensayo de tema histórico-social*. Peña is presently working on a book about historical memory and forgetfulness in Ocaña's travel account.

**Juan José Ponce-Vázquez** is a social historian whose research focuses on Latin America, the Caribbean, and the Atlantic world. He earned his PhD from the University of Pennsylvania. His current book project, entitled *At the Edge of Empire: Social and Political Defiance in Hispaniola, 1580–1697*, explores how local elites in Santo Domingo transcended their marginal location and status within the Spanish colonial world and took advantage of the intense imperial competition that engulfed the Caribbean during the seventeenth century, with the arrival of Northern European settlers to the region. He is an assistant professor at the University of Alabama.

**Marcella Salvi** is associate professor of Italian and Spanish at St. Lawrence University. She received her MA and PhD in romance languages and literatures from the University of Oregon. She has published a book *Escenas en conflicto: El teatro español e italiano desde los márgenes del Barroco* (*Staging Conflicts: Spanish and Italian Theatre from the Periphery of the Baroque*, Peter Lang, 2005) and several articles on sixteenth- and seventeenth-century Spanish and Italian drama in professional journals. Her current research interests include early modern Europe's fascination with sexual hybridism and with gender issues of the age as expressed in the Italian and Spanish theatre, and the politics of memory in contemporary literature in Spain and Italy. Salvi is currently coediting the anthology *Activism through Poetry: Critical Poems in Translation from Latin America and Spain*, which will be published in 2016.

**Oscar D. Sarmiento** is professor of Spanish in the Department of Modern Languages at SUNY Potsdam. His book *El otro Lihn: La práctica cultural de Enrique Lihn* was published by University Press of America in 2001. His articles on contemporary Latin American poetry have appeared in scholarly journals. Sarmiento was editor of the Chilean poetry chapter in the *Handbook of Latin American Studies of the Library of Congress* from 1993 to 2013. His translations of poems by poet Martín Espada were published as *La república de la poesía* in 2007. His translations of poems by Philip Lopate, Kathleen Sheeder Bonano, and Maurice Kenny can be found on the *Letras de Chile* literary website. His own poems have been published in literary magazines, and his book *Carta de extranjería* was published by Asterión in 1992.

**Liliana Trevizán** is professor of modern languages at the State University of New York in Potsdam. She is the author of *Política/ Sexualidad: Nudo en la escritura de mujeres latinoamericanas* (1998) and has numerous publications on Latin American women writers, such as Gabriela Mistral, Luisa Valenzuela, and Pía Barros. Her scholarship examines how cultural trends intersect gender, sexuality, and politics in Latin American fiction, poetry, and public discourse. Currently, she is working on a book on the influence of feminism on the public discourse of democracy in Chile. She earned a BA in Philosophy from the University of Chile, and a MA and a PhD in romance languages and literatures from the University of Oregon.

**Steven F. White**, professor in the Department of Modern Languages and Literatures at St. Lawrence University, has compiled anthologies of poetry from Nicaragua, Chile, and Brazil. He is also the translator of Federico García Lorca's *Poet in New York* and collections of poems by Rubén Darío, Pablo Antonio Cuadra, Gastón Baquero, Gioconda Belli, and Edimilson de Almeida Pereira. He has written and edited a number of books, including

*Modern Nicaraguan Poetry: Dialogues with France and the United States, El mundo más que humano en la poesía de Pablo Antonio Cuadra: Un estudio ecocrítico, Arando el aire: La ecología en la poesía y la música de Nicaragua* and *El consumo de lo que somos: Muestra de poesía ecológica hispánica contemporánea.* Recent books of his own poetry include *Escanciador de pócimas* and *Bajo la palabra de las plantas (poesía selecta: 1979–2009).* He is the recipient of two Fulbright fellowships as well as a translation grant from the National Endowment for the Arts.

www.ingramcontent.com/pod-product-compliance
Lightning Source LLC
Chambersburg PA
CBHW021818270326
41932CB00007B/238